THE MODERN WORLD

RUSSIA

THE MODERN WORLD
A SURVEY OF HISTORICAL FORCES

Edited by

The Right Hon. H. A. L. FISHER, M. P.

The aim of the volumes in this series is to provide a balanced survey, with such historical illustrations as are necessary, of the tendencies and forces, political, economic, intellectual, which are moulding the lives of contemporary states.

Already published:

GERMANY	by G. P. Gooch
IRELAND	by Stephen Gwynn
NORWAY	by G. Gathorne Hardy
RUSSIA	by Valentine O'Hara and N. Makeef

In preparation:

TURKEY	by Arnold Toynbee
IRAQ	by Gertrude Bell
INDIA	by Sir Valentine Chirol
CHILE	by His Excellency Don Augustin Edwards
ENGLAND	by the Very Rev. W. R. Inge
ARGENTINA	by Clarence H. Haring
AMERICA	by John Finley

RUSSIA

BY

NICHOLAS MAKEEV
PRESIDENT, ALL-RUSSIAN UNION OF ZEMSTVOS

AND

VALENTINE O'HARA
MEMBER, ANGLO-RUSSIAN COMMITTEE IN PETROGRAD

WITH AN INTRODUCTION BY
THE RIGHT HON. H. A. L. FISHER, M. P.

NEW YORK
CHARLES SCRIBNER'S SONS
1925

INTRODUCTION

THERE is no greater event in modern history than the Russian Revolution, whether it be considered in relation to the vast extent of the territory which it has affected, or the nature and quality of the changes which it has introduced, or the mass suffering of which it has been the parent, or the influence which it has exerted, and continues to exert, in international relations. The break with Confucius in China may prove to be equally far-reaching in its consequences; but we know far too little about China to be sure. The nearest parallel, and most helpful guide to the understanding of recent events in Russia, is the French Revolution; a movement which now, thanks to the efflux of time and the labour of historians, can be judged with comparative accuracy.

The French Revolution was an attack on privilege; the Bolshevik Revolution an attack on property. The one was the work of the *bourgeoisie*; the other of a knot of Communist sectaries working on the passions of a defeated army, and an ill-paid factory population. That revolution would occur in France, and in Russia, was a matter confidently foretold by many who visited the two countries under their ancient monarchies, but, while the particular course of the French revolution was unforeseen, the peculiarity of the Russian revolution lies in the fact that Lenin the communist had long predicted the nature of his opportunity, and had the plan of a Communist State ready formed in his brain.

Each revolution was formidable by reason of the fact that it was the triumph of a doctrine; but whereas the intellectual preparation for the French Revolution was the work of a great school of writers using the French tongue, the Bolshevik creed was made in Germany. The doctrine of the Dictatorship of the Proletariat, which is the distinctive feature of the Russian creed, was derived from the writings of Karl Marx,

v

a German Jew. It was exotic, not a native Russian product, and its *clientèle* was largely to be found among the persecuted Russian co-religionists of its author.

Both in Russia and in France the peasants, profiting by the general confusion, seized the lands of the nobles and gentry of the neighbourhood, and as no French government has dared to upset the land settlement of the revolution, so no Russian government will venture to annul the vast transfer of property which has been effected in the time of trouble. Indeed the principal security of the Bolsheviki will be found to consist not in the popularity of their communist doctrine, but in the wide diffusion of private property among the peasants which is associated with their *régime*.

Each revolution was anti-religious in character, and resulted in a scheme of lay schools supported by the public purse. In each case ambitious educational ideals, compounded of enlightenment and folly, were accompanied by a temporary paralysis of real education. There is, however, this profound difference between the French and the Russian revolutionary state. The French system is based upon the equality of all; the Russian upon the tyranny of a class. It is sufficient to observe that the son of the peasant and the artisan has a preferential claim to education in a Russian University.

Both revolutions were profoundly influenced by foreign wars. It was the failure of the Tsarist government to conduct war efficiently which gave the Bolsheviki their opportunity, just as it was foreign invasion which led to the execution of Louis XVI and the establishment of the Terror. In each case the revolutionary government was helped by the activities of foreign powers allying themselves with parties in the revolutionary state. There was, however, one important difference between the two cases. The Powers, who fought the French revolution, wished to restore the Bourbons. The Entente, in the recent war, accepted the Russian revolution;

but they entered into a war upon the Bolsheviki when it was clear that they were set upon a peace with the Germans.

Each revolution was doctrinaire and propagandist. Robespierre and Lenin had a cause in which they saw a promise for the redemption of humanity. The creed of France was Liberty, Fraternity, Equality; the creed of Russia, the Dictatorship of the Proletariat.

The French revolutionary government almost immediately reverted to the ancient French tradition of administrative centralization. Even so the Russian communists govern with the secret police of the Tsarist *régime*. In foreign policy, however, there is a difference. Revolutionary France swung back at once to the doctrine of the Rhine frontier which was the diplomatic tradition of ancient France, and so became involved in a war of conquest. The Bolsheviki, on the contrary, continue to pursue a policy of cosmopolitan conspiracy; and trust to doctrine rather than to guns to extend their rule.

The schism between revolutionary France and Europe lasted for more than twenty years, but though the doctrinal cleft between communist Moscow and the individualist societies of Western Europe is profound, Germany has already made a pact with the Bolshevist state.

The main outlines of French society to-day were traced by the thinkers of the French revolution. Civil marriage, secular schools, equality before the law, the abolition of privilege in finance, religious toleration, parliamentary government, all these conquests of the revolutionary spirit have been triumphantly maintained. In Russia large concessions have already been made to the principle of capitalism. The doctrine of Lenin has lost much of its vigour under the ineluctable pressure of events; but though Communism will fail, both at home and abroad, the old *régime* in Russia has gone once for all, and there is no power in the world which can restore it.

To the understanding of this vast and complex Russian movement, this volume makes an important contribution. Since Sir Donald Mackenzie Wallace published his famous book in 1887, I doubt whether any more substantial treatise on Russian affairs has been published in the English language. Of the authors, one is a Russian and the other a British subject long resident in the old Russian empire. Each has suffered imprisonment ; M. Makeev at the hands of the Tsarist Government, Mr. O'Hara at the hands of the Bolsheviki. Each collaborator writes with the authority of an eye-witness and an actor upon some phases of Russian history which are touched upon here. M. Makeev joined the Social Revolutionary party in 1904. Later he took part in the Co-operative movement and in the activities of Local Government. Early in 1917 he became a member of the board of the all-Russian Union of Zemstvos, of which he was elected president in succession to Prince Lvov, and in October of the same year he became a member of the Constituent Assembly of Vladimir. He left Russia in 1919. His collaborator, Mr. O'Hara, has also a long and varied experience of Russian affairs, gained in business and as a member of the Anglo-Russian Committee in Petrograd, and as taking part, at the invitation of the Foreign Office, in the British political mission to the Baltic States in 1919.

The attempt of the two authors to tell the truth about Russia, and to enable an accurate judgment to be formed as to the essential factors in the historical growth and political condition of this vast country is obvious upon every page. And since the reader is here invited neither to condemn nor to extenuate, but simply to understand, this volume should be read when thousands of polemical treatises on Russia, the fruits of anger, horror, prejudice, and spite, have passed into oblivion.

H. A. L. FISHER.

September, 1925.

TABLE OF CONTENTS

CHAPTER I

SOURCES AND ORIGINS

CHAPTER II

IMPERIAL RUSSIA

CHAPTER III

RUSSIA AT THE START OF THE TWENTIETH CENTURY

CHAPTER IV

THE RISE OF DEMOCRACY

Contents

CHAPTER IX

U.S.S.R. (THE UNION OF THE SOCIALIST SOVIET REPUBLICS)

CHAPTER X

ECONOMIC POLICY OF THE SOVIET GOVERNMENT

CHAPTER XI

COMINTERN AND PROLETCULT

CHAPTER XII

CONCLUSION

APPENDIX I

APPENDIX II

" The past of the Russian people is dark. The present is terrible. But they have a right to the future."—ALEXANDER HERZEN.

RUSSIA

CHAPTER I

SOURCES AND ORIGINS

THE deep-rooted differences to be found in the earliest evidences
of organized life in the east and west of Europe and their
persistence to the present day are nowhere more strikingly
illustrated than in the history of the Russian people. In
interpreting this history we must avoid the temptation of
adopting an exclusively western or eastern point of view, the
western generally taking but little account of conditions quite
peculiar to the early Slav settlements on the Russian Plain,
the eastern too often inclined to minimise the significance of
the reactions of other influences. On closer consideration in
the light of modern research such interpretations are found to
be confusing and misleading. The "Asiatic" formula for
solving the Russian problem is indeed as unsatisfactory and
unconvincing as that of President Masaryk, for whom Russia
is European but of the Middle Ages. It is in the combination
rather than the contrast of these two influences that we should
seek the solution of the problem.

Adventurous trade by all accounts seems to have been
responsible for the early settlements on the Russian Plain.
That this spirit was distinctively Slav is not so certain. That
the inspiration came from outside—incidentally we should not
forget that the early Slav settlements were mostly on sites of
older civilizations—is more probable. To this day Russia
remains a country of farmers, not of traders. The evolution
of the Russian State undoubtedly started from trading centres
and towns where popular assemblies (Veches), through their
elective magistrates, were the supreme law-makers and law-
givers. The towns engaged the services of foreign leaders of
military forces to protect their interests. These roving
" princes," as good business men as they were soldiers, gradually
succeeded in riveting their ascendancy over the Veches and in
consolidating their power over large tracts of territory. How this
process was quickened and intensified under the Tartar Yoke

which turned Russia into a land of slaves and slave drivers; how it led to the absolutism of the Tsarist autocracy, an oriental despotism where the will of the ruler was the supreme law; how under another name and in another guise this despotism survives essentially unchanged to our own times; and what are the prospects for the revival of native forces which far from weakening in the past have but gathered strength from the rude blows of adversity, it is the object of this work to examine.

Before dealing with the historical and cultural factors which have influenced the development of Russian civilization and national character, we should give particular consideration to natural conditions. That climate, not the accidents of history, according to Montesquieu, ultimately determines the character of peoples and of their institutions, is for many students of history an article of faith. It could hardly find a better testing field than Russia, with her very distinctive spiritual and intellectual culture spread over regions of greatly varying climatic conditions. If climate has determined the remarkable uniformity of this culture it can only be in so far as it has influenced the Russian mentality in its attitude to life and thought—that philosophic, imperturbable indifference to passing changes which never quite conceals a " true Promethean fire " burning within. Let us examine these conditions more closely.

Natural Conditions.—The Great Northern Plain, on which what was called Russia lies spread, is the largest in the World. From the line of the rivers Niemen and Danube on the west it extends for many thousands of miles to the river Yenissei on the east, and north and south from the White to the Black Sea, from the Arctic Ocean to the Hindu Kush Mountains. The greater part of its maritime boundary, 27,000 km. out of a total of about 50,000 km., lies in the tenacious grip of the Arctic ices. In respect of sea-trade routes Russia is the least favoured of any country in the world. The majority of the great Russian rivers bear their floods to the ice-bound Ocean from whose shores extends this veritable Ocean Continent, the area of which in 1917 was about 22,000,000 square kilometres.

The maritime boundaries on the land-locked waters of the Baltic and Black Seas did not exceed 6,750 km. and 4,400 km.

respectively. The Pacific Ocean is cut off by many thousand miles of wild mountain land from the Great Plain.

Level and smooth as a carpet the Great Plain spreads out from west to east, seldom rising above 350 m., the average height being 168 m. It is only in the middle of this plain that a slight folding-up of the surface is met, the Ural ridge.

Historical fancy has often given a special significance to this ridge as the wall parting Europe from Asia. Geographically, as well as historically, the significance is unimportant. The maximum altitude of the Ural Range rarely exceeds 1,500 m. From the point of view of climate, flora or fauna, the ridge forms no sharp dividing line between Europe and Asia. Rather does its great mineral wealth forge a strong link between them ; and the Great Plain stretches afar on either side as if no obstacle barred the way. Wave after wave of folk-migration found no difficulty in pouring to and fro over the Ural Range. And when in the sixteenth century the Russian colonization wave reached this point it overflowed with as little difficulty and fertilized the eastern part of the Great Plain.

It is only on the borders of this huge, dish-shaped valley that lofty mountains rise. As if to shade off the vast extent of rolling plain on the south-eastern European side the Caucasian mountain system spreads out, the highest in Europe, attaining to 5,360 m., with its prolongation towards the west, the Crimean Yaila.

On the Asiatic side the Great Plain is bordered by : the great Altai-Sayan mountain system rising to a height of 3,500 m., with its offshoots the Stanovoy and the Yablonovy Ranges, the Tienshan Range, the loftiest in Russia, rising to 7,500 m., and the Pamirs, the Roof of the World.

Rivers.—The Russian rivers as channels of trade, migration and colonization have had an immense influence on Russian national unity, economically and politically. The Russian river system, mostly fed by underground waters and the spring thaws, drains the Russian Plain to the Black, the Caspian and the Baltic Seas and to the Arctic Ocean. The principal rivers of Russia, the Volga, the Western Dwina and the Dnieper, all rise very close together in the central watershed of the Russian Plain, a slight elevation called the Valdai Hills. The double

Urals, for all their extensive coal resources, have not as in
the Don basin the materials for coke production. The Moscow
coal has but little commercial value, its friability and excess
of ash waste making it unsuitable for local industry. In the
north-west—the old Baltic provinces, Finland, the Archangel
and Vologda districts—there is no coal.

Russia has vast mineral wealth. It teems with abundance
of almost every known mineral, useful or precious. But these
minerals are mostly to be found on the borders of the Great
Plain and at considerable distances from the more populated
centres, as in the mountains of East Siberia, in the Altai
Mountains, on the eastern slopes of the Urals, in the Caucasus.
In consequence great obstacles had to be surmounted for the
development of industry. A considerable expenditure of
personal energy, initiative and organizing talent was called for.
No doubt Russia's natural wealth is not so boundless as many
Russians and foreigners believe it to be. But few other countries
possess such varied resources. She has at her disposal every
requisite for the harmonious development of her productive
forces. If only the national economy were properly organized
and a right balance struck between agriculture and industry,
production and distribution, Russia would more than amply
satisfy all her home requirements, and would soon become as
productive and self-supporting as the United States of America.
So much for physical conditions.

Pre-Slav Civilization.—The Slavs did not settle on bare,
isolated sites, but on sites of older civilizations steeped in the
atmosphere of eastern culture. However weak this culture may
have been, however lacking in originality and in values of a
creative character, it yet had a distinct significance for
Russia. For from this ground arose what is called the " Kiev
Civilisation."

To start with the history of Russia from the ninth century,
i.e., from the time of the Slav settlements, would be as misleading and unsound as to start with the history of England
from the period of its conquest by the Anglo-Saxons, or with
the history of France from its conquest by the Franks. " The
beginnings of cultural life in the Steppes of South Russia, on
the great Russian rivers, the Dnieper, the Don and the Kuban,

are inseparably associated with the three great centres of civilisation in the old world, the three cradles of humanity ; the western Asiatic, the Mediterranean and the mid-European " (*Rostovtsev*). Along the Kuban we may trace the remains of a high civilization at the time of the bronze age, a civilization linked up with the very earliest forms of culture in Mesopotamia, Turkestan and Egypt. In the same era there flourished on the Dnieper vigorous offshoots of the mid-European civilization considerably influenced however by the south-east. And lastly, the very first evidences of cultural life on the Mediterranean point directly to the civilization of the Black Sea. It was about this period that the first great trade routes intersecting Russia were established ; the Caravan route from the east to the Sea of Azov ; the sea route from the Black Sea to the Mediterranean, the Ægean Isles and the coasts of Asia Minor ; and the river routes to the Baltic Sea.

Two great Asiatic-European States in succession established themselves on the northern part of the Black Sea ; the Cimmerian-Thracian (tenth century—eighth century B.C.) and the Scytho-Iranian (eighth century—third century B.C.). They aroused much interest among the Greeks. Indeed, the Black Sea may be said to have rocked for a time the cradle of western European civilization. The Greeks had been attracted to the south of Russia by its great natural riches. It was the granary of the ancient Mediterranean world. If the Greek colonies did not succeed in Hellenizing South Russia, this may be ascribed to the strength of the cross-currents of the civilization coming from the east. Still the significance of Hellenism in the destinies of Russia was great. It certainly left its mark on the culture of South Russia [1], and helped on its association with systems of organized governments.

---

[1] Remarkable specimens of the purest Greek art have been discovered all over the south of Russia in the course of archæological researches. Near Odessa lie the ruins of the dead city of Olbia which has been called the Pompeii of the Black Sea. In the fourth century B.C., the inhabitants of this then thriving Greek settlement purchased a statue of Praxiteles' own handiwork for the embellishment of their town. Quite recently Professor S. Zusser has unearthed in Olbia more than 150 beautiful tombs dating from the period above referred to. They are in an almost perfect state of preservation. Coins, bracelets, earrings and trinkets of

The Scythian influences from the eighth century to the third century B.C. strongly swayed the Russian destinies. Well organized, with powerful armies under highly developed discipline, the Scyths eventually succeeded in subduing the majority of the various tribes between the Volga and the Danube, guaranteeing them peaceful economic development and every opportunity for disposing of their products and wares through the intermediary of the Greek colonies on the Black Sea. Their civilization was almost wholly eastern. Their religion was that of the Sun-worshippers of Iran. Their art was drawn from Central Asia. Their system of government was a despotic monarchy.

The Sarmatians followed the Scyths, and they brought but little change into the conditions of life in South Russia. The Greek influence, however, began to wane and its place was gradually taken by that of the awakening east.

In the third century A.D. the south of Russia was invaded by tribes of German stock. Their cultural level was considerably lower than that of the peoples conquered by them. They apparently developed nothing more than trade with the north and north-west, all Scandinavia and the north of Germany being induced to take advantage of the Dnieper route.

At the time of the first great folk-migrations the Huns overcame the German tribes, and South Russia became the main thoroughfare for the subsequent invasions. Fresh waves of eastern influences passed over South Russia. The so-called animal style in art, a development of purely eastern origin which flourished in China under the Chu dynasty, came into Russia about this period.

After the overthrow of the German tribes, South Russia did not long remain without masters. Ptolemy speaks of the Venetes, Slavenes and Antos, the undoubted forbears of the

---

every variety for personal adornment, as well as coloured pottery and wrought bronze and copper vessels and ornaments, all of exquisite workmanship, form a most interesting part of the treasure trove which incidentally includes a lady's fully equipped vanity bag.

The so-called filigree work in jewellery, for which Greece was famous at this time, was subsequently taken up and almost completely monopolized by Slav Russia.

Russian Slavs. At first they joined their lot with that of the Goths, but did not move on westwards with the latter. The settlement of these Slav tribes on the Russian Plain starts from the fifth century A.D. Everywhere they took the place of the more adventurous Goths, ever seeking fresh fields. The old trade routes now fell into their hands.

Slav Settlements.—The Slav race identified itself with the soil and with the political and economic development of the country. It took deep root along the Dnieper, advanced far on the east and the south, and stoutly defended its independence against new hordes of conquerors (*e.g.* the Avars). When the migratory fever began to abate in the south of Russia and tranquility was somewhat restored, the old civilization began to revive and the old trade routes were re-opened. In these conditions, not casually, not suddenly, the great trading state of Kiev came into existence.

The epoch just referred to has not yet been sufficiently examined and studied to enable us to get an accurate picture of the old Russian Slavs, and to measure with greater precision the varying degrees of the cultural influences which moulded their lives. This much, however, we can ascertain beyond doubt, that Russian civilization has not sprung from a desert soil, that it has had its period of antiquity and that it was of a composite type.

In the light of recent investigation in ancient Russian history we may distinguish in the ninth century A.D. three chief centres of cultural life in Russia : (1) Novgorod in the north-west, (2) Kiev in the south-west, and (3) Tmutarakan in the south-east. Of all these three centres, each politically independent of the other, each with distinctly differing neighbours, each living in different cultural economic and political conditions, it is only of Kiev and Novgorod that we can speak with a greater degree of knowledge.

Influence of Byzantium and the East.—So far as we know, the only common interests connecting these centres were religion, which brought in its wake the Byzantine culture, and trade which, while it gave greater scope to Byzantine influences, brought in its wake a strong Persian-Arabian influence. During this period of the Slav settlements on the

Great Plain the western European civilization which had been
almost completely destroyed in the fourth century barely
survived. It was the same in the towns with trade and
commerce. In this epoch, from the fourth century to the
eleventh century A.D., the old eastern civilization came to
its fullest expansion, as witness China and India and the
remarkable period of cultural and economic activity in
Byzantium, the Near East, Persia-Arabia, etc. Through Arabia
passed all the more important lines of communication between
west and east.

The Arabian world had then attained to something like
the unity now represented by the European world with its
enormous means of communication. It came into close contact
with the Great Northern Plain and embraced the Caucasus
(Georgia, Armenia and Azerbaijan) and the eastern shores of
the Caspian Sea. The Black Sea remained Byzantine.

From the fifth century A.D. the Greek settlements on
the shores of the Black Sea which had been destroyed by
nomadic incursions assumed a Byzantine type. Thenceforward,
especially from the seventh century when the Slavs entered
into direct trade relations with Byzantium, Russia seemed to
succumb to the infection of the Byzantine influence which soon
took the upper hand. It was not decadent, not a mere hybrid
Greco-Roman culture. In the light of recent research it now
stands out revealed as : " l'une des plus brillantes que le
moyen âge ait connue, et peut-être la seule civilisation qu'ait
vraiment connue l'Europe entre la fin du cinquième et le
commencement du onzième siècle " (*Diehl*).

In the making of the Byzantine culture full advantage was
taken of the triumphant progress of Christianity as well as of
the reviving spirit of eastern culture in its endeavour to
counter the supremacy of Greek influences. " In this very
mingling of two different influences, of two opposing traditions,
is to be found the mark of identity of the Byzantine civilisation " (*Diehl*). Indeed the most characteristic feature of
Byzantine History is its constant indebtedness to eastern
influences. The form of its government was absolute
monarchy, highly centralized and bureaucratic. The State
ruled the Church. Religion and art drew their inspiration

from the east. By contrast with the chaotic conditions holding in the feudal west the Byzantine state was admirably ordered. Its culture was attractive. Its towns, its trade, its movement of ideas were instinct with life.

Kiev State.—The Russian Slavs found themselves at the very centre of these cultural reactions, at the starting point of the great trade routes of the old world. The exceptionally favourable conditions soon showed results. The Slavs applied themselves earnestly and vigorously to commercial activities. They settled along the river routes linking the Black to the Baltic Sea. On the Great Plain at this time but scarcely populated and hardly touched by the plough-share, they created a great Russian dominion based on the commerce of the towns.

The fortuitous success of this almost purely foreign trade fed on the brief flame of the Kiev State (ninth—eleventh century A.D.) which on the loss of this trade soon became impoverished. Meanwhile, under the reaction of all these cultural forces and influences there arose a distinct, self-evolved Russian culture. Chronicles, legends and works of foreign travellers testify to the particular love of Russians for ornament, to the beauty of their everyday surroundings, of their arts, of their crafts. If the Kiev State was a willing captive of the Byzantine civilization in respect of religion, art, literature, education, even of dress, we yet meet further north-east in Novgorod and later in Vladimir-Suzdal with a remarkable originality and striving for self-expression when we investigate the earliest evidences of civilization in these two centres. " Byzantine art in painting, ornament and especially in architecture is undoubtedly the first inspiration here, the *point de départ*. The beauty and artistic finish of the Novgorod and Pskov architectural monuments created by primitive yet really great builders have strongly influenced all subsequent phases of Russian architectural development " (*Grabar*). Russian jewellery and carving were particularly prized in the Byzantine world of the twelfth century. The extraordinary perfection of detail attained at the same time in needlework with various kinds of silks may be noted as a creation of the Russian women. Indeed, at a period when one after another primitive forms of political and economic life were being built up under the greatest culture. Chaadaev, one of the most stimulating of Russian thinkers, considered that it was owing to corrupt Byzantium that Russia stood away from Europe and risked becoming fixed in a sort of Chinese immobility ; that it was through the fault of Byzantium with its narrow formalism that the living force of her great Christian ideals was cut at the very root.

The remarkable likeness we may observe between the Moscow State and Asiatic despotism is often traced to natural conditions just as the backwardness of Russia *vis-à-vis* of western civilization has been ascribed to the corrupting and destructive influence of Byzantium. But now that the significance and value of the Byzantine culture are placed before us in a clearer light, and that we are enabled to picture in greater detail the whole past of early Russian history, we realise that these explanations are not satisfactory and that the arrest of Russian progress must be sought rather in the historical and cultural setting of Russia after the Tartar invasion from the middle of the thirteenth century. About this time we may note great changes in the relative importance and influence of the civilizations of the east and of the west.

The civilization to which Byzantium was so much indebted was on the decline. China and India were the first affected. The great Arabian State followed next in the eleventh century A.D. In the twelfth century came the turn of Byzantium.

Western Influence.—Almost contemporaneously may be noted a revival, a renewal of western civilization. In the eleventh century it had penetrated into the territories lying beyond the German sway. In the twelfth century all the Mediterranean trade was centred in Italian towns and settlements. And at this period the influence of the west asserted its supremacy in Poland, Finland and among the Baltic peoples. Gradually it made its way to Russia. Western Europe was now the world centre of civilization. Kiev and Novgorod were trading with the west more than with Byzantium and the east. From the second half of the twelfth century could be met in Vladimir and Suzdal " craftsmen from all countries." A distinct Italian influence was at work, especially in architecture. Still earlier western culture had penetrated to Pskov and Novgorod which soon adopted the north Roman style.

But all these western influences did not at once succeed in ousting the already widely-spread influences of the east and Byzantium. The ground, however, was favourable, all the more so perhaps because of its previous cultivation by the Greeks. Indeed, we have every reason for believing that Russia would surely have been drawn within the sphere of western European civilization had not the course of events from the beginning of the thirteenth century changed the destinies of Russia and interrupted its cultural and political development. We refer to the terrible Tartar invasion whose repercussion on the west at the period when the old civilization of the east was almost completely swept away, dwarfs the events of the great folk-migrations into comparative insignificance.

Tartar Invasion.—The Mongolian hordes ravaged all Asia and eastern Europe, levelling towns, peoples and civilizations on their way. The west of Europe also would have shared the fate of the conquered had not these hordes exhausted their strength in the boundless steppes and plains of the east. A deadly blow, however, had been dealt to all the cultures of the east. The Near Asian civilization was almost completely destroyed. That of India and China took many centuries to recover.

The Tartar invasion was not a mere incursion of wild nomadic peoples. For centuries these tribes had been influenced by the civilization of China whence they borrowed not only their military and civil organization, but their elaborate bureaucratic methods of finance and assessment. Their army was the best equipped and disciplined and the most efficient of that time. They turned terror into a regular system which they made use of not only for military, but for administrative purposes. It was only by a system of ruthless repression and by the enforcement of slavery that they succeeded in completely disarming their enemies. They next proceeded to a regular census of the subject populations and to a methodical exaction of levies and contributions. Native princes were generally appointed tax gatherers. That the comparatively small numbers of these Tartar hordes were able for so many years to maintain their hold over Asia and eastern Europe is owing not only to the iron discipline of their armed forces with its strict and

deadening formalism, but to the efficiency of their financial
administration.

The Tartar conquest had an immense influence on the future
of Russia. It may well be said that the destiny of Russia was
decided in 1238 when she became an integral portion of the
great Mongol State, when in every sense she was one with the
ravaged east, when she was definitely cut off from western
Europe, which was now becoming the centre of world civilization. South Russia was a devastated area. In south-west
Russia after the collapse of the Kiev State civilized life revived
in Galich-Volhynia. Escaping from the Tartar yoke this part
of Russia formed for a while an independent Lithuanian
state.[1] The centre of Russian political and cultural life
was eventually shifted to the north-east—Vladimir Suzdal
and later Moscow—to the remotest corner from western
Europe of the great Plain where natural conditions were
particularly severe and trying.

Results.—The old lines of development were rudely altered
under the Tartar yoke. A definite stamp marked every
expression of life, every form of social and political organization. Former ideals had not indeed utterly perished. The
great promise of the earlier efforts and productions of Russian
art was fulfilled, and in one century we behold examples of
craftsmanship, no mere accidental instances, but ripe fruit
of a well-rooted growth, rivalling at times the art of the Italian
Primitives in beauty. But in the Ikons of the Moscow period
we no longer find that perfection of the Novgorod art with its
strength of colouring and its artistic apprehension, its elegant
simplicity of composition, its rhythmic lines and its general
feeling of grand art. The eastern influences already on the
wane began to take hold of Russian art. The Novgorod,
Vladimir and Moscow traditions degenerated and died out.

Russia had gradually become Christian and " was now being
transformed into ' Holy Russia,' the land . . . . . of
never-ending bell-ringing, of protracted fasts, of heads

---

[1] Later when the Poles entered into possession of the Lithuanian
territories and spread their influence over all south and south-western
Russia the problem of reuniting these lost territories was the chief
inspiration of Russian policy in the west.

devoutly bowing to the very ground."[1] This is the general impression one gleans from the observations of travellers to Muscovy, as Russia was then known, during the sixteenth and seventeenth centuries. The Church soon gave signs of becoming petrified by formalism, by an uncompromising nationalism, by intolerance, and by its too willing dependence on the State.

The Mongol yoke broke the back of this cultural life in Russia. During two-and-a-half centuries of Tartar oppression the intellectual and moral level of the Russian people was debased, their spiritual growth arrested, stunted and distorted. From being a country where the towns played a great rôle, Russia now became a loose aggregation of straggling villages attached to huge landed properties and unwieldy principalities. The peasants' loss was the prince's gain. The Moscow prince, trained in the Tartar school of politics and administration, dexterously exploited his position as tax gatherer, and gradually obtained complete mastery over his scattered possessions, grouped all the Russian territories under his dominion and established the formidable Muscovite State. The Muscovite ruler became an oriental despot, an absolute autocrat, moulding the rough material at his hand into an ordered state, holding it together by a strong bureaucracy. The Mongol yoke was chiefly instrumental in bringing about the complete enslavement of the Russian people.

Moscow Principality, 1280-1462.—By its geographical position Moscow was particularly favoured among the principalities of the north of Russia. Its central situation protected it against hostile assaults from all sides. The neighbouring principalities of Riazan, Smolensk, Rostov and Yaroslav were much more open to attack. The Moscow river connected the basins of the rivers Oka and Volga. It was at that time an important trade artery. The Moscow princes looked on the Tartar yoke in a light different from the other Russian princes. They did not think of armed resistance, but found it more advantageous to play a submissive rôle for the time being and to make the most of their opportunities. In this way the Khan eventually became an unconscious instrument of their own home policy. For his action in the

[1] P. N. Miliukov.

suppression of the Tver rebellion against the Khan the Moscow
prince " received " the Grand Ducal dignity in 1328. From
this time North Russia began to breathe more freely as the
Tartar oppression lessened. The Moscow Grand Dukes showed
themselves capable and clever masters at home. Their
political successes were consecrated in the popular mind by
the approval and blessing of the highest religious authority in
Russia which had acquired its own independence by means
very similar to those of the Grand Duke with the Khan.
Moscow became the religious metropolis and the seat of the
Metropolitan of Russia long before it became the capital.
Another fact to note is that elements of various ethnic origins
previously distinct now began to combine in one national
whole. They formed a solid compact mass, the Great Russian
block—Slavs with a considerable admixture of Finnish blood.
Born, bred and formed in conditions of constant danger from
outside they felt the need of a strong, centralized state power.
As soon as the people realized this the task of the Moscow
Grand Duke was easy.

   Moscow State, 1462-1598.—Muscovite Russia was now
passing through the difficult period of state formation. Cut
off from the cultural life of western Europe and completely
thrown back on her own resources, she awoke to a realization
of her powers. She prepared for a great rôle.

   From the second half of the fifteenth century the gathering
of Russian territories under the rule of Moscow became a
national-religious movement, a movement which was considerably accelerated by the gravitation to Moscow of many different
forces, social, religious and political. Territorial expansion
reacted significantly on the Muscovite policy. The great
Russian population now formed a political whole. The
Moscow principality alone survived among its fellows and now
became a national State. The Muscovite ruler realized the
growing importance not only of his possessions but of his
dignity. By the marriage of Ivan III with Sophia Paleologue,
the niece of the last Byzantine Emperor, Moscow was deemed
the successor of Byzantium, the second Rome. Moscow
must be the third Rome holding unsullied the truth of the
infallible Orthodox faith. There lay the Byzantine example

of an organized state. It was worth emulating. Muscovite Russia adopted the stately ceremonial, the sumptuous apparel of the Byzantine Court, as also the armorial insignia of the two-headed eagle. A proud national self-consciousness asserted itself as well as an ever-growing conviction of the inferiority of all other nations and a constant suspicion of all foreign influences.

The Muscovite rulers now set themselves to the task of assembling and putting together the material for their construction, of extending their domain and their dominion. Military colonies were established in the southern parts of Russia, and a penetration of many thousand miles to the east was made to Siberia. This penetration into the northern forests, the southern steppes and especially the Siberian plains, was very characteristic. From its start, just as in the earliest period of Slav historical life, it was a popular, spontaneous movement. The State hardly did more than follow up this popular wave. Towards the end of the seventeenth century Russian settlements had been made all over Siberia, even as far as the Pacific Ocean.

The terrible hardships endured by the masses of the people during the formation and establishment of the Muscovite power had driven them inevitably to such ways of escape. Many were urged no doubt by a spirit of enterprise and the call of the unknown. But the majority fled from famine, religious persecution, merciless government exactions and impositions, and from the strangle-hold of serfdom. No real effort, however, was made to advance to the seas or to control the great trade routes. The State absorbed in extending its territory and enforcing its authority needs men and money. It obtained these by temporary and conditional grants of populous territories to a military class.

Up to the end of the fifteenth century the State took but little interest in the relations existing between these newly appointed landholders and the peasantry. As to the latter, their relations with the State began and ended with the payment of taxes. The peasants themselves through their primitive communal system (sometimes called the *Mir*) organized settlement on the land, and were responsible not only for their own and for the

Trouble gave way and the State machinery was smashed, local connections and activities began to gain strength. The weakening of State power and at times its absence led to the strengthening of the influence of various social elements. Even in the sixteenth century the State power at times had recourse to an advisory body composed of : (1) the Boyar Duma, the permanent Council of State ; (2) the convocation of the higher clergy under the Metropolitan, the permanent organ for the Church and (3) of a group of local representatives (*Zemski*)— military men, landlords, officials and traders, all nominated by the Government. The growth of the State, the need of order and the problem of administration led to the summoning of such advisory institutions. They were called Zemski Sobors. But from the Troublous Time, not only the composition, but the rights and the range of activities and significance of the Zemski Sobors were changed. This third group, from being nominated by the State, became elective. In it we now see representatives of the peasantry. The Zemski Sobors acquired legislative rights. They elected Tsars, etc. (1598, Boris Godunov ; 1613, Michael Romanov ; and the Patriarch, 1619). They confirmed the right of the heir to occupy the throne (Alexei, 1645), and arrived at important decisions together with the Tsar and the Government. But as soon as ever the Tsar's power strengthened, the authority of the Zemski Sobors diminished. From 1653 they lost all significance. But in connection with general revival of national consciousness in the " Troublous Time " and in first years of the rule of the first two Romanovs, the Sobors did good work in educating the Russian people to a realization of their common interest and mutual interdependence, the understanding of the State affairs as a people's affairs. During the Trouble contact with the foreigner was constant and general. The intercourse with various foreigners resulted in some acquisitions of European military, technical and other knowledge. The spiritual and intellectual influences were considerable. Under these influences there was an exchange of outlooks on life. New European dress, Latin and Polish books, new religious and political ideas, now enter into Russian life. The loss of the Novgorod districts and the Baltic Sea determined the future foreign policy of Moscow.

Contacts with the West.—In the seventeenth century this vast agricultural state had no more than 250 towns, and notwithstanding the energetic measures adopted by the government to induce traders and artisans of all kinds to come to these centres the town population hardly amounted to more than two-and-a-half per cent of the whole nation. Internal trade was in a lamentable condition. Foreign trade could hardly be said to exist. Poland and the Livonian States fearing that Russia might draw on western Europe for war material, instructors and skilled labour were constantly on the look-out to prevent such relations from developing. They dreaded in their own interest the Europeanization of Russia. The Livonians closed the outlet to the Baltic Sea for the Moscow and Novgorod traders and did not allow them " to trade direct in their land with overseas peoples without suffering trouble." Against this enforced restriction of Russian trade and of free access to the sea Ivan the Terrible in 1558 had recourse to arms (the Livonian war).

The attitude of the Muscovite rulers towards foreigners was typically Asiatic : " to make use of the stranger in order to . . . send him to the devil." Ivan the Terrible in granting to the English Company free of all taxes and duties trading rights which he then withdrew, acted on this principle.

The old merchant community before the advent of Peter the Great were much perturbed in devising means for ridding the commercial centres within Russia of foreign traders, in securing that " as our Russian folk know nothing about the wares of these strangers, so also the latter should know nothing of our own products." Kilburger, a Swede, thus writes in 1674 : " It seems to me that for some inscrutable reason God Almighty still conceals from the Russian intelligence the great advantages that would accrue to this land from its being opened up to foreign trade."

The economic structure dating from the Kiev-Novgorod trade era was thus quite altered. A psychological change in the nature of the people took place. The old spirit of enterprise and initiative, and of Russian sociability, tended to disappear. Two worlds now met face to face as almost complete strangers, and even hostile to one another.

national unity had been achieved. Natural, historical and cultural conditions had moulded its forms and determined its character. Let us summarize results at this point.

(1) Of Aryan stock like the rest of European peoples, the Slavs from the very beginnings of their historical existence had been in contact with other European races and under the influence of western civilization. But at the very period when the peoples of the west were founding their historical existence on sites of ancient Roman culture, extending their contacts and strengthening their hold by blood admixture, the Slavs were cut off from such contacts. It was chiefly through Byzantium that they had accepted western civilization. But the Byzantine civilization was itself a very mixed one, strongly under the influence of the east. At the same time we should bear in mind that from the earliest period the cultures of the east had considerably influenced the Slavs on the Great Russian Plain. (2) The adoption of Christianity by the Slavs definitely linked them to the west, and severed them from the pagan and Mahometan east. But in taking Christianity from Byzantium, the Russian Slavs at the same time imbibed and assimilated prejudices peculiar to the Eastern Church, chief among which was an intense aversion to Latin Christianity and all that followed from it, a feeling at times engendering the bitterest hatred. Such an attitude created obstacles to the penetration of western civilization into Russia. The foremost influence of the Latin Church in the development of western civilization could not be forgotten. The Byzantine conception of the Church's dependence on the State was incompatible with that of Rome. Moreover, Byzantine Christianity had been very much under eastern and Asiatic religious influences, and from the time of the Tartar yoke when Russia was thrown on her own resources, these influences not only left their mark on public worship, but determined the religious as well as the national psychology of the people. (3) The Great Northern Plain is a part of the European Continent. But whereas in the west such physical features as the extensive coast-line, river courses, mountain ranges, peninsulas, etc., formed natural boundaries between distinct races, limited their territories and thus helped on the rapid formation of various States, in the east there were

too few natural frontiers and lines of demarcation to hold back the expansion of the population over neighbouring lands. The ordered life of a State had to be organized over an immense territory. Contacts with the west were difficult to establish. The east offered greater attractions. The severity of climatic conditions made great calls on the Russian's energy and endurance and brought out those characteristic traits of the Russian mentality, unquestioning submission to the inevitable, unlimited patience in the face of *force majeure*, imperturbable indifference to outward changes. (4) From the very start the Slavs settled on the Great Plain were in constant conflict with Asiatic nomads. The whole history of Kiev Russia is taken up with these incessant struggles. They brought about the fall of the Kiev State. The centre of political and cultural life was moved north-eastwards, to the sterner and climatically harsher setting of Suzdal-Vladimir and, later, of Moscow. The Tartar Invasion, however, dealt a deadly blow to a carefully built up structure of political and cultural development. The Lithuanians, and later the Poles, swayed the destinies of western and southern Russia for many centuries. North-east Russia had to construct its life anew. (5) The peculiar character of this structure should be noted. Self-governing towns with their Veche institutions, with their military forces under foreign princes, gradually combine to form a State whose organization develops at their expense. (6) The Tartar domination determined the form of state structure and altered the old conditions of sturdy local independence. Russia now became a country of villages ruled by a despotic Tsar. Russia was now definitely cut off from the west, but at the same time she was the sole defence of Europe against the barbarians of the east. Notwithstanding the effects of the Tartar domination on life and thought, the Russian people preserved a European type with their religion and their language and helped on the spread of western civilization to a certain extent eastwards. In the struggle of two-and-a-half centuries against the Tartar oppression from the east, before the menace of the foe on the west, amid the rigours of a severe climate, the State power of Muscovite Russia became more and more absolute. (7) The break-up of the Tartar domination brought forward which the State had hitherto taught them to reverence, and inculcated as inviolable truths and sacred traditions.

The Church.—We know that the great strength of the Russian Church in the sixteenth century lay in the conviction of its right, in the consciousness of its integrity. Thence had arisen that proud confidence in the historic world mission of Russian Orthodoxy. Even before Peter the Great it had become evident that the Church was less concerned with the question of the preservation of ancient traditions, and was more and more preoccupied with the development of a new religious idea on national lines.

In the eyes of the official Church such a movement betokened a deviation from the more regular path that should be followed by Orthodoxy. This it was that led to the divergences between the State and the popular worship. Under the Patriarch Nikon (1653-67) a reform of the liturgy and of ritual details had been introduced more in accordance with Greek originals and models. This at once led to the Raskol or Schism of the Old Believers (Old Ritualists) opposed to any alterations or emendations of the Church's traditional forms.[1] In the person of the Protopope Avvakum, Nikon found a fierce and tireless antagonist, and the Schism a passionate, single-minded leader.[2]

It would be unjust to trace this movement to undiscriminating conservatism or superstition. Religion is inseparably bound up with the texts and rites on which it is based. " The reforms of Nikon having a purely ritual character were interpreted as encroaching on the grounds of faith itself " (*Melgunov*). A no less important factor in this movement was the general dissatisfaction with the growing centralization in the administration of the Russian Orthodox Church.[3] The Heresies, usually grouped by Russians under the term Sektantstvo, were especially noticeable among the simpler elements of the population from the eighteenth century. They showed

[1] The Raskolniki were anathematized in 1656.

[2] *The Life of the Archpriest Avvakum, by Himself.*—(Hogarth Press, London, 1924.)

[3] The number of Old Believers in the sixties of the nineteenth century was about fifteen millions. The number would now be nearer twenty-five millions. The Old Believers have branched off in various directions.

originality of religious thought and forms influenced from the east and from the west. Even as early as the seventeenth century problems of social unrest inspired many of the Sectant movements. The great religious movement in Germany moreover had not passed unheeded in Russia, and the rationalistic " heresy " attracted many minds.[1]

Peter the Great ably exploited the predicament of the Church and completed the process of securing its absolute dependence on the State. By the establishment of the Holy Synod under the presidency of a lay government official styled the Procurator, the Church was transformed into a State administration. The clergy became a special class of State officials to whom was confided the moral and spiritual guardian- ship of the people. This nationalization of the Church structure, the transformation of the higher ecclesiastical governing body into an organ of the State, this transfer of outward authority, could be effected without particular hurt to the rights of the Church and of its dogmas. For the Catholic and Protestant Churches the question of ecclesiastical administration is fundamental, for behind this lies concealed another question, viz.: Where is to be found the highest authority either in the matter of development of Christian dogmas or in that of doctrine ? For the Greek Orthodox Church as also for the Russian Church such a question could not arise. In the eyes of the Orthodox believer the treasury of the Church is sufficiently full. The spiritual content of Christianity is complete and its soundness is guaranteed by the seven General Councils whose decisions are irrevocable and binding on all Christians. The supreme ecclesiastical

[1] Among the better-known Russian Sects are : (1) the *Beguni* (Runners) for whom the world was permeated with evil. They looked on Tsardom as the Apocalyptic beast. Only by ceaseless wandering could one escape from sin and evil—" leave town, village, house," was their guiding principle ; (2) *Khlysti* (flagellants) who reject all Church rites and authority. Man himself is " a living Church," and the Holy Ghost dwells in every deserving one. The body must be cleansed and purified, sinful desires uprooted ; (3) *Skoptsi* who practise self-mutila- tion, an extreme development of the previous sect ; (4) *Dukhobori* (soul-wrestlers), offspring of the Khlysti abandoning the asceticism of the latter became prominent in the nineteenth century ; (5) *Molokanie* an Evangelical sect.

the west. However, it was only the higher strata of Russian
society which were immediately affected. A new outlook, new
forms and expressions of life and of thought were created.
New tastes and needs arose, unknown in the not-so-distant
past and in sharp contrast with the needs and tastes of the
rest of the people.

The Peasantry.—The peasantry, reduced to serfdom, were
but little touched by these influences. This class was more
than ever the dumb patient of the tax collector and recruiting
agent. During the reign of Peter the fiscal burdens increased
almost fourfold. As far as the peasantry were concerned,
the westernizing process expressed itself first and foremost in
Peter's attempt on the Swedish model—an attempt which was
attended with but little success—to introduce a system of
individual taxation and to levy men for the army and navy.
These burdens increased after Peter's reign and became
almost unbearable. According to official statistics the number
of peasants escaping from taxation was about 200,000 from
1719 to 1727. From 1727 to 1736 this number more than
doubled. The means and methods employed for exacting the
fulfilment of these obligations were ruthless. State Commissars
accompanied by military forces, for whose maintenance the
local peasantry were responsible, inaugurated a systematic
terror on all sides. In 1731 the State found it advisable to
withdraw these Commissars and to leave the immediate
responsibility for the collection of taxes and for the raising
of levies in the hands of the local landed proprietors. In this
way the peasant was now definitely placed under the absolute
and arbitrary power of his landlord.[1] From this period the
abuses of serfdom are particularly noticeable : corporal
punishment ; sale and barter of peasants as ordinary goods
and chattels, family ties and relations being of no account ;
penal servitude and exile to Siberia for any crime, etc., etc.
The Senate about this time, in giving its reasons for certain
decisions taken with respect to these serfs, argued that it was

[1] In 1858, two-fifths of the peasantry were landowners' serfs. The
remaining three-fifths consisted of State peasants, Cossacks, Free
Settlers, Colonists, etc., who did not bear the full measure of the serfs'
burdens.

guided by the desire of "discovering the easiest means of pleasing all the *pomeshchiki* (the landlords)." It was, however, considerably owing to these heavy burdens that the peasantry developed and perfected their primitive communal organization with the object of adjusting and apportioning them fairly among their members. The landowners responsible for the payment of taxes and the fulfilment of services by their serfs did not in their own interests take it on themselves to destroy the communal organization or to interfere overmuch in its working. And in regard to its own peasantry (the State peasantry), the State for a long time, owing to its lack of organization and to its ever-growing fiscal exigencies demanding immediate satisfaction, could not, and indeed found it better not to, deprive these of their freedom of action within their own organization.

Meanwhile, to satisfy their economic needs which began to increase noticeably from the second half of the eighteenth century, the peasantry relied on the products of their own home industry (*Kustarnoe Proizvodstvo*)[1] which they greatly developed. Climatic conditions and the financial needs, especially in the centre and north of Russia, favoured the development of what were in origin essentially side activities and additional occupations. On the one hand there was the enforced abstention from the labours of the field during eight months of the year ; on the other hand, the returns from agricultural work could not cover the heavy burdens of taxation.

Industry.—The factories established by Peter the Great— about 200—worked almost exclusively for the Government. Up to the reign of Catherine II, the Government favoured the system of Government monopolies. It looked on manufacture as a kind of service to the State, and at times visited laxity in this direction with severe penalties. Catherine II, however, put an end to this system, declaring that "private factories are a property which each one should be free to develop without

[1] In the Kustarny industry the populations of particular villages and districts specialized in distinctive forms of production according to local conditions. One district would take up boot-making, another would take up the making of wooden spoons and similar work. Clothes would be the speciality of one village, Ikons of another. Kust—shrub, bush.

special permission of the State." But her well-meant wish that " the private interest of each should be the best and most reliable incentive," long remained no more than an aspiration. The factories throve on Government orders, on serf labour, and on high protective tariffs. At the end of the eighteenth century their growth, according to contemporary observation, corresponded more with the multiple requirements of the army and navy than with those of the general consumer. Intellectually and spiritually the mass of the people lived their own life in their own way. Lay education could hardly be said to touch them. Even at the end of the eighteenth century for a population of 26,000,000 there were no more than a dozen village schools with an attendance of 300 pupils. Indeed, the total number of lay schools of every kind within the empire did not exceed 300 with less than 19,000 pupils.

Church and the People.—The Church was standing more and more away from the people. " Invested in the scholastic apparel of the middle ages Russian theology of the eighteenth century began to speak by imitation in a strange tongue, Latin, and in ceasing to be the possession of the people it became the property of a school."[1] Ministers of religion carried out their duties perfunctorily. " We were born, we were each of us christened in due form. We grew, we grew up, we grew old. All our lives we spent in going to Church. And what of it ? Let us speak the truth. We stood there utterly wearied, and like the rest could not understand that complicated, difficult book language especially in its rapid hastily-swallowed utterance. And thus millions of souls are led to God. . . . . How much better it would be for the people if hundreds were spent on explaining to us our own selves, the formation of the world and of God's Holy Word, instead of thousands being squandered on the erection of huge stone churches and on their splendid decoration."[2] These are the simple words of a Dukhobor from Ekaterinoslav, written in prison in the year 1791.

In such conditions, the creative genius of the people continued to nourish itself from the old sources, from the Russian epos which was carefully preserved for later transformation

[1] P. N. Miliukov.
[2] Declaration of the Ekaterinoslav Dukhobors, 1791.

and re-creation, or else it threw itself earnestly into the study
of Christian teaching and of its development. This self-
evolved spirit of religious inquiry sought the resolution of its
doubts in all directions, in the development of outward forms
and ceremonials, in the repudiation of the doctrine of grace,
even in ascetic self-denial carried to extremes.

Process of Westernization.—In the upper sections of Russian
society western culture during the whole of the eighteenth
century would seem to have been accepted merely passively,
and on the surface. Driven on at first by Peter's stout oak
stick, and later caught in the general stream of influences, the
upper classes endeavoured to copy the life of the European
Courts. Gilded ornament at times succeeded in concealing the
dirty, smoky walls of the Muscovite period. The Boyars of
yesterday decked out in court shoes, lace ruffles and French
wigs, did their best to emulate the exquisites of Versailles.
But even under this surface imitation a serious purpose could
be discerned. In giving up further resistance to westernization, in laying aside her old national pride Russia accepted the
new culture as being not only inevitable but indeed the best.
Yesterday was dead. A new day was at hand. So forgotten
were the high achievements of the old Russian painters that
even in our own days it is difficult to restore their neglected
works to their proper place in art. The beautiful old Ikon art
has had to be discovered anew.

It has been said that the imaginative, creative faculty of the
artist was held prisoner by the Church in Muscovite Russia.
The foundation of the Imperial Academy of Arts on the
western model opened up an epoch of even more bitter captivity,
introducing subjects of Greek mythology quite foreign to
Russian mind and thought. Notwithstanding all this, Russian
pupils showed themselves as capable as ever in a new school.
A great tradition had quite evidently not died out. At the end
of the eighteenth century Russian painting and architecture
were not below the western European level, as testify the works
of Levitski, Borovikovski, Kazakov and Bazhenov. This was
the period of the formation of a new literary language in
Russia. The old literary speech—that of the Church—soared
far beyond the ken of the ever changing popular dialects.

It was too stilted, too remote, too detached for the expression of living emotions and new ideas. The new literary language taking definite form towards the end of this century was nearer to the spoken language. It was now, moreover, the language of the average reading public which came into existence about this time. On the establishment of a clear-cut, comprehensible literary speech, literature found a good ground for closer contact with real life and for exerting an influence on the same. In other walks of life considerable activity was to be seen.

Catherine the Great.—From the time of Catherine II a lively interest in foreign politics was to be noted. The possibility of taking an active part in European affairs was not far from realization. A new self-reliance manifested itself. A new era was started in the foreign relations of Russia. The " colonization " policy took a great extension, and established a firm footing in the Caucasus. The settlement of the Lower Volga and Novorossyisk districts proceeded apace.

A revival in the economic life of the country arose about this time. As already indicated a distinct increase in the exchange of commodities and in home consumption was to be observed especially in the latter half of the eighteenth century. Import and export figures of 5,700,000 roubles and 6,900,000 roubles respectively in 1750, were already 50,000,000 roubles and 65,000,000 roubles respectively at the end of this century. It was by the imposition of high protective tariffs and by similar artificial means that the Government was enabled to maintain a favourable balance for the country.

Although, notwithstanding the Government efforts, Russia still continued to be a purely agricultural State with a town population hardly amounting to 4 per cent of the total population, still a fairly considerable development of industrial activity in the reign of Catherine II gave occasion for growing antagonism between industry and the landed interests. Traders and artisans were beginning to realize the necessity of looking after their own concerns, " striving for freedom " as Catherine expressed it. It is easy to understand this striving at the time when Russia reached the highest point in the development of serfdom and privilege. The nobility were granted a considerable share in the provincial government system, in the control of the police and in the administration of justice. A privileged class thus gradually gained ground. Diderot when visiting Russia in Catherine II's reign, was surprised, notwithstanding his slight acquaintance with the country, at the evident lack of organic cohesion in this great empire, at the startling contrast between enlightened rule and arbitrary government where personal freedom meant nothing, at the splendour of palaces surrounded by wildernesses, at the strong power absorbed in schemes of conquest, at the impassive, silent serfdom of the masses whose distrust and reserve were the result of long standing oppression.

End of a Century.—This glaring contrast was bound to lead to reaction. The mute slavery of the peasantry at length found voice in the Pugachev risings and in the Pugachev manifestos demanding freedom and a share in the land. This movement was a direct outcome of centuries-old peasant repression, and was the first definite expression of a rising social and political consciousness among the people. The contrast created a new, more critical attitude towards life in the more cultured circles. It brought about a severance between the most representative elements of these circles and the Government. The pioneers of the borrowed culture had relied too confidently on its utilitarian, mechanical character. The younger generation, however, was more absorbed in the development of ideas coming from the west than in their mere technical application to practical needs. But at the same time it failed to recognize the connection between the advanced ideas of the time and the real setting of Russian life with its particular problems. The glaring contradiction between the reality and the ideal, between the Russian religious outlook and the French intellectual movement after 1754, began to trouble the finer minds. Freemasonry tried to find a basis of reconciliation between these opposites. It offered a faith enlightened by reason and a convenient formula for uniting all intellectual forces on the ground of a common idealism. Freemasonry had a great significance in the history of social development in Russia. It took the form of a private society concerned with social problems, strong in its convictions and its influence.

From the last decades of the eighteenth century may be said to start that unbroken continuity of intellectual activity we associate with the " Intelligentsia " movement, essentially a critical and independent attitude towards all practical applications in social and political movements. The Intelligentsia stood out against that evil of many heads, serfdom, where might was the only right. In the period of Catherine II's militant policy it protested against wars of aggression. It was especially in cultural and educational activities that it endeavoured to find an outlet for its energies. These activities, however, were confined within a limited circle of the progressive Russian Intelligentsia. Among the social and educated *milieus* nationalistic tendencies had a greater influence than the latest advanced political and philosophical ideas. The State did everything in its power to plant and extend its own political concepts and to encourage their growth in this field.[1]

The outward growth of the State and of its prestige coupled with the increasing power within, offered a good basis for the development of this nationalistic movement. The lack of adjustment of the borrowed culture to the prevalent conditions, the artificiality and even distorted character of its manifestations at times could not help provoking comparison and compelling reflection. It led to a genuine endeavour to strengthen the national basis and to justify the old traditions. Such essentially are the phenomena to be noted in Russian life during the eighteenth century as resulting from the sharp change brought about by Peter the Great. The interests of the State continued to push all other considerations aside. Every individual was looked on as being under the guardianship of the State, as its docile, obedient servant. Gradually, however, under the political and philosophic influences from the west of Europe, a new movement of ideas began to stir the Russian conscience.

The Intelligentsia and Western Influences.—In the first half of the nineteenth century the spread of western culture was

[1] Catherine with the characteristic zeal of the " new " Russian gives the tone here and expresses it vehemently. For instance, she is deeply interested in demonstrating that " the ancient Russian Slavs had given the names to the majority of the rivers, valleys and plains in France, Scotland and other countries."

already more deeply felt. It captured larger sections of Russian society. The extension of the frontiers, the establishment of relations and the strengthening of influence with foreign states, the Napoleonic wars and the triumphant march through Europe, all these things brought about a closer contact and more intimate acquaintance with western culture on the part of a widening circle of Russians.

Russian thinkers were deeply concerned with the question of the destiny of Russia and of her national welfare. The problem of Russia and the west became a growing pre-occupation. Serfdom on the one hand and lawlessness on the other engendered among the Intelligentsia a great compassion and love for the weaker brother, even a combative spirit. Forming gradually into what seemed to be a special class, it had, however, no class interest. Developing in some sort as an " order " it asked no more than to give of its best to the service of humanity and justice and to the promotion of higher ideals. This trait of idealism was to be found in all the activities of the Russian Intelligentsia. When at one time the liberal bourgeoisie of France inscribed a definite principle on their banner they were actuated by the desire of securing a definite recognition of their own rights. On the other hand the Russian Intelligentsia started forth with the distinct object of securing the unqualified recognition of principles and ideals on their own merits. It stood up as the defender of the rights of others.

Dekabrists.—A number of years spent by the Russian forces in direct contact with peoples who had grown up under the influence of the ideas of the French Revolution, in new social conditions and new forms of political institutions, were bound to leave an impression on the Russian mind. What did Russian officers find on arriving home ? Absolute contempt for the idea of the rights of man, serfdom firmly established, education and the press almost non-existent or existing only for the very few. " We spilled our blood for our country and now we are again forced to toil and sweat for our task masters ! We freed our country from the tyrant and yet our own despots oppress us," wrote one of these (*Alexander Bestuzhev*) reflecting the opinion of many. The impossibility of taking any open part in political activities led to the creation of " circles " and secret societies formed by men of advanced liberal ideas. The Union of Salvation formed in 1816, was broken up later into the Northern Union and the Southern Union. These were followed by the Union of Federated Slavs. The secret societies aimed at introducing radical alterations in the form of Government. The abolition of existing privileges, the liberation of the serfs, the securing of independent justice and of equality before the law, the mitigation of the rigorous military service were among the immediate objects of their policy. The officers of the Guards and the educated nobles who formed these secret societies were prepared to realize their objects by active means. On the death of Alexander I, who left no children, they attempted a *coup d'état*. Some Guards regiments appeared on the Senate Square in Petersburg on December 14, 1825, and demanded the grant of a constitution. This " Dekabrist " rising as it was called was summarily crushed. Many of the conspirators had foreseen its failure from the start but were convinced of the need of a " shaking up." " We shall give a lesson to others by our failure." They had acted quite openly, relying on general sympathy and support. Their hopes and their calculations were not justified. High idealism and a conviction that only self-sacrifice could benefit the Russian people urged them on to action. This characteristic of the Intelligentsia became more definitely pronounced later, in the second half of the nineteenth century.

Even here during the " fixing " process of the Slavophil and Westernizing ideas, the Russian Intelligentsia was anchored to theories and principles.[1] This theoretical " mise au point " of a problem led to the affirmation by the Slavophils of the originality and distinctiveness of Russian spiritual and economic development, and to the efforts they made to protect it from westernization. It also brought about the idealization of the old Muscovite Russia. On the other hand, it led to the affirmation by the " westerners " that the paths of Russian development were in no wise to be distinguished from those of the

---

[1] " This is the sin of the Slavophils that we understood neither the Russian people nor their history. Their Ikonlike ideals and the smoke of incense prevented us from beholding the real life of the people and the foundations of their social structures " (Herzen).

west, and that Russia should pass through all the stages of western experience from the very beginning. Later we shall see how these two divergent tendencies affected the Russian political and social movement. But if the tentative efforts in these directions but feebly translated the will and aims of the country, we must attribute their failure to the fact that the real needs of the country and of the people lay in a very different direction and were to be found where the amazing contradictions between the social structure and the " constitutional " edifice had not yet been fully realized.

State Structure.—Arbitrary administration, serfdom, lack of independent justice, of self-government, of elementary civil rights and of law, and of schools, in a country which was more and more being drawn into international life and into closer contact with the west, all these things were impossible. Hardly any progress was to be observed in the building up of the State within. The latter was too absorbed in enforcing and confirming its absolute sway. It led to that Asiatic half-slavish attitude of State officials to the Tsar and to his primitively patriarchal attitude to them. A minister became " le grand domestique."

To Paul I's sick mind came the thought of liquidating all State institutions, of concentrating all the State administration in his own hands. Besides all this, political plans and military aims as before overbore all other considerations. Any other problems took a back place.

Military requirements continued to be the chief concern of the State. At the death of Peter the Great, the army numbered 200,000. At the time of the Turkish War (1787–91) it numbered 400,000. In the Napoleonic period it numbered 800,000. At the time of the Crimean War this number was already 1,600,000.

Economic Life.—Military resources and means quite evidently continued to be the State's first and chiefest need. Military expenditure was the basic calculation in all government schemes. Although the internal trade and commerce steadily increased, it suffered very considerably up to the middle of the nineteenth century from the general lack of organization. The isolation of the local markets, the predominance of the Great Fairs system when at stated periods all flocked to particular centres, the unsatisfactory state of land and water communications, the lack of means of transport where caravan-like conditions for transit of merchandise prevailed, all these were unfavourable conditions for the development of trade. Access to the international money markets, the reform of the national money system, with the consequent improvement in credit, brought about, however, a revival of economic life. Foreign trade developed considerably, the import figures in the middle of this century attaining 131,500,000 roubles and the export 151,700,000 roubles. This progress may be explained by the fact that western Europe needed Russia's low-priced raw materials. The Russian Government was not behindhand, meanwhile, in extending its relations with other States by means of trading and shipping agreements.[1] It showed a great interest in developing trade with Asia, realizing that only there could it reckon on an extensive and constant market for its produce.[2]

But political, and especially fiscal motives were constantly upsetting more reasonable schemes for trade development. For example, as late as 1865 exports of corn, flax and hemp were heavily taxed. Fiscal considerations led to the granting of what was in effect a privileged position to " big industry " which had been artificially grafted on to the economic organism of Russia. This protection was given to an inconsiderable minority, and was at times a much too powerful brake on individual or corporate initiative among the mass of the people. For industrial enterprise and healthy trade it was indeed no more than the guardianship of particular interests.

Capitalistic Industry.—Big industry itself began to realise that its future depended considerably on the adaptation of production to mass consumption.

In this connection the most remarkable success was achieved by the textile industry which set out to meet directly the vast

[1] In 1828 Russia concluded a trade agreement with Sweden, in 1838 with the United States of America, and in 1842 with England.

[2] *N.B.*, the large plan of Alexander I for the great trade routes to the East and his effort to develop the Transcaucasian trade as a means for further trade penetration into Persian and Central Asia. In 1822 a trade agreement had been concluded with Persia, and a similar agreement with China was successfully carried through in 1852.

popular demand. The remarkable spread of the textile industry in Russia was immensely facilitated by this adaptation. Another not less important factor in this success was the large use of " free labour." The liberating struggle dating from the eighteenth century was making itself felt everywhere. In their own interest the industrialists strove to free themselves from Government intrusion and interference in their more intimate concerns, from the system of fiscal sops and grants, from the special privileges granted to nobles under Catherine, and last, but not least, from the imposition of enforced serf labour. The extent to which this forced labour had become an obstacle rather than a source of profit may be gauged from the fact that in the beginning of the nineteenth century one half of the industrial workers in Russia did not form part of the legally constituted and registered forced labour. The newer industrialism was gradually driving out not only the so-called " Possession " Factories of Peter the Great's time with their regularly ascribed quantum of serf labour, but the Landlords' Factories of Catherine's time.

The growth of capitalistic industry in Poland resulting partly from the great privileges granted by the Russian Government and partly from the object lessons of the great capitalistic developments in Germany, was a stimulus for a corresponding development at home. The undoubted growth of capitalistic industry in the first half of the nineteenth century [1] was accompanied by a great revival of Kustarny production. The latter created a keen competition with the textile factories. Clever craftsmen and skilled workers introduced the latest improvements of mechanical production into their villages. The looms of the factory were now to be found in their homes. The people were soon being supplied with goods turned out cheaply and more suited to their immediate requirements. The Kustarny activities extended to other branches. They scored technical successes. But the Government while constantly preoccupied by its politico-economic reasons for

[1] In 1804 there were 2,423 factories employing 95,202 workmen. In 1850 there were 9,843 factories employing 517,671 workmen. (This does not include factories coming under Excise category and the smaller undertakings.)

protecting the interests of private capitalistic initiative, showed no sympathy for this national domestic industry and made no attempt to develop it, or to add to its growing strength.

State Policy.—We have already seen how little attention the Government in general bestowed on national economy and sound constitutional development. This was even more evident in the sombre period of the Nicholas I reaction. The lack of any sort of guiding plan or programme during the reigns of Catherine the Great's three successors, Paul I (1796-1801), Alexander I (1801-25) and Nicholas I (1825-85), and the absolute dependence of State policy on personal caprice, which was often mainly concerned with destroying what had been achieved in the previous reign, combined to weaken not only the inner stability of the State but its inter-national significance. The previous systematic and methodical foreign policy of Peter the Great and Catherine the Great, as also the course of events in western Europe during the early part of the nineteenth century (the French Revolution, the Napoleonic Wars) had considerably helped in strengthening Russian influence abroad. Yet never did Russian foreign policy undergo such unexpected changes as during the succeeding reigns. Paul I reversed the policy of Catherine, and twice changed his attitude to western powers. Alexander I was at first the enemy of Napoleon, then his ally, and later stood at the head of the anti-Napoleonic coalition. Nicholas I intervened in Greek affairs when his predecessor had obstinately held aloof. The whole of Russian foreign policy during this time was dictated not so much by national interests as by the desire of preventing the penetration of revolutionary ideas into Russia. It was based on the principle of maintaining intact the existing absolutist regime against all aggression from the new order. At home the State was faced by definite problems : (1) the liberation of the serf ; (2) the granting of some measure of civil rights for the individual ; (3) the education of the masses ; (4) the organization of the administration of justice, and of local government. Something had already been done by Catherine the Great on these lines. Paul I, however, com-pletely upset all this. Alexander I inaugurated his reign by promising to give effect to his grandmother's plans but ended by Arakcheevism [1] and by acting directly against his earlier convictions. The whole reign of Nicholas I was but a continuation of this reactionary policy. He brooked no compromise, blindly devoting himself to the single idea of preserving the existing form of rule as divinely created and enlightened. He endeavoured to introduce the autocratic principle into every relation of life, and looked on himself as the supreme guardian of the people, ever watching over their ideas, opinions and activities.

The Crimean War (1853-6) ruthlessly exposed the internal situation. The financial resources of the State were exhausted. The national economy was on the border of dissolution. The " System " as it was then called was destroyed under the walls of Sevastopol. The imperative need of change, of a renewal of the very bases of the State's economic organization was urgent. The abolition of serfdom, the reform of the judicial system, the establishment of schools, the freedom of the press, the introduction of municipal and local government were urgent necessities. At the end of the '50's a large body of opinion was in favour of the abolition of serfdom in the interests of the nation. Some landholders began to realize how unprofitable this serfdom was. In the second half of the nineteenth century, the defects of the system became very evident. It was necessary to start at the construction of railways, to encourage the development of various branches of industrial activity and to discover new sources of State revenues.

Abolition of Serfdom.—The further maintenance of serfdom with its meagre labour results was plainly a hindrance to the realization of these plans. Alexander II stated the case clearly : it was better to effect the abolition of serfdom from above rather than let it start of itself from below.

At the period of the Abolition in 1861 the landowners' serfs in Russia numbered about 22,000,000 souls of both sexes. The relations between landlords and serfs were uncontrolled by legal sanctions. The indefiniteness of this mutual relation was

[1] Arakcheev, friend, evil genius and chief agent of Alexander I in the latter part of his reign. He was responsible for the introduction of mercilessly oppressive measures in government administration, aimed at crushing all freedom in spiritual and intellectual activities. His military " settlements," his methods of fostering morality and worship officially, have made his name a byword in Russia.

a condition of things which the nobility in its determination to maintain its hold over the serfs were desirous of preserving from interference on the legal side. But it turned to the advantage of the serfs when the question arose of liquidating this relation.

A stroke of the pen was sufficient to destroy this rotten structure of arbitrary despotism. The new law came into being in the complete absence of any juridical constitution. But tó grant the peasantry merely personal liberty while leaving all the land to the landlords was clearly impossible. When we remember how this land and the peasantry thereon came into the absolute possession of the landowner we can understand why the peasant could never be reconciled to this solution. The interest of the State required the allotment of land to the liberated serf. Vigorous opposition to this was shown by the nobility. In consequence the peasantry received very inadequate grants of the least profitable land, for which at the same time they were compelled to pay more than it was really worth, an overcharge which all their toil thereon would never suffice to clear off. The practical application of the well-meant Reform and the heavy taxation brought on fresh troubles and anxious problems with which we shall deal later. Already in 1862 the liberal-minded nobility of Tver had declared in an address to the Tsar : " It is an unjust state of affairs where the poor man pays a rouble and the rich man not one kopek. We consider it, Your Majesty, a capital sin to live and to enjoy the advantages of social institutions, at the expense of other classes."

Introduction of Local Government.—The Abolition of Serfdom brought about the problem of organization of local government. By the law of January 1, 1864, the first serious attempt was made to decentralize the old control over affairs of purely local (*Zemski*) importance by handing these over to competent locally-elected bodies. Matters of such local significance as health and sanitation, education, communications and assistance to agriculture, also such affairs as the levying of state and local taxes, were now to be administered by bodies called Zemstvos. These institutions were established one for each government or province and one for each of its districts

(*Uézd*). The members were elected councillors who themselves elected an executive body called the Zemskaya Uprava. The electorate in the district Zemstvos was composed of three groups : (1) the nobles and landlords ; (2) the peasantry, and (3) the rest (townspeople, merchants, etc.), each of these groups electing one-third of the members. The members of the Government Zemstvos were elected in the district Zemstvos, the peasantry forming about one-tenth of the whole represen-tation.[1] The local Governor exercised state control over the activities of these Zemstvos. Town local government on very similar principles was introduced in 1870. These two reforms helped considerably to bring the varying social elements of the state together. They made for co-operation among all classes in economic cultural relations.

Judicial Reform.—The judicial reform of Alexander I, by the law of 1864, made a clean sweep of the old inquisitorial system where the procedure was carried out in secret and in writing, where the clerk (*pisar*) held justice in the palm of his hand, where no distinction was drawn between judiciary and administrative functions. By this law these functions were separated. The independence of the judges and courts and the equality of all before the law were secured. Judicial proceedings were to be public and the procedure oral. The jury system was adopted. Two orders of tribunals each with its own court of appeal were created : (1) courts corresponding closely to English Petty Sessions courts with justices of the peace (*Mirovye Sudy*) for trying minor civil and criminal causes; (2) ordinary tribunals (*Okruzhnye Sudy*) for more serious causes, where nominated judges with or without juries decided. From the first courts appeal lay to the Mirovye Siezdy, a sort of Quarter Sessions, and in final instance to the Senate. From the second courts appeal lay to a higher tribunal, Sudebnaya Palata, and in final instance to the Senate. For the peasantry there was a special judicial institution, the Volost court, for which the statute law was not binding.

---

[1] The proportion observed in the land taxes levied by the district Zemstvos about this time is worth noting : 40 kopeks a dessiatine (2¼ acres) on peasant's land, 21 kopeks a dessiatine on the noble's land, 12 kopeks a dessiatine on Crown and State land.

Great Reforms.—The fundamental reorganization of the constitutional and administrative system in Russia during the period between the Crimean and the Turkish Wars, *i.e.*, from 1856-77, brought about a great cultural and economic revival. If full political freedom and democratic institutions did not follow up the great reforms of this period still a certain amount of liberty and recognition of civil rights was obtained. The rapid development of railways,[1] trade banks, commercial undertakings, joint stock companies, etc., although accompanied by unhealthy phenomena, was bound to help on the growth of industrial activity in the country. By means of protective tariffs the Government encouraged more obstinately than ever the development of big industry and its extension to other fields of production. The immense development of industry in South Russia during this period is an illustration. Russia was rapidly being drawn into the international mart. Although in the general turnover of world-trade that of Russia was about 3.5 per cent at the end of the century, the absolute yearly value attained the figure of one milliard, 195 million roubles (1891-1900).[2] The capitalistic form of production throve exceedingly in the neighbouring countries, especially in Germany, and soon took a firm hold in Russia. The returns from industry began to take a larger place in the national revenue.[3] The number of workers including women and children engaged in industry was now about three millions. The Government engrossed in its policy of protecting large scale industry, in its military

[1] In 1838 there were in Russia   27 versts of railway.

„	1858	„	„	„	1,092	„	„
„	1878	„	„	„	21,476	„	„
„	1898	„	„	„	43,803	„	„
„	1901	„	„	„	53,064	„	„

[2] In 1800 it was 107 million roubles.

[3] According to official data the value of agricultural and industrial production in :—

	Agric. Prod.	Indust. Prod.
1883 ..	2,981 mill. R.	1,167 mill. R.
1901 ..	3,394 „	3,950 „

The statistics however on which these data are based are defective, the value of raw materials, fuel, etc., being partly included under " industrial production."

schemes, and in its aggressive colonial policy, gave but little attention to agriculture and to the peasantry. The Russian people had now won personal freedom, but at the cost of bureaucratic tutorship and pressure. However, they soon began to find outlets for their energy.

Effects of Abolition on Peasantry.—In this period, the second half of the nineteenth century, we may observe the revival of the communal organization peculiar to Russia. The Russian Commune with its periodical redistribution and levelling up of the land tenure, with its unwritten common law, is as unusual and strange for Europeans as the peculiar form of agriculture in China. It is not in fact an ancient form of Russian land tenure, developed, as is generally imagined, from the forms of a primitive communism. We now know that it must have arisen in later ages of Russian history. Its revival and expansion only date from the Abolition of Serfdom in 1861. That form of land ownership so prevalent in mediaeval Europe, which is usually styled communal by westerners, viz., individual possession in cultivated land and collective property of uncultivated and common land is often contrasted by Russians with their own communal system. It corresponds to the Russian Podvorny (Homestead) system. The basic principle of communal property in Russia is the right of the Commune, not to the land alone but to the tillage, in other words to the land with the labour put into it.

The dissatisfied peasantry tried to extend their inadequate allotments by renting more land or by buying it outright ; their yearning for the land also led them to seek new fields for their activities by means of unauthorised emigration.[1]

In this period the peasantry manifested a great desire for higher spiritual development. The Sectant doctrines of the Dukhobors, Stundists, Tolstoyists with distinct social, political and philosophical elements made headway. The peasantry

---

[1] Of the 100 million dessiatines of land held by the nobles at the Abolition only 53 millions of this remained in their hands in 1905. 16 millions had been acquired by the peasantry. During the 25 years from 1860-85, 300,000 Russians settled in Siberia. During the 20 years from 1885-1905 the number was almost 1½ million.

allied with police persecution of other religions. For her,
" freedom of conscience was an absurdity,"[1] and it was declared
that cultured people seeking for religious truth outside official
guidance, devoting themselves to free inquiry and obstinate
spiritual questioning, striving to reason and argue instead of
humbly submitting to authority, were acting reprehensibly.
The contribution of the Church and the monasteries to culture
was very much a thing of the past. They had never enjoyed
the influence exercised by the Church in the west. The control
of the spiritual life of the people had long slipped from the
hands of the Church. A well-known Russian religious thinker,
V. Rozanov, commenting on the excommunication of Tolstoy,
writes : " The Holy Synod is an institution without any soul
of its own, without any of the elements of religion : inspiration,
conscience, free will. To speak in the name of God it cannot
and could not—it cannot give expression to what is wanting
within, the image and the likeness of God." When a Procurator of the Holy Synod could write to the Tsar the blas-
phemous words we may read in the letter of K. P. Pobedonostsev
—the Grand Inquisitor of Russia—to Alexander III concerning
the proposed pardon of the assassins of Alexander II, we can
understand the reason of that peculiar attitude among Russians
to religious experience and inquiry, that moral nihilism which
so surprises the stranger when he at the same time recognizes
the undoubted religious feeling of the Russian soul with its
resoluteness in matters of conscience and convictions.[2] In all
its historical life the Russian people has displayed a very great
attachment to Christianity. Beneath the official surface of
Russian orthodoxy flows a deep stream of religious feeling and
thought, which gives a but too little known picture of the
immense influence which religion has had on the Russian
national character.

Even the Slavophils called the Russian people Holy Russia.

[1] Nikanor, Bishop of Kherson.

[2] " For God's sake forgive me for troubling you and worrying you so
often. People have become so vicious that some think you ought to
spare these wicked men. Is it possible ? No ! No ! a thousand times,
No ! it cannot be. The whole country demands revenge and murmurs
abound that there is delay. Believe me, your Majesty, it would be

A contemporary observer, the Catholic Professor Grivets, who knows Russia well, thus writes of Russia : " If we turn to the simple Russian people, look at their cottages, follow their pilgrimages and examine their literature, we can see how this name is not undeserved. The Russian people excel all other Orthodox nations in their religious feeling and faith. If the Russian people were to become Catholic they would excel all others in religious zeal." Orthodoxy has indeed left an indelible mark on the religious character of the Russian. A certain passiveness, a tendency to introspection, a humility at times not far removed from self-abasement, a conviction that religious truth is a very simple thing to be attained only by simple faith, a mystic longing for the Kingdom of God, the idea of the universality of the Church's foundation—all these distinctive features of Orthodoxy developed under the strong influence of the east are to be met with in every variety of Russian religious thought. Not one literature in the world has given so high a place to the problems of religion as that of Russia. Hardly one of the great Russian writers has passed these problems by without deep heart-searching and mental anguish. Some like Chaadaev, Gogol and the Slavophils Samarin, Khomiakov, etc., strove to revive the dying spirit of the Church by restoring its independence and the old elective Sobor system. Others like V. Soloviev, allured by the theocratic ideal of the Middle Ages insisted that " the State should be the political organ of the Church, and the secular ruler should be the word (*i.e.*, the mouthpiece) of the spiritual ruler." They were very much under Catholic influence and aimed at reorganizing all social and political life on the basis of Christ's teaching. Others again like Tolstoy would throw away all outer religious forms, seeking to attain perfection from within. The revolutionary movements in Russia have always had, as they still have, an almost religious seriousness. The Narodnichestvo movement of the '70's " could hardly be

---

considered a great sin and will break the hearts of all your subjects. All thirst for revenge." (*v. K.P. Pobedonostsev and his Correspondents* (Moscow, 1923, two volumes) and the interesting review thereon in *Times Literary Supplement* of August 21, 1924.)

called political. It was more like a crusade distinguished by
the all-embracing, all-absorbing character of a religious
movement. Socialism was its faith, the people its God." A
Sectant writing to Merezhkovski said: " If we carefully examine
our Sectant problem, not excluding that of the Dukhobors[1]
we can only conclude that we never were rationalists. We have
always been and still are mystics of the purest water. We are
mystics of a special sort, of the Russian build. We are indeed
men of the earth since we believe that our blessed millennium
will not be beyond the grave, not in heaven, but on this earth."[1]
And yet as previously noted, hardly any other people can show
greater indifference to religious feeling. If, as says Miliukov,
the educated Englishman still loves his religion, if the educated
Frenchman still hates it, only dreaming of it at times as of a
paradise lost, the vast majority of educated Russians are quite
indifferent. And Miliukov rightly seeks the explanation of
this in Russian history, especially in the history of the Russian
Church.

Such were the essential lines of development in Russia towards
the beginning of the twentieth century. She had become a
Great Power. Her spiritual culture was very high. Her music,
her literature were not merely national, they were universal.
It is sufficient to mention the names of such writers as Pushkin,
Lev Tolstoy, Turgenev, Dostoevski, Chekhov, of the composers
Chaikovski, Musorgski, Rimski-Korsakov, the philosopher
Soloviev, the scientists Mendeleev, Lebedev, Siechenov,
Pavlov, Mechnikov, Pirogov, Lobachevski, and the explorer
Przhevalski, to remind the western of the significance of
Russian culture in the course of the nineteenth century.
Almost forgetting her own past, Russia had now joined the
concert of European civilization. To understand modern
Russia, to distinguish the lines of her development one must
remember that the old cultural life of Russia is held in solution
in its present, and that not only her spiritual culture, but the
economic and political forms of her development, and, indeed,
her civilization in general continue to be a peculiar combination
where the mark of western civilization is not always to be
discerned.

[1] *v.* A Blok *Russia and Intelligentsia*, Berlin, 1920.

The twentieth century revealed the weakness of the old regime and the strength of new forces it had unconsciously called forth. Some of these features may here be indicated. State administration and political organization had not kept pace with economic and cultural development. By contrast with conditions in western Europe with which Russia was now in contact, her backwardness was very evident. The autocracy was accustomed to look on the necessity of State as the first and foremost consideration, and on itself as the sole judge of any disputable point in this connection. The people were merely there to accept its decisions unquestioningly. Haltingly and with difficulty the autocracy had dealt with such problems as serfdom, legal reforms and the recognition of civil rights. The great reforms of Alexander II not only came rather tardily, but they were ill-applied and misused from the very start. Indeed, the State subsequently did its utmost to annul these reforms. Meanwhile the struggle against arbitrary authority, the long-sustained efforts to secure elementary civil rights and some share in the control of State and local affairs grew more determined. Ever-widening circles of the population were drawn into active sympathy with the advanced political ideas. Political and economic troubles sapped the strength of the Russian autocracy during the twentieth century.

CHAPTER III

RUSSIA AT THE START OF THE TWENTIETH CENTURY

THE complex variety of interests in the modern, social, economic and political constitution which we call the State makes considerable demands on the foresight and wisdom of its pilots. While a large measure of personal and social liberty is one of the first requisites of a well-ordered State, a vigilant control is at the same time indispensable. The modern State cannot be based on absolutism, cannot depend on irresponsible government. Its legislation and laws must be as binding for the rulers as for the ruled. Its administrative apparatus must be efficient and readily answer to the exigencies of the time and the moment. In the midst of the problems associated with the ever-changing forms of social inter-dependence, with the conflicting relations between the various social classes, national groups and the State, the latter cannot hope to maintain its power and authority without the confidence, support and co-operation of its organized social elements.

The Autocracy at the Start of the Twentieth Century.—At the start of the twentieth century Russia offered a remarkable example of a State not satisfying any of these requirements. Its political structure—absolute monarchy—did not respond to the real interests of the country. An economic system out of relation to the complicated social problems was being developed. The State was incapable of adapting itself to the needs of the time and to its spirit, and yet too absolute to brook compromise. It was powerless to inspire any respect for its authority. The monarch himself did not obey his own Constitution.[1] He violated its fundamental principles, hampered its administration and overrode its ordinances in every direction. There was no law defining the power of the

---

[1] Count Witte in his Memoirs mentions that when he was Minister of Finance in 1897 he received the Imperial Order to include the estimates of the Ministry of the Court in the current State Budget, which was, in fact, more than an alteration of the Constitutional law. At the same time the Emperor insisted on the Imperial Order not being divulged " so as not to excite comment." In the next edition of the Constitutional Code " the paragraph in question was accordingly altered."

Tsar or determining the rights of his subjects. There was no Parliament for the expression of the wishes of the people, for the expression of the wishes of even the privileged class. The will of the Tsar was the supreme law. He was the head of the administration. All the Government Ministers were strictly subordinate and there was no priority of place among them. There was no Prime Minister. The Russian autocrats jealously guarded their absolute power against encroachments on it from outside. The old Boyars and the newer aristocracy might succeed for a while in gaining economic privileges and personal advantages, but they never succeeded in gaining power for any length of time. The Tsar ruled the country by means of a huge bureaucracy which formed a special class personally interested in the permanence of the absolutist principle. In the ranks of the bureaucracy every class of the people was to be seen. The favour of the Tsar was the only qualification for entry. Up to 1861 these loyal adherents of the autocracy had been won over by grants of land and of the status of nobility. Later bureaucratic rank (*Chin*) and money rewards, constituted the greatest attraction. Here we find the explanation of that spirit of servile opportunism so characteristic of the Russian Chinovnik. After the Abolition when capitalistic industry began to spread in Russia, the gradual impoverishment of the middle and lower sections of the nobility brought many willing recruits to Government service, keen on exercising even in a subservient capacity a personal authority they were fast losing elsewhere. The lower classes of the bureaucracy were very ill-remunerated and were compelled to make the most of opportunity and occasion in order to advance their own interests. The higher classes of these officials held the real power for the exercise of which they were responsible only to the arbitrary power of the autocrat whose disfavour was the only thing to be feared. Thus, a talentless, and in general poorly educated bureaucracy, highly centralized, ruled over a population of 150,000,000 spread over a sixth part of the earth's surface. Abuse of authority and corruption were rampant.

The strongest weapon of the autocracy for keeping the people in subjection was the police, especially the gendarmerie and the secret police exercising an almost unlimited control in political matters. Under an elaborate system of espionage and provocation no citizen was safe from denunciation. The people had not even the minimum of political freedom necessary to acquire civic experience. Meanwhile the growing interest of all classes in State affairs was manifest. Towards the end of the nineteenth century every one seemed to be bent on giving expression to long-restrained energies. Public opinion was becoming a power to be reckoned with, and the more the State persisted in ignoring this the greater was the menace to the existing order of things.

When Alexander II came to the throne in 1855, he seemed to realize the inefficacy of absolutism in the new conditions of life, the necessity of a radical change of policy. His fundamental reforms, despite the fact that the State hindered their full realization by every means in its power, produced unexpectedly good results. The remarkable cultural and economic achievements of Russia at the end of the nineteenth century, and beginning of the twentieth century, are mostly to be ascribed to the release of strangled energies from the grip of serfdom after 1861. At first it seemed as if the authorities were definitely committed to the policy of enlarging the scope of the reforms already initiated. But it was not so. On the contrary, a speedy and methodical liquidation of much that had been already accomplished followed. Alexander III began his reign, 1881-94, by attesting his " belief in the reality and strength of the autocratic power which we are called upon to secure and maintain for the good of the people against all aggression." Already in 1881 a measure for strengthening the hand of the Government against revolutionary activity (*Usilennaya Okhrana, i.e.*, enforced protection) had been introduced whereby Governors and Prefects of Police were empowered to prohibit at will all meetings and assemblies, to arrest, dismiss from office or position, court-martial and exile any individual, and to close down universities and schools. All citizens and institutions of Russia were now placed under the absolute control of single administrators. This measure, which was at first put into force for one year was automatically renewed from year to year in some places (*e.g.*, Petersburg) even up to 1905. Freedom of the press and the independent course of justice were especially restricted. In 1889 the institution of justices of the peace was abolished, exception only being made for the capital and larger towns. To replace the justices in the country the Government appointed new officials called Zemskie Nachalniki (local prefects) chosen from the nobility, with combined judicial, police and administrative functions. There seemed to be no limits to the authority of these officials who were highly unpopular, especially among the peasantry. They were empowered to control the village communal institutions and the expenditure of their funds, to annul the decisions of their assemblies, to dismiss the elected members of the latter, to enforce decrees for the preservation of public order, good conduct and morals. The old rough-and-ready self-government of the peasant communities was almost destroyed. Yet, with all their wide powers of intervention and interference the Zemskie Nachalniki, under the direct control of the local Governors, who were in turn under the direct control of the Home Office, exerted no real authority. In 1890 the law of 1864 was modified, and the local government rights of the Zemstvos were restricted. By the new law the nobles were entitled to three-fifths of the whole representation on the Zemstvo councils. Moreover, instead of being all elected, some members were to be nominated by the Government and others, such as the Marshal of Nobility, were made members ex officio. The aim of the Government was to turn the Zemstvos from being organs representative of the opinions and wishes of the local population into instruments of the Government administration. The Governor exercised complete control over all Zemstvo activities. The president and members of the executive organs (*Uprava*) of the Zemstvos now ranked as Government officials responsible as much to the Government as to their own Councils. It was in such an atmosphere of reaction that all the Government measures concerning education were inspired. Higher courses of instruction for women were hardly allowed. The new university regulations, 1884, brought an end to the independence of the professorial body in Russia. The Government appointed the professors and also special inspectors whose duty it was to keep the students under close observation. Greater restrictions were created against the admission of children of the poorer and lower classes to secondary schools. Strong measures were adopted to curtail the activities of the Zemstvos in spreading lay education among the peasants. For the opening of public libraries and for permission to open evening and continuation schools and classes the signed agreement of three Ministers was necessary. Tsarist absolutism in its endeavour to maintain unimpaired its prerogatives, tried in every way to escape from the lessons of history and the realities of life. All this naturally led to such chaos in the administration that, at one and the same time, a President of the Council of Ministers might have in hand, to be used at his discretion, three simultaneous Imperial ukases on one essential question of government. It even led to State reforms being carried through in direct contravention of the law.[1]

International Relations.—In view of the complex international relations at this time it is easy to understand how such forms of misrule inevitably led to irresponsible action in foreign affairs and to serious misunderstandings and conflicts. The aggressive policy in China in 1895–8, the occupation of Port Arthur and of the Liautung Peninsula, the criminal enterprise of Yalu where General Bezobrazov exploited the private concession of the Romanov family, all these things arousing the hostility not only of Japan, but of other interested nations, were only possible under an irresponsible autocracy. The Russian policy in the Balkans, the long-continued distrust between England and Russia, the compromising and dangerous relations with Germany, can only be explained by the organic defects of the Tsarist government system.[2]

[1] Witte's financial reform was effected in direct violation of the rights of the State Council. Again, the legislative right granted to a committee for the construction of the Trans-Siberian Railway was another infringement of the law.

[2] *N.B.*, General Kuropatkin in his Memoirs under date February 16, 1903, refers to: "The grandiose plans in the head of our Emperor . . . to proceed to the annexation of Korea . . . to take Tibet under his sway, to seize Persia, to capture not only the Bosphorus but

The so-called Björkö Treaty of 11/24th July, 1905, between the Emperors Nicholas and William II of Germany is a very good example of such an irresponsible and dangerous policy.[1] Already in early October (14/27th), 1904, William, by wire, had raised the question of an agreement between Russia, Germany and France " against the Anglo-Japanese group." Nicholas fell in with the suggestion, and on 16/29th October wired to William, " Please formulate a draft project of such a treaty and inform me." Next day William sent on his project in three articles which, as he writes, " we (*i.e.*, William and his Chancellor, Prince Bülow) have drawn up according to your wish secretly, without letting it be known to anyone." However, the projected treaty was so clearly directed against the interests of Russia's ally, France, that Nicholas himself could see through this. His private comment was, " I could not help laughing on reading it. There are only three articles, but they are chiefly concerned with France." Nicholas then sent on his own plan for a defensive alliance " to localize the Russo-Japanese War." From the further correspondence it is evident that Nicholas had realized how awkward it was to make such a treaty behind the back of his Great Ally. He wired : " I believe it would be wise to show the French a rough draft of the Treaty before we sign it." William, however, believed that " preliminary notification to France would lead to a catastrophe." France should only be notified " when our Treaty would have previously become a *fait accompli*." When Count Lamsdorff, the Russian Minister for Foreign Affairs, heard of the negotiations and correspondence over the proposed treaty, he at once raised the alarm and insisted categorically on its previously being notified to France. Thereupon the correspondence on this matter between the monarchs almost dropped. Suddenly, the 11/24th July, 1905, the Björkö Treaty was signed by the Emperors in secret on the Tsar's yacht,

---

the Dardanelles." As regards Persia the Anglo-Russian relations suddenly changed in 1907 owing to the British Government's realization of the growing German danger in the Balkans and the Near East.

[1] Full details of this Agreement were but little known hitherto and have only recently been brought to light by the publication in Russia of documents in the secret archives of the Ministry of Foreign Affairs.

was not to be hindered by all the obstacles put in its way by the autocratic regime. The successes achieved proved that the Russian people released from a bondage of centuries possessed sufficient intelligence, initiative and energy to make the most of their resources. Meanwhile the absence of political and civil rights, the granting of larger class privileges, the determined policy of the Government in creating hindrances to every form of progress, embittered political and class antagonism and intensified the deep distrust of the existing regime in an ever-widening circle of discontented elements. One has only to compare statistics for 1900 and 1913 in order to see how the expansion of the national economy may be measured not only in agriculture and industry, but in trade and transport.[1]

National Income (Thousands of Pounds Sterling) in Fifty Governments of European Russia.[2]

	1900. £	1913. £	Increase. Per cent.
Agriculture	312,572	592,694	88·5
Industry	146,837	268,753	83·0
Transport..	55,625	110,481	98·9
Trade	58,836	102,710	74·6
Forestry and Fisheries ..	65,567	76,437	16·6
Building and Construction	49,539	88,237	78·1
Total ..	£688,976	£1,239,312	79·4

Of course, allowance should here be made for the general increase in the price of commodities during the twentieth century. The total value of the national income for 1913, based on the prices holding in 1900, would still be £960,246,000—so remarkably had the national productivity grown. Agriculture as we see easily takes first place here. At the same time it should be noted that while the share of industry in the national income increased from 21·3 per cent in 1900 to 24·9 per cent in 1913, that of agriculture decreased from 54·9 per cent in 1900 to 49·7 per cent in 1913.

[1] In 1897 the population of the Russian Empire exclusive of Finland was 125,640,012. The figure 1·7 per cent represents the yearly increase of population before the War.

[2] Based on a calculation by Prof. S. N. Prokopovich, Moscow, 1918.

Industry.—A standard of economic development may be found in the statistics of fuel consumption of a country. At the end of the nineteenth century Russia consumed 65 per cent of her fuel supplies for domestic purposes. Already, at the beginning of the Great War, industry and transport were responsible for about 70 per cent of this consumption. At the end of the nineteenth century wood and charcoal formed about 73 per cent of available fuel, but from 1913 coal and oil took first place. The output of coal in Russia for 1885 was about 4,260,900 tons, for 1905 about 18,391,400 tons, and for 1913 35,686,500 tons. Notwithstanding her rapidly-increasing coal output, Russia imported a good deal of foreign coal, especially English, to satisfy her industrial needs. In 1900 these imports amounted to about 3,500,000 tons, and to 7,641,000 tons in 1919.

With respect to iron, the position of Russia was very good. From the second half of the seventeenth century to the end of the nineteenth century the Urals were the chief source of this production. From the end of the nineteenth century the south-west of Russia became an important centre of the iron-mining industry. This development is particularly associated with the name of an English concessionnaire, John Hughes, the founder of the Hughesovka Works near Krivoy Rog. Natural conditions in this part of Russia were particularly favourable for the development of the iron industry. In 1895, South Russia had an output of about 550,000 tons from its smelting furnaces. The figures for 1905 and 1913 were respectively about 1,662,000 tons and 3,058,000 tons. But the total production of about 3,870,000 tons was insufficient to cope with the demands of the metallurgical industry in Russia. Large quantities of metal had to be imported from abroad.

Progress was also to be noted in regard to machinery for industrial purposes. In 1900 £3,360,000 worth of such machinery was manufactured in Russia. In 1913 the amount was about £10,000,000. The manufacture of agricultural machinery in Russia increased nearly eightfold from 1900 to 1913. The growing demand was also met by imports from abroad which in 1913 exceeded in value more than £5,500,000.

By comparison with the mining and metallurgical development in England, Germany and U.S.A., during the period just referred to, Russian development lagged far behind for obvious reasons. In the textile industry, however, this development was not inconsiderable. In this industry mass consumption was catered for. From 1900 to 1913 the cotton industry showed an increase in production of 103 per cent. Imports of foreign manufactures in this branch (mostly of the dearer sorts) covered only 9 per cent of total requirements. The total consumption of cotton in Russia for 1913 was 2,508,000 bales. Very remarkable was the development of cotton culture in Transcaucasia, and especially Turkestan, during this period. Cotton culture in Turkestan goes back to very early times. The methods of culture up to a fairly recent period were extremely primitive. The particular species in cultivation there, was one of the worst kinds known, viz., *gossipum herbaceum*. The introduction of the American cotton plant, *gossipum hirsutum*, came only in the nineteenth century. Already in 1913 Turkestan supplied the Russian cotton mills with 12,664 thousand poods of cotton. In the '90's, cotton seed in Turkestan had been almost exclusively used for fuel. In 1913 Turkestan had already thirty well-organized factories for oil-pressing from this seed. The total production of home-grown cotton in Russia during 1913 was about 13,101,000 poods, covering about 55 per cent of the demands of the Russian cotton industry. As regards the flax industry, it increased 108 per cent from 1900 to 1913. About three-quarters of the raw material grown in Russia was exported.

It would be erroneous to assert that the great success of Russian industry was solely attributable to the Government protective policy. The textile industry was the most flourishing of Russian industries, yet 50 per cent of its raw material, highly taxed, came from abroad. On the other hand, the linen industry, despite the great surplus of raw material at home, was not correspondingly successful. The rubber industry, exclusively dependent on imports for raw material, was very successful and increased its production threefold from 1900 to 1913. Again, Russian sewing machines made from foreign half-manufactured material sold well. The chief factors determining the growth of Russian industry were to be found in the agricultural and economic welfare of the peasant.

Home and Foreign Trade.—Under the influence of this general economic revival, and in a considerable degree owing to the development of the railways, trade changed in character. There was a remarkable increase in the number of syndicates, joint stock companies, agencies, etc., exclusively engaged in trade. The Great Fairs trade gradually lost its predominant importance. The Nizhni-Novgorod Fair, for instance, was no longer the All-Russian mart of the past. Up to the present we do not possess reliable statistics of Russian trade, and it is impossible to calculate the capital engaged in it. It may, however, be estimated on the basis of trading licences registered in Russia that from 1900 to 1913 the number of trading undertakings increased by at least 50 per cent.

In foreign trade an essential change and a considerable increase were to be seen. In the period 1891–1900 the average annual value of exports was 659·8 million roubles. In the period 1909–13 the average annual value was 1,501·4 million roubles. The corresponding import figures for the same periods were 535·4 million roubles and 1,140 million roubles. At the beginning of the nineteenth century raw materials formed the largest part of the exports. In the twentieth century a change took place and foodstuffs, chiefly grain, occupied the first place. In the following table the proportions per cent under various heads in imports and exports are indicated :—

| | Percentages. | | | |
| | Imports : | | Exports : | |
	1802 to 1804.	1908 to 1912.	1802 to 1804.	1908 to 1912.
Foodstuffs	39·0	19·1	19·4	60·8
Raw materials and partly manufactured articles	24·0	48·5	70·1	33·1
Animals	1·8	0·9	2·1	1·7
Manufactures	35·2	31·4	8·4	4·4
	100·0	100·0	100·0	100·0 [1]

The remarkable development of Germany, her proximity to Russia and her untiring enterprise brought about great changes

[1] M. Sobolev : *Foreign Trade of Russia.*

in the respective shares of other countries in Russia's foreign trade.   In the middle of the nineteenth century about 33·6 per cent of this trade was in the hands of England.   In the beginning of the twentieth century England had no more than 17·9 per cent and Germany 34·2 per cent.   The change was still greater in 1913, when England's share in the total imports was only 12 per cent, whereas Germany's was 47·4 per cent.   In the same period England exported from Russia 17·5 per cent of the total exports, whereas the figure for Germany was 29·7 per cent. This change reacted adversely on Russian industry and on the national economy when, during the critical period of the War, the urgent need arose to make up for the loss of the German markets by the finding of new ones.

Siberia.—The outlook for Russia's national economic revival was still more favourable by relation with prospects in the more distant parts of the Empire, especially in Siberia and Turkestan.   We have already referred to the vastness and variety of Asiatic Russia's natural resources, and to how little these had been investigated and exploited.   The construction of the Trans-Siberian Railway and later of the Orenburg-Tashkent Railway (1906) in the Turkestan direction, and the consequent great increase of immigration, brought considerable prosperity to the regions in question.   The land hunger, and more especially the ruin of hopes founded by the peasants in European Russia on the Revolution of 1905, intensified this movement.   Four millions of Russians had settled in Siberia in the early part of the twentieth century.   In twelve Governments and Provinces of Siberia[1] in 1897, the population was 8,184,000. Twenty years later, in 1917, this population already exceeded 14,400,000, showing a total increase of 76·6 per cent, an average annual increase of 3·8 per cent.   In these twenty years the amount of land under cultivation almost trebled.   The figures below explain :—

(In Thousands of Acres.)

1897.	1911.	1917.
11,156·1	24,078·6	32,433·4

[1] Siberia before the Revolution was divided into thirteen Governments forming four large Provinces : Western Siberia, the Steppe Region, Eastern Siberia, and the Far East Region.

Siberia's internal trade, as well as its trade with European Russia and abroad, developed rapidly. Its export of corn increased from 80,600 tons to 2,420,000 tons. The export of butter (almost exclusively produced by the immigrant peasantry) was 80,000 tons at the beginning of the Great War. As a result of this remarkable development the Trans-Siberian Railway from being at first an unprofitable undertaking was enabled in 1913 to show a net profit of 13 million roubles. In 1895 the output of coal in Siberia was 38,000 tons, in 1913 1,993,000 tons. The development of industry in general was not, however, so considerable, although favourable conditions prevailed.

Lack of Trading Initiative.—Russian industry grew more and more dependent on mass consumption, on its adjustment and adaptability to the demands of the consumer and his buying capacity. The vast majority of the consumers consisted of the peasantry whose general welfare was essential for the normal development of industry. The existing political conditions, the lack of foresight on the part of the State, and even at times its ill-considered or too-precipitate intervention, however well-meant, were all obstacles in the way of industrial progress. In order to realize its significance in the national economy, to create a better organization for its production, industry needed to be freed from its swaddling clothes, to hold its own in free competition, to acquire a more practical knowledge of the real requirements of its clientele. Instead of this, we find the Russian industrialist not only timid and lacking in the spirit of enterprise, but ignorant of his own rôle in the development of the national economy and of his personal interest and advantage therein.[1]

Labour Conditions.—Another result of this Government protection was the remarkable concentration already referred to of large-scale industry and of great numbers of workmen in particular centres. This concentration of workers with a strongly-developed class-consciousness was not likely to make the labour question less acute. The Russian State meanwhile was firmly convinced that in matters affecting the interests of

[1] Foreign initiative and capital played a considerable rôle in the development of Russian Industry.

labour its patriarchal benevolence excluded all possibility
of economic conflict, that " in Russia, thank God, there was
not, could not be, a labour question " ; that under the paternal
regime, standing as it did over the people and acting
independently of all, the labouring class had constant protection and could always look to it, the State, as to an unbiased
judge for a just settlement of conflicting interests.   At present,
in view of all that has happened in Russia within recent years,
it is difficult for us to believe that as late as 1903-4 this
opinion was stoutly maintained by the Government and
firmly believed in by many in Russia even up to the very last
days of the autocracy.   The whole history of the labour
movement in Russia is a living contradiction of this curious
conception.   It shows us the hard realities of the labourer's
lot, his outcast status, his moral and material misery.   It was
the consciousness of this constant neglect that created the
class solidarity to be found among all Russian wage-earners.
The growing dissatisfaction with all-powerful injustice
expressed itself at times in the worst excesses.   Strikes were
an ever-recurring phenomenon in Russian industrial life.   It
should be here noted that the whole of the Russian factory
and labour legislation owed its existence to labour strikes and
disorders.   Whereas in the west labour movements took
organized form, in Russia, where labour was long forbidden
to organize, up to the latest times strike movements have had
a turbulent and destructive character.

Labour Legislation.—The real object of the Government
was " to make the State authority responsible for the protection of the interests of the labourers." Translated into
fact these words meant something very different.   Armed
police and military force, arrest, exile, these were among the
protective measures most favoured by the Government—
against strikers.

Up to the '80's of the nineteenth century, there existed no
definite regulations for protecting the interests of labour or for
controlling relations between employers and workmen. The
position of the workers was such that inspectors of factories
appointed from about this time, frequently expressed their
astonishment at " the inhuman, merciless exploitation and

the crying injustice of the manufacturers." According to reports of these inspectors, " the extreme arbitrariness in the infliction of fines in some factories, was unbelievable ": 40 per cent of wages was often deducted in fines. There was great irregularity in the payment of these wages. Thus in the central industrial districts these reports show only 11 per cent of cases where the workers were paid weekly, 5 per cent where payments were made twice or three times a month, 41 per cent once a month, and 43 per cent even less regularly. In this way, the workman was at the mercy of his employer, who supplied him with goods from the factory " stores " in part payment. In the great majority of cases these stores were a source of considerable profit for the employers, and instances are given of prices exceeding market quotations by 10, 20, 50 and even 100 per cent. Reduction of wages, increase of working hours, dismissal, etc., against the terms of contract were of everyday occurrence. In the light of these facts it is not difficult to understand the origin of many of the strikes from the '70's of the nineteenth century. They assumed such a formidable character that the Government was at length compelled to intervene. In 1882 a law was put into force to regulate the employment of minors in factories and workshops. Children under twelve were not to be engaged in such work. Eight hours a day in two shifts was the limit for children between twelve and fifteen. By the law of 1884 this limit was fixed at six hours a day without shift. In 1890 the limit was nine hours a day in two shifts of four-and-a-half hours each. On the petition of the textile manufacturers night work for women and children was prohibited in 1885, the object being " to diminish production which had reached such a point that all the markets were overstocked." In 1886 another law was enacted dealing with the relations between employers and workers and with conditions of work. The initiative came from the Minister of Home Affairs, who declared, among other things : " Investigation by the local authorities of the present strikes show that they threaten to take a serious turn [1] . . . and are the result of the lack

[1] From 1881 to 1886 there were about fifty strikes where more than 80,000 workers took part.

of proper legislation for defining the mutual relations of workers and employers . . . The necessity of having recourse to the army for stopping strikes is sufficient evidence of the urgent importance of proceeding to establish regulations which to a certain extent will limit the arbitrariness of manufacturers and help to put an end to the lamentable occurrences of this time." The law of 1886 was aimed at preventing the arbitrary abuses by the manufacturers of the conditions of labour contracts, such as the imposition of unjust fines, docking-off of wages, withholding payments, paying in form of goods supplied and all other kinds of undesirable exploitation of labour. In view of the lack of previous legislation on the subject this law was undoubtedly a great advance. Yet, essentially, it did not much improve the position of the workman, for its whole tendency was to differentiate in favour of the employer. For example, the workman was held criminally responsible for an infringement of this law and liable to imprisonment, whereas the employer was held only civilly responsible and liable to the penalty of a fine, except in such cases where his actions constituted a menace to public order, rendering him liable under other laws to more severe administrative measures. In actual practice the law of 1886 was not strictly enforced or observed. For instance, despite the regulations concerning the payment of wages, the reports of factory inspectors in 1901 show that on this score alone 20,000 individual and collective complaints were recognized as founded. In 1902 the number of these complaints doubled.

A great step forward in labour legislation was made by the law of 1897, regulating the working hours of factory hands (adults). This law, the result of fierce strikes in 1896 and in the early part of 1897,[1] limited the working hours of a day to $11\frac{1}{2}$. The limit for a night shift or for the eve of a holiday was to be ten hours. This regulation according to the Ministry of Finance of that time " established the limit beyond which the exploitation of the worker was useless for the employer." The law, however, in indefinite terms made allowances for the employment of overtime labour by special agreement, thus opening the door

[1] The number of strikers during 1895-99 was about 434,000.

to many abuses. These were particularly noticeable in the following years when the overtime working hours limit—not more than 120 hours a year—was abolished.

From this short survey we see how ineffective was labour and factory legislation in Russia up to 1905. Labour had not the right to organize unions for the defence of its economic interests. Up to 1906, strikes were looked on by the Government as criminal acts. Strikers were not only liable to imprisonment of 16 months in Russia, but to exile in Siberia for indefinite periods. Labour conditions were, indeed, thoroughly abnormal. The reports referred to of inspectors of factories, Government officials, do not disguise the appalling misery of the mass of the factory hands at this time, the dirt and filth of their working and home surroundings, the overcrowding, etc., etc. It may be noted here that these inspectors were appointed by the Government from the year 1881 with the excellent intention that they should act as mediators between the workers and the employers, and see to the fulfilment of regulations affecting factory labour. Their number, however, was very limited. In the Moscow Government, for a long period, there was only one inspector and one assistant inspector for 2,000 factories. Moreover, the original purpose of their appointment was too soon forgotten. Collective organization among the workers was not allowed " as not being in accordance with our State structure " (opinion expressed in State Council, 1897). Factory inspectors had to take on the ungrateful rôle of mediators and arbiters between irreconcilable opponents—the haves and the have-nots before the law. This was a most undesirable state of affairs for growing industry. From 1896 the inspectors were required to inform the police of any revolutionary and criminal propaganda coming under their notice, and to keep a strict watch on strike movements. In 1903 the factory inspectors whose activities within the limits imposed on them had been on the whole without reproach, came under the direct control of the local Governors. From that time the inspectors lost their relative independence of action and became the mere agents of the local administration.

"A peculiarity of the Russian factory legislation was the

prominent place given to considerations of a political and police character in the enactment of these laws." (*Prof. Tugan-Baranovski*). Two motives were always at the base of this legislation : the maintenance of peace and order and the protection of the interests of the manufacturer as far as possible. In Russia, where the right of assembly and of forming unions did not exist, stoppage of work was the only means left for drawing up and presenting even the simplest economic demand. The organization of a special factory police force " on whom as well as on the owners and managers of factories was placed the responsibility of keeping a careful watch on dangerous propaganda and disturbing rumours of any kind," shows how far the Government went to protect the interests of the labourers. Meanwhile, the working class lived almost exclusively in an underground atmosphere. In such conditions it was quite natural that labour not having any possibility of openly forming organized associations and unions, not having any incentive to take a greater interest in the development of the national economy, should lend a willing ear to the persuasive eloquence of the missionaries of revolution.

Agriculture.—When we come to consider the position of the peasantry and the agricultural question, the contrast between the political system and the needs of the country is still more glaring. Dangerous symptoms in this field were certain to head to most serious results in view of the place held by agriculture in the national economy. The vast majority of the Russian population cultivated the land ; even at the period of the Great War the town population did not exceed 17·5 per cent of the whole. In the national income, agriculture's contribution was the highest. Exports, and in consequence the financial prosperity of the country, were almost exclusively based on agriculture.[1] Notwithstanding the significance of all these facts the State neglected the

[1] In 1900 Russia produced about 63 million tons of cereals, in 1913 about 78 million tons. From the beginning of the twentieth century Russia exported yearly about 10·6 million tons of cereals, including 5 million tons of wheat and rye. Russia supplied more than one quarter (27·4 per cent) of the total imports of cereals in Western Europe.

greatest source of its wealth. Its trade and tariff policies placed agriculture in an extraordinarily unfavourable position (*cf. Russo-German Trade Agreements*). The weight of taxation lay heaviest on the farmer. Even in 1913 a considerable part of the Russian territory never had a natural surplus of cereals. The huge exports of these were, indeed, artificial. They were drawn not from real surplus but from the very needs of the peasantry. The chief concern of the State in this field seemed to be to squeeze out of the peasants agricultural products for export, regardless of the real position of affairs.[1] The Government, in fact, paid no heed to developing and increasing agricultural productivity, to organizing easy and cheap credit for such development, still less to providing education for the peasantry. Anything that was accomplished in this direction was effected without Government help, indeed, in spite of Government hindrance and opposition, by the Zemstvos (especially in the period immediately preceding the War) and by co-operation, a new factor in the economic life of Russia to which we shall return later.

Isolation of the Peasantry.—The wide dispersion of an agricultural population in comparison with the closer contacts of a town population is everywhere to the economic and social disadvantage of the farmer. Country folk, and especially the peasantry, have not the same opportunities as town folk for benefiting from the material and other advantages of our time, for securing their rights and for exercising higher activities and finer responsibilities. The formal obligations may be the same, but there equality ends. The inequality between town and country was particularly noticeable to Russia.

When we contrast the returns of national income drawn from agricultural and town centres we realize the insignificant proportion of the amounts allocated by the State to the former. The Russian mujik, according to the saying, " had to get everything out of his head," relying almost solely on his own hardwon, time-worn stock of experience. The poverty-stricken, unenlightened peasantry had not only to find the

[1] In this connection it is worth noting that the State spirit monopoly just before the War yielded a yearly revenue of over £75,000,000.

wherewith and the whereby to develop their own farming and to raise their own standard of culture, but at the same time they had to supply from their own scanty means the needs of the rich and comparatively educated towns. Their isolation was such as to arrest the attention of all serious thinkers. After the Abolition, in consequence of the strong opposition offered by the nobility to the reforms of Alexander II, very little improvement had been effected by the State in regard to the peasantry. The abyss between them and the rest of the population broadened and deepened. Up to the War and the Revolution the special administrative and juridical system set up by the State to control the activities of the peasantry, as well as the unhappy land relations, constantly brought them back to conditions and facts reminding them but too bitterly of their old servitude. The introduction into the local administration of the Zemskie Nachalniki, who were drawn from the ranks of a but poorly-educated resident gentry, was in the eyes of the peasantry a revival of the former power and privileges of the landlords and serfowners. The peasant was prevented from forming a definite conception of law and rights in general and particular, and from acquiring a clearer understanding of his own legal position. The effects of this cleavage of Russian society were to be seen at work in every direction, in the Government, in the administration, in the army.

The healthy basis of co-operation and mutual assistance which existed in the peasant Commune, the Mir organization, and which developed considerably in the second part of the nineteenth century, was constantly being upset by Government interference. The Government had bound the peasant to his Commune by prohibiting his leaving it at will. It merely exploited the Commune as a means " extremely convenient for administration of public finance . . . . and collection of regular payments," [1] and for recruiting purposes. In these respects, however, the collective responsibility imposed by the law was a heavy burden for the peasantry, hindering the natural development of its economical interests. Up to the

[1] *v.* Count Kokovtsev, Minister of Finance in the Tsarist Government, in the *English Review*, September, 1924.

very period of the Stolypin reform[1] the Government persisted in this course as offering the best solution of a fiscal problem. We shall not enter here into a detailed discussion of the question of communal collectivism and communal ownership of land in relation to agricultural progress, a question which, for long, divided public opinion in Russia into two camps. This much, however, can be said—it is the considered judgment of one of the best authorities on small holdings—" communal ownership did not in any way hinder essential technical progress." [2] The communal form perhaps acted as a brake on the initiative of the more advanced members of the Commune. On the other hand it must be borne in mind that it was more often engaged in pushing on the backward. For agricultural developments on modern lines, knowledge and credit were just as needed as a clearer conception of individual rights and personal liberty, not only in social and economic relations but in the still more difficult questions involved in the very definition of the term property. In Russian law there was no clear interpretation of the civil rights of the communal institution or of the private rights, interests and relations of its members.

The Russian peasant, now tied by law to his Commune, needed most of all to be freed from this restriction, to have the right of choosing for himself the best form of land usage, individual or communal. He also needed a larger portion of land without which it was impossible to attain satisfactory economic results. A sound policy of peasant emigration was wanted to cope with the problem of overpopulation on the Black Land belt.

Problem of the Land.—All these problems were fraught with the gravest menace to the existing order. The danger of the situation could be gauged by the more positive expression of

[1] It should be noted here that the communistic theory of the Bolsheviks does not derive from the peasant communal institution. As a matter of fact, the Bolsheviks have always been hostile to the latter as being essentially a bourgeois development. They were in favour of any measures of the Tsarist Government which aimed at destroying this communal organisation. On the other hand, the peasants under the present Bolshevik regime have clearly demonstrated their anticommunistic sentiments.

[2] A. I. Chuprov: *Small Holdings and Their Essential Needs.* (Moscow, 1907.)

the peasants' attitude to the land. Serfdom had ceased to exist, but the old conditions when the peasants had worked the whole of a property—" Our work is the master's, but the land is ours," ran the peasant saying—were still very present in their memories. They never forgot how their land had become the property of the landlords, the origin of the grants of their land to soldiers of fortune. The land hunger should be appeased at once. The land should belong to those working on it and to no one else.[1]

After the Abolition the peasantry of each local landowner formed one body, a distinct community to which was allotted a portion of the landlord's property. Its own organization saw to the fair distribution of the land among the members of the community. These allotments were on the whole quite insufficient, working out in the average at about 6¼ acres per family. Landlords exploited to their own advantage an interpretation of the allotment law enabling them to choose which part or parts of their property they would give over to the peasantry. Thus the peasants in many cases not only received dwarf allotments, but land least fitted for cultivation, at inconvenient distances from their villages, and often split up into strips scattered indiscriminately over the whole property. There was evidently method in this disposition. For in order to save themselves from economic ruin the peasants were practically compelled to rent intervening parcels of land held back from the allotment by their landlords, very often absentees who had no other interest in their property except that of extracting money from it in the form of high rents. In many instances these rents were exorbitant, being out of all proportion to the economic value of the land in cultivation. It often happened that the peasant's labour on the landlord's domain was much more remunerative than that expended on their own miserable holdings. The peasant, however, was ready to sacrifice everything if only he could have more land.[2] Meanwhile he jealously nursed his ancient grudge against the landlord who stood before him as the embodiment and personification of a great injustice.

[1] *v*. Korolenko's interesting Memoirs in this connection.
[2] On the eve of 1905 the peasantry rented about 105,000,000 acres.

Overpopulation and the Land Hunger.—A still more serious consequence of these unsettled conditions was that as the result of a 79 per cent increase of the agricultural population from the Abolition up to the beginning of the twentieth century, the average size of a family's share in the original allotment diminished considerably. The problem of overpopulation, especially in the Black Land belt, at this time called for urgent solution.[1] The land hunger assumed formidable dimensions, quite ignored, however, by the authorities. A proper land reform, an active agrarian policy based on augmenting the peasant allotments from the landlords' and the State lands, and on increasing productivity ; a carefully-considered scheme for encouraging emigration to the rich unoccupied tracts of land in Siberia and the south-east, would have relieved the situation. But the Government hardly did anything. From 1861 to 1904 the Government even hindered emigration by creating all kinds of restrictions. For instance, the written consent of two Ministers was necessary in order to obtain permission to emigrate. Poverty and land hunger drove many to clear out of the country secretly and seek refuge elsewhere often at a very great material sacrifice. When we take all these facts into consideration it is not difficult to understand the cumulative effect of all the forces at work in the turbulent peasant insurrections of the early years of the twentieth century.

Problem of Nationalities.—In this brief sketch of the social, political, and economic contradictions in Russia at the beginning of the century, we cannot omit reference to one of the saddest pages of the Tsarist past, concerning the question of the minor nationalities within the Empire. From a theoretical point of view the national problem should have been the central, the key problem of Russian life.

In the following table the racial and national elements included in the Russian Empire in 1897 are indicated according

[1] In 1916 statistics show that in Denmark for one hundred of the population there were 338 acres of tillage available. The acreage for France was 283. For European Russia it was only 227. Dana Durand, the American economist, is of opinion that the agricultural overpopulation in Russia was the chief of her evils, greater than all the others taken together. (*v. Quarterly Journal of Economics*, February, 1922.)

to official census returns. From this calculation it will be seen that the great Russian element, forming a little more than 43 per cent of the entire population, was numerically predominant in the State :—

National Elements in the Russian Empire according to the Russian Census of 1897, within boundaries of 1914.
(Figures represent Thousands.)

	Russia in Europe	Poland	Caucasia	Siberia	Central Asia	Finland	Totals	Per Cent
Great Russians	48,559	267	1,830	4,224	588	6	55,574	43·3
Little Russians or Ukrainians	20,415	335	1,305	223	102	—	22,380	19·4
White Russians	5,823	29	20	12	1	—	5,885	4·5
Poles	1,110	6,756	25	29	12	—	7,932	6·2
Other Slavs	213	7	4	—	—	—	224	—
Lithuanians	1,345	305	5	2	1	—	1,658	1·3
Letts	1,422	5	2	7	1	—	1,437	—
Iranians	2	—	418	—	364	—	784	—
Armenians	77	—	1,096	—	5	—	1,178	0·9
Moldavians	1,122	5	7	—	—	—	1,134	0·9
Germans	1,312	407	57	5	9	2	1,792	1·4
Swedes	14	—	—	—	—	350	364	—
Other Aryans	132	1	105	6	1	—	245	—
Semites	3,715	1,267	40	33	8	—	5,063	3·9
Finns	143	—	—	—	—	2,353	2,496	1·9
Karelians	208	—	—	—	—	—	208	—
Lapps	2	—	—	—	—	1	3	—
Mordvinians	990	—	—	21	13	—	1,024	0·8
Other Finno-Ugrians	1,090	—	—	32	—	—	1,122	0·9
Estonians	990	4	4	4	—	—	1,002	0·8
Kirghiz	264	—	—	33	3,989	—	4,286	3·2
Tartars	1,953	4	1,510	210	60	—	3,737	2·9
Bashkirs	1,488	—	1	1	3	—	1,493	1·1
Sarts	—	—	—	—	968	—	968	0·7
Chuvashes	838	1	—	4	—	—	843	—
Uzbegs	—	—	—	—	726	—	726	—
Turkomans	8	—	25	—	249	—	282	—
Osmanli Turks	69	—	139	—	—	—	208	—
Other Turko-Tartars	—	—	205	227	623	—	1,055	0·8
Mongols	171	—	14	289	—	—	474	—
Other Uralo-Altaians	4	—	—	82	—	—	86	—
Georgians	—	—	1,352	—	—	—	1,352	1·0
Other Caucasians	—	—	1,092	—	—	—	1,092	0·8
Hyperboreans	—	—	—	39	—	—	39	—
Chinese, Japanese	—	—	—	86	—	—	86	—
Total	93,479	9,383	9,356	5,769	7,723	2,712	123,332	

The ethnic diversity in the composition of the Russian Empire, the variety of the cultural and economic standards of different nationalities ought to have induced the State to give much more particular attention than it did to this question, especially at the end of the nineteenth century and the beginning of the twentieth century, when the national consciousness of the peoples within the Empire began to make itself felt.

The tragic fate of the Polish people partitioned between the Russian, German and Austrian Empires, the no less tragic fate of Armenia split up between Turkey, Russia and Persia ; the virulence of racial and national antagonism in the Caucasus where the bitter enmity of the Mussulman and the Armenian in Turkey found favourable soil, the ambiguous policy in Finland, the self-contradictions in the Baltic provinces, the very position of nationalities on her borders numerically important and with old traditions—all these things presented most difficult problems for Russia, which required the most careful handling. It was necessary to strengthen the bonds of state by meeting and helping rather than by turning the back on the growing revival of national consciousness. There was all the more reason for adopting such a policy when we remember that the various peoples of the Russian Empire were loyal to the State, realizing that their economic interests might best be served in this connection. If only the Russian administration could also have realized that there was no need of the artificial methods of fostering Russian culture to which they had recourse among the non-Russian subjects. The influence of Russian culture was felt everywhere and would have been much greater in normal, healthy conditions.[1] Russian public opinion stood for the development of a sense of responsibility, for peaceful co-operation of each with all.

[1] " All of us (Caucasians) nurtured in the Russian culture have always had a longing for it. We have caught at all possibilities to maintain our connection with Russia," declared the representative of the Mahomedans in the assembly of the Caucasian Seim, 1918. Similar declarations were made by prominent Armenians and Georgians (among the latter Mr. Jordania, late chief of Independent Georgia). Contemporary Polish nationalists speak with a certain amount of dissatisfaction at Russian influences on Polish literature and social movements.

communal institutions which enjoyed comparative freedom from Government interference as long as State obligations were duly fulfilled, the practical application and working out of many of these theories. In the religious teachings we often meet with the negation of unjust power. "All were created alike and equal by God. God never created rulers." Social teachings of every kind found justification here. The peasantry chafed at the burdens imposed by the State, especially military service. The opposition, however, was mostly passive, expressed hardly otherwise than by resigned submission to punishment for holding these convictions. Amid all these teachings another element gained in significance, the principle of co-operation, an attempt to establish peasant social and economic relations on the most democratic basis. But in spite of these developments the peasantry could not be counted as an active political force up to the beginning of the twentieth century, when industrial labour had already begun to make its strength felt. The factory workers drawn mostly from the peasantry had never cut off relations with the latter. Labour dissatisfaction was expressed in the most turbulent and anarchistic forms, directed as much against the local administrative authorities as against the oppression of employers. It was only towards the end of the nineteenth century that labour began to form political centres closely linked up with the political movements of the more educated *milieus* of the Intelligentsia.

Reform and Revolutionary Movements.—The political activities of the latter had already manifested themselves in the eighteenth century through masonic lodges and cultural societies for the dissemination of liberal ideas (*Novikov, Radishchev, etc.*). In the face of merciless persecution these movements were forced to take refuge underground, giving birth to all kinds of secret societies and conspiracies whose definite aim was the complete overthrow of the existing regime. The French Revolution and its consequences in western Europe had an immense influence on the development of political activities in Russia. The *Dekabrist* rising of 1825 revealed the first clearly defined anti-Government political organization of a secret society. Its failure was foreshadowed and foredoomed in the very attitude of its leaders, mostly of the educated nobility, high-minded but impractical men, convinced from the very start of the impossibility of overthrowing the firmly established military despotism by their own desperate action. None the less the rallying note had been struck, the call to action sounded.

Meanwhile the serf system had proved itself to be an economic failure, to be incompatible with the development of capitalistic industry. Gradually the political movement began to attract new elements, keen on reform. Education was spreading its influence among large sections of the people. This was particularly to be noticed in the rising generation of the smaller official, clergy and merchant classes. The German idealistic philosophy, especially that of Hegel, exerted an irresistible attraction. According to Herzen the absolute contradiction between the words of instruction and the facts of life around could not help striking the young generation. Teachers, books, the universities said one thing which appealed as genuinely to the head as to the heart. The family and the *milieu* said another, to which nor heart nor head could give assent. The contradictions between ethics and conduct, between education and morals, were never so sharply contrasted as in the Russia of the pre-Abolition days. The formation of small circles among young students was the answer to an urgent requirement of that time. Some dreamt of creating a new secret organization on the Dekabrist model. Others were more concerned with purely philosophic and theoretical arguments. Meanwhile all the cultured *milieus* were deeply interested in the problem of Russia and the west. The romantic movement was responsible for the remarkable idealization of the traditions and customs especially in the simple life of the people. For the Slavophils Russia was a country quite distinct from Europe. The Slavs, they asserted, were a race apart where communal life and sociability were the leading characteristics. The Orthodox faith had left a particular stamp on their mind. Russia should not blindly follow Europe. Her ways, the ways of all Slavs were different from those of the west. It would be a great error to try to rebuild Russian life on the western model.

system the Russian people would surely arrive at that new organization of society towards which western Europe was tending through other routes. It was a long, a slow route. Russia must adapt herself to the ways of political democracy, must pass through the commonwealth stage. But it would be a crime for her to destroy her traditional land system, and to plant there instead the institution of private ownership, thereby destroying those elements of democracy in economic relations, which have taken form and shape in Russia. If Chernishevski laid the economic basis of the Narodnichestvo movement, Lavrov, on the other hand, was the creator of its historical and philosophical school of thought. For Lavrov, history, development and progress were not mere mechanical processes. Individuality, especially in its critical aspect and attitude, played a very great rôle in progress. " The ideal springs up in the mind of an individual, then travels from his brain to others, gaining in quality by the greater intellectual and moral values of these individuals and quantitatively by their ever increasing numbers. It becomes a social force when these individuals become conscious of their unanimity and readiness for concerted action." The realization of a certain sense of responsibility for what was taking place around, the moral conviction of the prevailing injustices urged on the advanced political thinkers of the '70's and '80's to redoubled efforts on behalf of the submerged masses by the propaganda of their liberative and educational theories. Young men abandoned their homes and left the universities in order to " spread the light " among the village folk and factory workers, to share in their toil and live their simple life. " Nothing like it was to be seen before or after. A new revelation, not so much a propaganda, seemed to move all. . . . Everyone whose soul was awakened gave himself up to this movement with an exalted enthusiasm and ardent faith knowing no obstacles and counting no sacrifices." [1] This movement would hardly be called political or revolutionary. Many historians liken it to a religious movement. The cruel methods of repression applied by the Government, arbitrary arrest, imprisonment, exile, etc., only intensified the fervour of its adherents, and drove

[1] Kravchinski *Russia of the Underground*.

the younger heads to frenzied revolt and conspiracy. The ground had been but too well prepared for such developments. The autocratic regime showed not the least desire to give valid effect to the Reforms of the '60's. No change whatsoever was to be noted in the form of government, the social structure, the attitude of the ruling classes. Whatever had been won for progress in the decade following the Crimean War was altered or curtailed. From 1866 the reaction of the nobility took the upper hand. The land allotment scheme for the freed serfs had been carried out, as we have shown, to the great profits of the landlords, and to the detriment of the peasants. The harsh persecution of all engaged in any work of social endeavour or public utility among the poorer masses, the ruthless suppression of the Polish insurrection (1863) definitely destroyed the illusions of many still holding to their faith in progressive evolution. The ruling classes of the '70's only dreamt of the restoration of the " happy times " of the Nicholas I reaction. *Nechaiev* is the most striking example of the special type of conspirator produced by the terrible conditions of life in Russia at this time when political activity of any kind could only find refuge underground. Endowed with an iron will and indomitable nerves he stopped at no means in order to turn the youth of Russia into the malleable material from which he forged the blind instruments for his revolutionary aims. No means were left untried, even lies, deceit, the foulest slanders of those leaders whose influence on the radical and democratic Intelligentsia he most feared. Murder was no bar to the realization of his immediate object in this respect. Although Nechaiev himself had no great influence on the revolutionary movements—his organization was small and short-lived—his attitude, his faith in the power of conspiracy left lasting impressions on all subsequent movements of the kind. For *M. Bakunin* revolt was the quickest means to attain the end, and " blind submission to one all-knowing yet secret committee " was the best, indeed, the only, method of controlling a revolutionary movement,[1] a precept

---

[1] Engels wrote thus to Marx in 1870 *re* Bakunin : " Splendid idea ! to establish discipline and unity among the proletariat of Europe by subjecting them to Russian orders ! "

section of the community. The Japanese War (1904-5), just as the Crimea War half a century back, revealed but too poignantly the tragic reality of existing conditions, the false illusion of the power of the autocracy, the disastrous consequences of leaving the destinies of the country in the hands of a small group of the higher bureaucracy and a court clique. It was not so much the reckless, senseless character of this clique's amazing adventure in the Far East as the humiliation endured by the whole of Russia in honouring the gambling debt incurred which stiffened the sinews of resistance against this unreal mockery of autocracy. Some members of the Government actually reckoned on the War's distracting the attention of the nation and of the people from social and political evils at home. They were mistaken. The Japanese War only intensified a burning resentment and a spirit of opposition which the old methods of repression could no longer succeed in stamping out.

Even among the very nearest to the counsels of the last autocrat Nicholas II, the premonitions of impending disaster were strong. Too well they realized that all was not right. Deadly disease was undermining Russian life. The future held no hope of good. On the eve of the Japanese War, General Kuropatkin notes : " The people will understand the danger of leaving the destinies of one hundred and thirty millions of a population in the hands of one autocratic power when the autocrat's decision may at any time be influenced by such crooks as Bezobrazov." (*Diary of Gen. Kuropatkin.*)

" The general dissatisfaction with the existing regime has seized all sections of society. . . . . Things cannot continue in this way for long." (*Diary of Count Muraviev, Minister of Justice.*)

" It is a protest against brutality and arbitrariness. We must have respect of law and right," said Adjutant-General Richter to the Tsar after the assassination of the Minister Sipiagin.

" Has the Russian Government friends ? " asks the ex-Secretary of State A. A. Polovtsev in 1901. He answers thus : " Most decidedly no. Who can be friends with fools and louts, with robbers and thieves ? "

So great was the alarm that in 1905 one of the leaders of the monarchist movement wrote to one of his political adherents : " The destruction of the dynasty is getting to be so unavoidable that every Russian should look ahead and think over the consequences of such an event, in order that it should not take him unawares." (*From corresp. of B. Nikolski, with Bishop Antoni, of Volhynia.*)[1]

Revolution of 1905.—The Revolution of 1905 was the Russian autocracy's last warning. In the large towns it was prefaced by manifestations and meetings of protest in connection with the War failure. Social and political questions immediately came to the forefront. Peasant risings started all over the country. The ferment was not less noticeable among the industrial workers. Indeed, so considerably had the labour movement grown in the towns that even in 1902 the Government made efforts to control it by creating special unions organized by men in the service and pay of the police department. On January 9, 1905—" Red Sunday "[2]—an immense number of men, women and children of the working classes headed by the priest Gapon, marched in solemn procession through Petersburg, bearing their ikons and sacred pictures, and singing hymns. They made for the great square facing the Winter Palace with the object of laying a petition of their grievances at the feet of the Tsar. The unarmed mass was met at the approaches of the Winter Palace by fully armed police and military forces, who could not stem the irresistible stream of people soon covering the whole of the vast square. In vain the Cossacks used their knouts and the soldiers their swords and rifles to disperse the kneeling crowds who were unable, indeed unwilling, to escape. Then began the formal massacre by the military of the helpless seething mass. It lasted several hours. In those few hours the Little Father of his people lost beyond all hope of recovery whatever authority was still to be found in the autocracy.

By the summer of this year the anti-Government movement had united all the progressive parties in open and determined

---

[1] *v.* interesting sketch of M. Vishniak *Fall of Russian Absolutism*.

[2] " The year 1905 began in Russia with the most terrible massacre of modern times." *v. Annual Register*, 1906, *re* Russia.

opposition. Already at the start of the Japanese War the representatives of the Zemstvos had met in Moscow and Petersburg to organize help and medical assistance for the wounded. Among the resolutions of their assembly in Petersburg early in November, 1904, certain definite reforms were insisted on : (1) the immediate abrogation of the restrictive measures put into force by the administration against the Zemstvo activities ; (2) freedom of conscience, speech, assembly, union ; (3) organization of the State on fundamental laws binding on all Russians from the Tsar down to the peasant ; (4) equality of all before the law, and civil and criminal responsibility of State officials ; (5) abolition of power of arbitrary arrest without decision of independent judicial authority ; (6) it was hoped that " the sovereign power would summon freely elected representatives of the people so that with their assistance it might be enabled to lead the country into a new path where the State would develop in accordance with the principle of co-operation between that power and the people." In April, 1905, the General Assembly of the Zemstvos drew up a scheme of State reorganization on the basis of a two-house Parliament : one house with representatives of all the people, the other house with representatives of the Local Government institutions. Universal suffrage, direct vote and secret ballot should be guaranteed, as also the abolition of the Reinforced Protection system which had given occasion for grave abuse of State authority, and of the Zemski Nachalnik institution. But the autocracy would listen to no counsels of wisdom and foresight, would take no definite stand. At one moment it sought to quell the rising spirit of revolt by drastic measures ill-executed and applied, at another it sought to win the people by concessions, promises and half-measures or reforms never carried through. In this way the autocracy was merely undermining its own authority. The people were now convinced that force was the only effective means of obtaining reforms.

A series of political assassinations, among them that of the Grand Duke Serge in Moscow, February, 1905, forced the hand of the Government. On 6th August, the Tsar issued a rescript declaring that " while preserving the fundamental law concerning the autocratic powers," he had in accordance with the policy of his predecessors decided to " summon elected representatives from the whole of Russia to take a constant and active part in the work of legislation. For this purpose a special consultative body was to be attached to the higher State institutions, entrusted with the preliminary discussion and elaboration of measures and with the examination of the State budget. This body, the State Duma, was to assemble for work in January, 1906. It was clear that according to the rescript the Duma had no other right than that of expressing opinions in no way binding on the Government. Three categories of electors, landowners, townspeople, and peasants were to return 412 members for the whole of the Empire with the exception of Finland. The landowning element was specially favoured. Ministers and Chiefs of Departments could not be members of the Duma.

Instead of appeasing public opinion the Government's half-hearted measure only fanned the flame of revolt. In direct contravention of the existing laws people of all classes in the larger town centres began to form Unions—labour, professional, etc. In Petersburg a Union of all these Unions was created. Soon there appeared the Central Soviet (*i.e.*, Council) of Workmen's Deputies, the leading members being Khrustalev-Nosar, Trotski and Avksentiev. This Soviet became the centre of the extreme radical influences. Its aim was to destroy the Monarchy and to replace it by a Republic.

The Revolution of 1905 was not merely the revolt of the Russian people against the existing order of things. It was the signal of the general awakening of all nationalities and races within the Empire. In their clearly formulated programmes the various nationalities freely expressed the need they felt for autonomy, especially in cultural and economic matters. There was no reference to separation from Russia. Their protest was against the narrow nationalism of the Government and the oppressive centralized administration. The voice of the Great Russian in Siberia was as clearly heard here as that of the Ukrainian or the Lithuanian. The nationalities were looking to the reconstruction of Russia on new democratic lines and in this their wishes coincided with those of the real Russian.

The Manifesto of October 17.—The whole country was becoming paralysed by the general strikes. On October 17 the Tsar issued another manifesto declaring his " inflexible will : (1) to grant the people the immutable foundations of civic liberty based on inviolability of the person and on freedom of conscience, speech, union ʻand association ; (2) without postponing the elections to the State Duma already ordered, to bring into participation in the Duma, as far as is possible within the brief time available before date of assembly, those classes of the population now quite deprived of the suffrage . . . ; (3) to establish the immutable rule that no law can come into force without the approval of the Duma, and that it shall be possible for the members elected to take a real share in the supervision and control of the legality of the acts of the State authorities." [1] Count Witte, who had inspired this manifesto was forthwith appointed the first Prime Minister. He had only just returned to Russia after the conclusion of the Treaty of Portsmouth (August 23). New electoral regulations considerably enlarging the franchise as proposed in the rescript of August 6 were drawn up in December. In February, 1906, the constitution of the Duma was finally approved, and the State Council was reorganized as a Second Chamber exercising a certain control where, beside certain members nominated by the Government, were to be found representatives of the nobility, clergy, merchants and industrialists, Zemstvos and such corporations as universities, etc. A new era of peaceful progress seemed to open out for Russia.

The manifesto of October 17, 1905, the promise of reforms, the summoning of the first Duma, the restoration of the Finnish Constitution, the abrogation of the laws prohibiting the use of the Ukrainian, White Russian, Lithuanian and

[1] In Witte's report appended to the Manifesto it was recognized that " The unrest which has seized various sections of Russian society . . . cannot be considered as the result of organized action of extreme parties. The roots are deeper. They are to be found in the want of equilibrium between the ideals of the Russian educated classes and other forms of life. Russia has outlived the forms of existing structure. She aims at a constitutional structure on the basis of civil rights and of freedom."

other languages, the relaxing of the intense Russification regime in Poland and elsewhere gave good ground for hope that the new constitutional changes would bring about the restoration of the State to health. But it was not to be. Autocracy soon came back to the old ways of centralization and political repression. It crushed all attempts at social reform. Its nationalism narrowed to the utmost.

Even the very first steps of Witte's premiership showed that he was not only unable, but did not want to face all the consequences of the act of October 17. He certainly did not want to break away from the reactionary court cliques which soon began to reassert their influence and to take the upper hand. His efforts to secure the collaboration of such prominent liberals as Prince G. Lvov, Shipov, Prince Trubetskoy, Miliukov, etc., met with the response that they were ready to join in a government willing and able to give full effect to the promised reforms. They could not join in any other government. In Witte's own memoirs we realize how unwilling Witte himself was to take a firm stand on the constitutional basis. As a matter of fact he could not. His premiership was only tolerated by the Court and the reactionary elements for as long as his personal influence among financial circles was actually necessary in order to bring off the urgently needed loan on the European market. As soon as ever this operation was effected in France, Witte was dismissed, on the very eve of the summoning of the Duma.

The support given by Europe at this time to the autocracy, notwithstanding the warnings of Russian public opinion, proves how little was known abroad of the real state of affairs in the Russian Empire. The German support was quite comprehensible. Of the French Loan in 1906, Baron S. Korff says : " The money France loaned to Russia only helped to support a decaying and degenerate autocratic government which was fated to fall sooner or later." [1]

---

[1] His general conclusion in this connection is pertinent : " This might be also a lesson as to the great dangers of government interstate loans, of one government supporting another with selfish motives and not minding the interests of the people at large." (*Russia's Foreign Relations*, Baron S. Korff, 1922.)

who uphold despotic government ? " In the complete lack of political foresight in the last Tsarist Government we find an eloquent answer to this question. The alarming state of affairs in the capital and the danger of the general situation seemed to be quite unrealized. The Tsarist autocracy was absolutely bankrupt of authority and did not know it.

Historians of the French Revolution often point out that if the Bourbons, instead of committing so many grievous mistakes, had honestly and steadily followed the path of concessions they would have escaped the disasters which overtook them, and would have maintained their power. Future historians of the Russian Revolution, on carefully examining the real facts of the autocracy will, one feels, draw less optimistic conclusions, will rather incline to fatalism, and will abide by the conviction that the path of compromise was out of the question for the autocracy. Its whole policy was essentially self-destructive and tragically absurd. Its sole aim, grimly and deliberately pursued through all the centuries of its existence, seemed to be to level to the ground the very pillars on which it had imposed its by no means welcome authority. The autocratic superstructure has now crumbled to dust. The fallen pillars lie low and can hardly take their stand once more in a sound State structure.

It would be a great mistake to ascribe all the misfortunes which have brought about the complete collapse of Russian autocracy to the evil genius of the last of the Tsars. The recent publication of the diaries of Nicholas II, and of his correspondence with the Empress Alexandra, makes it easier for us now to understand his character and form a picture of his personality. The last autocrat of the Russian Empire was a weak-willed, obstinate man of very moderate abilities, whose education had been sadly neglected, ever striving to cover the defects of an otherwise sympathetic nature by distrust of his servitors, and shallow cleverness. With his deep and strong family affections he represented the ideal husband and father. In ordinary intercourse his affability and charm won over the most recalcitrant. As Emperor he was extremely jealous of his authority. Maurice Paléologue, the last French Ambassador of the Tsarist regime, has well observed : "As is often the case with weak characters, his jealousy is of the silent, obstinate, suspicious and resentful variety. By nature he was passive and quite submissive to fate." From the very beginning of his reign the Emperor's footsteps were dogged by misfortune. In the grip of fatalism he sought relief and the appeasement of a naïve curiosity in abject superstition. On this propitious soil the rank charlatanism of worthless individuals like Monsieur Philippe, Rasputin, Bishop Barnabas, and others of less ample rascality, struck root and flourished. " I've no luck at all. And anyhow the human will is so impotent "—this is typical of Nicholas II's philosophy. Of all the ineluctable and inexorable necessities to which he had to yield in his life perhaps the chiefest and the most trying for him was to be the Tsar of Russia. In his memoirs Paléologue quotes the following words attributed to Nicholas II by Sazonov : " I have a presentiment, more than a presentiment—a secret conviction—that I am destined for terrible trials. But I shall not receive my reward on this earth. How often have I not applied to myself the words of Job : [1] ' Hardly have I entertained fear than it comes to pass, and all the evils I foresee descend upon my head.' " One has only to read the diary of Nicholas II in order to realize how little Russia, her future and affairs of State and policy meant for him. His every interest was centred in his family life, in his wife and children. The entries in his diary are almost wholly concerned with the greater or lesser happenings around the domestic hearth. For him, it may be truly said, duty to the State was an onerous and distasteful responsibility. Here assuredly lies the reason of his ready submission to his lot both before and after his abdication. The caprice of history and the accident of birth made him autocrat of an immense empire at the most critical stage of its existence. Without any will of his own he easily fell under the most casual influences. Without faith in himself he had no confidence in others. All reasonable counsel and support he deliberately put aside. The more troubled the horizon became the more he had recourse to the auguries and prescriptions of his soothsayers.

[1] The Emperor Nicholas II's birthday was the Feast of Job.

and nationalism. He stood out prominently among the higher officials of the Tsar's entourage by his strength of will and purpose, character and determination. He clearly understood that the autocracy required much more than the support of a police organization to enforce and ensure respect of its authority. Stolypin did his best to win this support from the countryside by encouraging the growth of reactionary, monarchical organizations among the masses of the people, the utmost use being made of the police to stimulate by very questionable means an artificial loyalty to the throne, where the quality of mercy to political opponents entered not at all. Stolypin's agrarian policy was a distinct bid for peasant support of the autocracy and of its Government. This policy merely succeeded in replacing a very real solidarity among the peasantry by unsettled conditions which led to great internal disorder. His " national " policy inflamed the passions of the oppressed minor nationalities, sharpened race antagonisms and turned " patriotism " and " loyalty " into contempt and derision among the more cultured elements of society. The constantly recurring scandals revealing the corruption of the police and the increasing demoralization of political life did not stop the Government.

The reforms conceded were gradually withdrawn, the promises broken. Once more the Finnish constitution was violated. The Ukrainian movement was declared to be " not in accordance with the Russian State interests." An intense policy of Russification in Lithuania and the Baltic Provinces was inaugurated by means of colonization. There was not one nationality that was exempt from humiliation and insult by the new system. Unfortunately at this time the more moderate and influential circles of Russian society did not take a sufficiently resolute attitude against this system. At first even the land reform of Stolypin was favourably received by a portion of the Social Democrats. The doctrinaire Marxist saw in it the quickest means for the " proletarianization " of the peasantry !

The Land Reform.—We have already referred to the complexity of the land problem linked up as it was with the question of agricultural development and with that of the significance of the peasantry in the social structure. Stolypin already understood that autocracy had no solid support in the country. Taking a leaf from the examples of the west of Europe, he wanted to form a basis for it on a strong class of small landowners.[1] As such a class did not exist in Russia outside of the nobility, Stolypin thought to create it by a policy of which " the axis " (his own expression) was the destruction of the communal system and the artificial planting of individual peasant proprietorship.[2]

Apart from the fact that such a land policy was a complete novelty among the majority of the peasants who held to old custom and tradition, we know that it was not so much dictated by concern for the interests of the peasant as by political motives.

In the two forms of landholding among the Russian peasantry, the communal and the homestead (the latter especially in the western governments), the system of open fields and intermixed strips still survived. This was one of the great evils of Russian peasant agriculture. Whereas under the communal system the disadvantage to individuals might to a certain extent be remedied by periodical redistribution, in the homestead system, owing to frequent sub-division, sale, purchase, etc., it led to an uneconomical splitting up of holdings. The Stolypin reform, instead of curing this evil and putting an end to it, created more confusion. Moreover, according to agricultural and hydro-technical experts, it undoubtedly hindered the application of up-to-date methods of agricultural improvements, irrigation, etc., where a certain amount of co-operation was needed.[3]

[1] The old Russian weakness—we see it even in Peter the Great's time—for rushing after foreign models, copying the stranger and making experiments on the back of the peasant, is just as peculiar to the Bolsheviks of our own days as to the extreme reactionaries of the Stolypin period.

[2] According to the Stolypin law if one communal holding was converted to a homestead property, the rest of the Commune in question was, *ipso facto*, recognized as having changed over to homestead property. (*Ukaze of November* 9, 1906, *and the law of June* 14, 1910.)

[3] *v. Report of Second Congress of Hydro-technical Engineers*, and *Problems of Tver Zemstvo in Flax Growing*, V. Kurochkin.

(cattle, farming requisites, etc., etc.). Meanwhile, during the forty years following the Abolition, the peasantry was becoming more involved in debt over payment for the land allotments of 1861. It suffered greatly from the lack of means to develop farming by the introduction of improved methods, new machinery, etc. This was especially noticeable after the Revolution of 1905.

CHAPTER V

THE WAR AND DOWNFALL OF THE AUTOCRACY

THE Revolution of 1905 did not attain what was expected of it by the liberal and progressive *milieus* in Russia. The promised Constitution did not materialize. Freedom of the press, civil rights and justice were still unsecured. The Revolution, however, was not without lasting effects on public opinion and on the national economy. The long stagnation of Russian provincial life came to an end. Closer contacts were established between the villages and the towns, and between all classes of the community. All classes, with the exception of the great landowners and the higher bureaucracy, were now united in one common aim, the securing of civil and political rights. They had discovered that the immovable autocracy could be moved, that it was now impossible for the latter to take back all that had been wrung from it. The Duma curtailed of its rights and powers was yet the nucleus of a people's representative assembly. It was no longer possible to return to the old censorship, to the old control over public activities. The peasantry aroused at last from its long sleep by the activities of the Zemstvos in education and agriculture, and by the energy displayed by the leaders of the co-operative movement, was now becoming conscious of its own significance in the future of Russia.

Zemstvo Activities.—The work of the Zemstvos in raising the level of culture among the peasants, in improving methods of farming and bettering conditions of life in every way was a remarkable example of organized effort. The following facts and figures speak for themselves. In 1873 the budget of the then existing thirty-four Zemstvos totalled about £2,600,000. In 1915 the amount was £30,700,000, showing a twelvefold increase. The increase in the State budget for the corresponding period was only sixfold (from £51,000,000 in 1873 to £336,000,000 in 1915). It was more particularly in the spread of education and in the development of a scheme of medical relief and assistance that the Zemstvo organization distinguished itself. In 1871, 13·3 per cent of the total expenditure of the Zemstvos went out in medical service, 7·7 per cent in

the nineteenth century—credit co-operatives date from the
'60's and consumers' co-operatives from the '90's. Up to the
Revolution of 1905 the movement was almost exclusively
confined to the towns and the Intelligentsia. After this date
the movement rapidly spread to the village despite the great
obstacles put in the way by the Government. The rapid
growth of the movement showed that it had found a good
ground. By 1911, it was so strong that it was able to establish
its own bank, the All-Russian Co-operative, under the name
of the Moscow Narodny Bank, with a capital of one million
roubles, mostly paid in by village centres. In 1914, the
co-operatives were a big feature in Russian economic life.
The number of vigorous co-operative societies was about 20,000.
Up to 1915, they had a strenuous struggle with the Government for the right of organizing their societies.[1]

From 1905 the general direction of the co-operative movement was clearly marked. The consumers' co-operatives up
to 1917 had their headquarters in the Moscow Union of
Consumers' Societies. The number of these societies in 1914
was over 2,000. The agricultural producers' societies developed
mostly on lines of dairy farming. Up to the War, two of these
were immense organizations, the Vologodsky and the Union
of Siberian Dairies' Artels.

The following figures for the Siberian Union speak for
themselves :—

Year.	No. of Artels and Societies.	Turnover (in thousands of pounds sterling).
1908	65	305
1913	563	1,481
1916	722	7,732

No less successful were the co-operatives for flax-growing.
The great development of these societies led to the formation

[1] In many cases it took six years to get permission from the Government to form such unions.

in 1915 of the Central Association of Flax-growers. Remarkable success was also achieved by the introduction of the co-operative principle in the Kustarny industries.

Co-operative credit also developed greatly after 1905. The following figures are telling :—

Year.	Credit Associations.		Loan and Savings Associations.	
	No. of Associations.	No. of Members.	No. of Associations.	No. of Members.
1905	537	181 thous.	894	383 thous.
1910	3,610	1,768 ,,	1,784	822 ,,
1914	9,552	6,224 ,,	3,528	2,038 ,,

These were almost exclusively village societies. The growth of capital and the extent of the business done in these societies were very remarkable. From 1905 to 1915 the amount of capital engaged increased from £1,800,000 to £14,000,000, the deposits from £3,400,000 to £42,000,000, the credit advances from £5,400,000 to £60,000,000. More than 70 per cent of this credit was advanced for rent of land, agricultural improvements, purchase of agricultural implements, seed, cattle, etc. In addition these societies, helped by the Moscow Narodny Bank, undertook to purchase directly all the peasant requirements, to dispose of all agricultural and Kustarny products, finding the best markets for these operations. They established grain elevators, grading and packing centres, stores, etc., and even studied the export markets. In 1913 these co-operative societies spent over £2,000,000 in the purchase of agricultural implements and seed.

The special significance of the co-operative movement in Russia was not so much in its eliminating the middleman, in its increasing productivity through facilitating credits, as in

might have warded off the conflict for some time by rallying
all classes and sections of the people in defence of the commonwealth, but one could foresee that as in the past (*Crimean War,
Japanese War*) the tension of a new war would only make
these questions more acute.   The opinions similar to the one
expressed by General Sukhomlinov, just before the War:
" Russia wants peace, but is ready for war," were not merely
the flippant commonplaces of the bureaucracy of the period.
They were expressions of their overweening self-confidence.
They did not realize the alarming nature of the internal state
of affairs politically and economically.   They were absolutely
convinced that war would never bring such serious changes in
purely agricultural countries as in highly industrialized
countries with highly developed industry.   Indeed, in circles
near to officialdom economic backwardness and " patri-
archalism " were looked on as distinctly advantageous by
contrast with advanced industrialism with its complex and
delicately adjusted organization in time of war.   But public
opinion not infected with this official optimism, looked on the
possibility of war with alarm and frequently pointed to the
dangerous consequences that would inevitably follow the
Government's ill-considered foreign policy and rash militarism.[1]
In no respect whatsoever was Russia prepared for war.   She
was moreover divided into two camps : (1) official Russia and
(2) the rest [2]—the Intelligentsia and the people—irreconcilably
opposed to the existing system.   There was little hope in
Russia of arriving at that National Union of hearts between
Government and country which alone could give the endurance
and the strong nerves necessary for such a long protracted
struggle.

Effects on National Economy.—The financial prosperity of
the country was based, to a great extent, on its foreign trade.
The very first economic effect of the War was the closing of
the chief frontiers through which passed almost the whole of
Russia's foreign trade.   In pre-war times the frontier stations
which still remained open, barely let pass 5 per cent of the

---

[1] *v.* Speech of A. F. Kerenski in Duma, 1914, in debate on the
" great " military and naval programme.

[2] " We and they " to use the expression of the Minister Krivoshein.

total exports, and 25 per cent of the total imports of Russia. These, moreover, were not adapted for greater transit of goods. The Government had not seen in proper time to the construction and development of the new means of communication (Archangel, Murmansk, the North Sea Route, etc.).

In consequence of all this, Russia was almost completely blockaded. Her exports two-and-a-half years after the outbreak of war fell to one-ninth, and even imports, notwithstanding every effort made to bring in munitions, fell to four-fifths of the pre-war totals.[1] This sharp decline in the trade balance could not help reacting heavily on the exchange value of the rouble. The fall was catastrophic. The War was making enormous demands, beyond all prevision, on the State treasury. Already in 1915, these exceeded 10,000 million roubles. According to Prof. Prokopovich, over 12,870 millions had been spent during 1916. Meanwhile, the State revenues rapidly decreased. The decline in foreign trade alone was responsible for a huge deficit. The prohibition of spirits, wine and alcoholic liquors was another terrible blow to the exchequer. This well-meant measure was no doubt highly desirable, but not at this moment. The immediate result from a practical point of view was calamitous. The yearly loss to the Treasury was £75,000,000. " In the whole history of the world there never was such an instance of a state in time of war renouncing its greatest source of revenue." [2]

The revenues from the railways almost exclusively engaged in military transport and from the large territories in the hands of the enemy also ceased. The fiscal machinery could not adapt itself to the demands of the time and devise new means of increasing the revenue by sound taxation.

It was only in the second half of 1916 that the Income Tax law was put into force. The Government had recourse to indirect taxation, especially on articles of mass consumption. But in the general collapse of economic life, in the general

---

[1] *v. War and National Economy of Russia* (Prof. Prokopovich, Moscow, 1918) and *After-War Perspectives of Russian Industry* (Prof Grinevetski, Moscow, 1919).

[2] From a speech of deputy Shingarev, 1915.

of overtime labour, the introduction of night work, etc., the non-regulation of workmen's wages, the rise in prices ; all these things combined to produce strain, exhaustion and increase of social antagonism. This was felt all the more that there were no legally constituted and organized workmen's unions which might have helped to solve some of the problems in question.

If " Russian technique on the whole grappled with the situation and carried out what was necessary for the defence of the country on a considerably wider scale and more rapidly than could be expected," [1] and private initiative and more especially social endeavour (All-Russian Zemstvos and Town Unions, War-Industrial Committee, etc.) displayed remarkable organizing ability and immense energy in supplying the needs of the army, we must chiefly attribute all this to the great enthusiasm of the first years of the War, and to the great responsibility before the country felt by all classes. This enforced concentration of industry on war needs deprived it of the possibility of satisfying the popular demand, especially of the peasantry. The colossal requirements of the army brought about a " goods famine." The absence of any plan on the Government side for regulation of the consumption and the price of production, the lack of system and the contradictions in the local administrations—every government had its special regulations—only added to the general disarray in the national economic life.

Agriculture.—It seemed as if agricultural interests should not be so severely affected during the War. In the first place the calling up of 7,400,000 of the agricultural population towards the second half of 1915 was hardly felt—there was already overpopulation before the War. Secondly, the former great exports of cereals now went in part to satisfy the huge demands of the army. Thirdly, the prohibition of alcohol undoubtedly had a favourable reaction on the agricultural productivity as indeed on that of labour.

The improvement in conditions of life in the village is confirmed by data of the first year of the War. But soon the general confusion in the national economy resulting from the

[1] **Prof.** Grinevetski.

War began to make itself felt in agriculture. The want of system and method in the requisitioning of horses and cattle, no account being taken of the needs of farming, and the renewed intensive recruiting of levies (in second year of the War, eleven million men were called to arms) were bound to react on agriculture. The maintenance, repairing and replacement of inventory and the supplying of stock alone got to be more and more difficult owing not merely to rise in prices, but to the very dearth of the necessary material on the markets. The production of agricultural implements, which it must be said was but little developed in Russia before the War, was completely disorganized by the War Department, which turned the factories in question to war purposes.

We have before pointed out that the huge export of corn from Russia was in reality detrimental to the economic interests of the country and of the peasantry. To satisfy the growing foreign demand, these exports flourished at the expense of the peasants' own consumption. In the first years of the War, however, it is to be noted that the peasants' requirements began to increase.[1] It was very considerably, owing to this, as also to evident wariness on their part, that demand soon outran supply. Already in 1916 the sowing area had very distinctly diminished. From the second year of the War the village began to feel acutely the emptiness of the markets. In exchange for his own products the peasant received back only paper money, and with this he could buy nothing. The village "swelled" with money the value of which was rapidly falling. The peasant soon realized the nonsense of parting with his products in this way. So he held these back.

The impossibility of replacing the worn-out inventory and the constant requisitions of horses and cattle were weakening productivity. The village was getting impoverished. In the northern and central governments, where even in peace time the peasantry could not gain their livelihood without supplementing their labour on the land by extra work and occupations, the War was greatly felt. The fall in productivity was much

[1] " So, notwithstanding the very great exodus from the village of men joining up for the army, the consumption in the village increased rather than decreased."—Prof. Prokopovich.

more serious in its consequences here than in the richer self-supporting corn districts. The destruction of trade and transport and the absence of organization for food supplies following up on the refusal of the more productive governments to send corn to the markets, led to food crises in the towns as well as in the northern and central agricultural districts of Russia. The State, which before the War had exported about 11,000,000 tons of corn yearly and was proud of its place in the world export trade, was now unable to satisfy the demands of its own people.

The position of the peasantry in the north and the centre was bad enough. Still worse was the position of the labouring classes who depended entirely on wages for their livelihood. In 1915 the price of articles of first necessity rose 50 per cent, whereas wages had hardly increased 20 per cent. The allowances for soldiers' families granted by the Government might somewhat ease the situation in the country. In the towns they were quite insufficient. It was quite natural, therefore, that economic strikes, which had practically ceased during the first years of the War, soon became of frequent occurrence.

But the worst position of all was that of the middle classes and of the Intelligentsia, mostly composed of professional men and women, teachers, etc., whose incomes were out of all proportion with the increased cost of living. The difficulty of procuring even the most ordinary necessities led to their gradual exhaustion.

Minor Nationalities.—The War also had tragic results for many of the nationalities struggling for emancipation in the Empire. The question of nationalities appears in quite a new light. At the start of the War, the fact that the autocratic Government was fighting in alliance with the democratic states of the west, roused great hopes of a radical change on the nationality issue. But soon the ambiguous policy of the Government in Galicia, the persecution of the Ukrainian press, the handling of the Polish question and the never-ending Jew-baiting[1]—all these things showed how little was to be expected

---

[1] In a number of circulars issued by the Police Department, the Jews were blamed for all the evils visiting Russia, for the prevalent speculation, for artificially raising the prices of goods and for lowering the purchasing value of the rouble.

from the continuance of the present power. While the most elementary and basic rights of nations and nationalities within the Empire were being constantly violated, the Government's official declaration about the liberating aims of this War was more like derision than a serious programme to be translated into practice. In such contradictions the German and Austrian intelligence service found excellent material for " information " purposes, especially among the prisoners of war. The subject peoples deprived of the possibility of organizing their own national divisions in the Russian army were supposed to be fighting as much for their own independence and rights within the Empire as for the safety of the Empire itself. The lack of enthusiasm so necessary for carrying on the War successfully was consequently not to be wondered at. Over and above this the War had revived national hopes all over Europe, and many thoughts were turning to the possibility of achieving complete independence from Russia. The national problems thus took a new form. Extreme separatist tendencies were everywhere in evidence.

Failure of the Regime.—In this rapid survey of the changes which took place in Russia under the direct influence of the War, we have endeavoured to give in brief summary a general idea of the intense dissatisfaction and growing alarm among the vast masses of the Russian people. Within this frame of rapidly-evolving changes must be included the psychological feature stamped on the Russian character by the war failure and the moral collapse of autocracy.

The first war reverses in Eastern Prussia had already sown the seeds of doubt in Russia as to the ability of the Ministry of War to cope with the military situation. Prominent members of the various political movements, whose views were far from being dangerous, urged the Government to invite the co-operation of many hitherto unrecognized forces of social progress. The efforts were fruitless. The retreat of the Russian army from Galicia in April of 1915 revealed much. The tardy realization of the dangerous situation forced the Government to certain concessions. The general enthusiasm and willingness to help in every way immensely facilitated the new efforts of organized forces and initiative to supply the army with war material and inspire it with confidence and assurance.

But a brooding fate seemed inevitably to drive absolutism to its destruction. The dissolution of the Duma, September 3, 1915, was proof that the Government had decided not to rely on the support of the people. Meanwhile a conviction gradually gained ground among men of moderate opinions and even among strong monarchists, that " if the German General Staff had got the mastery over our life, and that of our army, they could not have created conditions more to their own advantage than those created by the Russian Government."[1] Among the very chiefs of the Russian General Staff the doubt arose : Treachery or stupidity ?

Isolation of the Tsar.—On the exit of Nicholas II for Head-quarters after assuming supreme command over all the military and naval forces, the Empress on her side assumed a leading rôle in the centre of the stage. Her influence was soon evident not only in the general administration and in the nomination of Ministers, but even in military appointments and military matters.[2] In her intimate circle, where Rasputin was the leading figure, every sort of political intrigue was schemed or unravelled. Although we have no ground to suppose, no reason to believe that treachery showed its head in the Court itself, there is no doubt whatsoever that it had harbour and refuge in *milieus* very near the Emperor.[3] All over the country and " in the army rumour loudly, persistently and unrestrainedly spread the news of the Empress's insistence on separate peace, of her treachery in connection with Field-Marshal Kitchener, of whose journey she had, forsooth, informed the Germans, etc., etc."[4] The effect of all this on the army in the highest as in the lowest ranks can only be imagined.

The breaking up of the army had already started in 1916. Insubordination, refusal to obey orders and desertion on a

[1] A. I. Guchkov, Conservative member of the Duma.

[2] *v.* Correspondence of Nicholas II and Alexandra Feoderovna Romanov, State edition, Moscow, 1923 ; and M. Paléologue.

[3] The fact that there existed in Petrograd a serious pro-German organization composed of Russians in close contact with Rasputin is beyond all doubt. It is confirmed by many proofs.

[4] *v.* General Denikin's *Russian Turmoil.*

vast scale were rife.[1] Even the introduction of special police sections among the regiments were of no avail to stem this current. Authority was giving way to merciless discipline. Exasperation became general. The frequent change of Ministers, the haphazard and senseless nomination, and still worse the appointment to office of persons whose honour was far from bright, whose Germanophilism was, indeed, their only reputation, led to still greater isolation of the Court and to the final loss of all prestige on the part of absolutism. Those nearest in blood to the Emperor now realized the danger of the situation in all its bearings. More than once members of the Imperial family individually and collectively pointed out to the Tsar the seriousness of the danger for the monarchy. Their representations were in vain. They only resulted in personal disfavour or disgrace. Rumours of the planning of a palace revolution in high circles soon took hold of Petrograd. The atmosphere was tense with excitement. We now know that this conspiracy actually existed. A number of secret organizations were at work in Petrograd whose members were mostly monarchists and included certain well-known Grand Dukes. The fate of Paul I was in everybody's mind.[2]

The assassination, or rather murder, of Rasputin, December 17, 1916, showed that these preparations were well forward and were not merely idle exercises. The question of arresting the Empress was seriously discussed among some of the chief generals of the High Command. The isolation of the Tsar and of his Government was complete in 1917. In these conditions the autocracy existed and carried on more by inertia than by its own authority and strength. The Government alone were convinced that this turmoil raised by the revolutionaries could be quickly crushed. The best way was to skilfully provoke it and then nip it in the bud. The old police system of provocation was for them the only method of safety.

[1] According to some accounts the number of desertions from the Russian army reached one million in 1916.

[2] *v.* Maurice Paléologue, Purishkevich (*Extracts from Diary* with Preface by V. Maklakov, *Revue de Paris*, October 15, 1923, Miliukov— *History of Second Russian Revolution*).

In the surcharged atmosphere of Petrograd this certainly precipitated events and provoked the masses to street demonstrations. But not all the feverish efforts of the police and gendarmerie, not all the machine guns placed by them on the tops of buildings commanding strategical points, could avail to put a stop to the now open revolt. The conspiracy and the *coup d'état* were too late. The people were up and doing. The army could not be relied on. Even the " staunchest regiments " could not be reckoned on as before for the work of pacification. The soldiers began to take the side of the insurgents and soon went over *en masse*. The Government orders had lost all force. The authority of the Tsar had come to an end.

The isolation of the Tsar was now complete. So little did he realize the significance of the course of recent events that on the evening of the 27th February, 1917, he telegraphed his categorical refusal to the request of the President of the Council of Ministers for a change in the composition of the Government. On that very same day power was actually in the hands of the Provisional Committee of the Duma, which had already appointed its Commissars over all the Government Departments. But the next few days showed that the insurgents were not to be satisfied with a mere change of government or even a change of monarch. They were already bent on the complete abolition of the autocratic system. The fate of autocracy in Russia had now been decided, and yet the Tsar's chiefest concern was that the Ministers should be responsible to him and not to the Duma.

The Duma by this time began to lose control over the revolutionary movement, which fell more and more into the hands of the Council (*Soviet*) of Workmen's and Soldiers' Deputies organized on the model of 1905-6. On March 1, when the power of the autocracy was definitely at an end, the Tsar expressed " agreement with the appointment of a responsible ministry, the choice and nomination of which was to be wholly in the hands of the President of the Duma." On March 2, the Provisional Government, under the premiership of Prince G. E. Lvov, was in power.

The revolutionary movement had now seized the whole country. A certain amount of resistance had been shown in

Petrograd, but in the provinces, the country, and on the front, the Revolution was effected with hardly any trouble.[1]   On the night of March 2, took place in Pskov, the abdication of Nicholas II, in favour of his brother, the Grand Duke Michael Alexandrovich.[2]   In view of the unyielding obstinacy ever displayed by the autocracy, the efforts of some members of the Duma to save the monarchical constitutional system at the last moment were not only hopeless—they sowed distrust and suspicion of moderate political opinion among the masses. The Grand Duke Michael realized this, and on March 4, took " the firm resolution to assume the supreme power only in case that such were the will of our great people, on whom it rests to decide the form of rule and the new constitution of the State through its representatives elected by universal suffrage to the Constituent Assembly.   In begging God's blessing I ask all citizens of the Russian State to submit to the Provisional Government created on the initiative of the State Duma and fully empowered to act until the Constituent Assembly summoned within the shortest possible time on the basis of general, direct, equal and secret voting expresses the will of the people by its decision." [3]

In this way the autocracy, which had existed for 300 years in Russia, came to an inglorious end, abandoned by all its adherents, admirers and friends.   Neither in Europe nor in the New World did its fall excite any pity.   Among the Allies there was a general sense of relief.[4]   Autocracy had outlived its time.   The last pillar of absolutism in Europe lay in the

[1] In Tiflis the Grand Duke Nicholas declared that he would permit no " counter-movement," and that any officials not recognizing the new Government would be dismissed.   The Governor of Ekaterinoslav issued this order : " I require all persons and officials to submit to all orders from the new Government.   Any act of resistance against the new Government will be punished with the severest penalties."

[2] On the eve when already forsaken by all, he wrote in his diary : " Around me is treachery, cowardice, deceit."   Only two generals, Keller and Khan Nakhichevanski, offered their services to the Tsar for a fight against the Revolution.   (Denikin, *Russian Turmoil.*)

[3] From the abdication message of the Grand Duke Michael Alexandrovich.

[4] It was only after the fall of autocracy in Russia that America decided to enter the War on the side of the Allies.   *v.* President

dust. The revolt of Petrograd that was to have been nipped in the bud was now the Russian Revolution. The former mighty Russian Empire was now to enter a new stage of existence.

Wilson's message to the Senate in connection with the declaration of war on Germany, April, 1917. " For the United States the possibility that a new and liberal Government in Russia might now develop was a welcome factor in removing previous American hesitation at association with a Russian Government which we had rightly judged to be tyrannical and corrupt," writes Alfred L. P. Dennis, Professor of History in Clark University, U.S.A. (*v. The Foreign Policy of Soviet Russia*, London, 1924.)

CHAPTER VI

REVOLUTION

Now that we have before us a number of memoirs, reminiscences and notes of leaders and active participants in the Russian Revolution, and that we are in a position to study the facts of the case more closely, we must come to the conclusion that the movement was not so prepared and organized as is generally supposed. The inflammable material was there in abundance. The general conflagration was indeed foreseen by everyone, but when it did come it came so suddenly that it caught unexpectedly even those who were convinced that there was no other way out of an inextricable position except by revolution. The socialist and some of the nationalist revolutionary organizations, which had been broken up after the reaction of 1907, could not see any favourable issue by constitutional means on lines of peaceful and healthy development in Russia. Their secret centres were too weak and scattered, and their connections too inconsiderable to enable them to exert any active influence on the masses. Undoubtedly their ideas interested the people immensely, and the " parties " made full use of this sympathy after the revolution began. It was during the revolution of 1905 that this influence had been attained. Those, however, who are inclined to ascribe to the revolutionary parties the leading rôle, in the preparation and calling forth of the revolution, forget the real facts of the case as regards these parties before March, 1917. They also forget the fact that for the majority of the revolutionaries the revolution never was an end in itself, but a last means. The executive committee of the People's Will Party (*Narodnaya Volya*), an organization which was well known for its terroristic activities against the autocracy, wrote to Alexander III, on his accession : " The conditions which are necessary for replacing the revolutionary movement by peaceful work have been created not by us, but by history. We need not insist on them—we would merely remind you of them." The committee further solemnly declared that " it would not henceforth engage in forcible counter activity the general enthusiasm, swept along by the great stream, only vaguely conscious of their aims and wishes.

The movement was not, therefore, a mere revolt at the centre, Petrograd, which might easily be checked and stopped by a change of Government. It was a revolution capturing the immense majority of the people, especially the peasantry. Its force was irresistible. Social wrong was its inspiration.

Not only foreign observers, but even foremost Russian leaders of opinion were mistaken in their diagnoses of events in the spring of 1917. They were convinced that the explanation of the sudden collapse of the autocracy was only to be found in its inability to cope with the problem of carrying on the War. Many seemed to think that a change of Government would soon restore order. But we know now how great was the variety of the motives and forces at work in the Revolution, how complicated was the condition of affairs in the country at the time when the break with the past definitely took place.

The peasantry naturally were ready to seize every opportunity for acquiring the land. The memories of the past were for them very vivid. The soldiers, the army, could not help feeling exhausted not only by the War itself, but by its senseless direction, by the hopeless conditions under which it was being waged. How could one expect from the people a consciousness of duty based on right and justice, a respect for discipline developed from political experience when all their past was one continuous story of subjection to arbitrary will and power ? All the heaped-up contradictions of centuries of misrule had at length combined to put in motion the elemental forces of a revolutionary reaction even within the iron ring of war with all its exacting demands at home and abroad. Furthermore, the Revolution broke out in a country where no ready moulds of forms existed which might have been made of use for establishing, maintaining, and strengthening the right relations in the right way. New forms of constitutional life and intersocial relations had to be created to meet the changed conditions brought about by the release of long suppressed forces. The Revolution broke out in a huge Empire with scattered populations having conflicting interests, where communications of every kind were poorly developed.

First Effects.—Every revolution is accompanied by an intensive process of " mass " changes. Former distinctions and differences tend to disappear. The new cannot immediately take definite form. Old points of view and standards of conduct vanish. Other obligations impose themselves on an unwilling obedience. Social, political and economic forms must of necessity be remodelled and readapted quickly to the requirements of the time. Therein lies the weakness of a revolutionary government when we compare it with a military one. We have examples of this in the French Revolutionary government, 1789–92, and in the " 1848 " government. Karl Kautski well points out that " this phenomenon is not accidental and is not the result of the weakness of individual members or parties, but is in the very nature of things. Revolution is a consequence of the break up of an old administrative machinery. The new machinery cannot at once adapt itself to the new requirements. Without this apparatus a Government is but ' hanging in the air ' and is less capable than any other to produce a dictatorship."

That is why in such periods of great social crises the various formations of groups, classes and established parties whose roots are deep in the past, which have experience, relations, and consequently the possibility of calculating and weighing the facts of the situation, play a considerable rôle, and have a special significance in the revolutions of our days which are taking place in societies with delicate and highly complicated organizations.

In Russia there were no such things as trade unions, groups and class organizations with practical experience which could in some way be made use of when the need arose. The existing workmen's economic organizations, such as the labour sections in the War Industrial Committee, and their medical relief societies, could not exert any influence. They were immediately drawn into political activity. The trade unions, which arose from these organizations and developed vigorously at the time of the Revolution, were unable to oppose their influence to that of the previously formed Soviets of the workmen's and soldiers' deputies enjoying a certain political authority.

Municipal Organizations.—The Russian municipal organizations, especially the Zemstvos—although in the eyes of the of the Government and of the police there was but little chance for anyone or any party to acquire political experience, to put their opinions and theories to the test of practical application. All parties, conservative, liberal, radical and socialist, were seriously handicapped in this respect.

Conservatives.—That is why conservatism in the English sense did not exist in Russia. What other tradition could it preserve here than that of national and political repression, of arbitrary power, of privileges of a favoured caste ? The guardians of such traditions and privileges seemingly found no better use for whatever political talents they possessed than in such creations as that of the Black Hundreds organization and in the support of reactionary policies of every kind initiated by the ruling bureaucracy. Their narrow nationalism and shameless self-interest became repulsive to the finer intelligence among convinced monarchists. When on the Emperor's downfall the opportunity came of translating their noisy patriotism, their fierce and provocative loyalty into action, these champions of the utterance maintained an almost unbroken silence. It was only much later that they recovered some semblance of their old courage. During the whole period of the Provisional Government the fullest liberty of the press and of political activity was assured to all parties. The old monarchist organs like the *Novoe Vremia* appeared regularly. The former monarchist leaders had every freedom of action. They seemed to have forgotten their own principles. They were unable to effect a consolidation of the conservative forces by constitutional methods. Indeed, their activities were more apparent under the old familiar guise of intrigue and conspiracy.

Later we shall see that the whole tragedy of the so-called White Movement against the Bolsheviks during 1918–21 under Denikin, Kolchak, Wrangel, etc., was to be found in the fact that the struggle for the restoration of the old system of privileges, for the recovery of losses of property, etc., incurred during the Revolution, took precedence over all other considerations. The " Black Hundreds " of the old regime were but too much in evidence, bringing to naught the efforts of a few sincere and earnest patriots.

The moderate reform party of the Octobrists offers another

instance of how unfavourable were the conditions in Russia for the development of sound constitutional practice. Under the demoralizing influence of the " system " the party rapidly lost its significance and became a tool in the hands of the Government. During the War its more progressive elements sided with the Revolution and even took an active part in it, but were unable to form a conservative constitutional party.

Opposition Parties.—It seemed as if in Russia were to be found a good soil for the growth and spread of liberal ideas. In the first Duma it was evident that in Russia there were considerable bodies of people ready to put their trust in the hands of the liberal parties. But the reaction of 1906–7 once more convinced the majority of the hopelessness of reform on the basis of evolution. A radical and immediate change in the system of government was necessary, and those striving to effect this were naturally in favour. As regards the political organizations, in opposition to the Tsarist regime, they could hardly be called political parties; they were not recognized by the Government, and had to work underground. They were not in a position to know the actual extent of their own membership, to form regularly elected bodies, to maintain a proper control over their activities. They were no more than secret, organized groups, small in the number of adherents, scattered about all over the country, but poorly linked together, their real centres being abroad. Their object was to spread propaganda. The sympathies they won in the eyes of the great masses of the people proceeded rather from a strong antipathy to autocracy than from willing acceptance of their programme.

Constitutional Democrats.—Of all these, the Cadets alone had recognized legal standing. They had, moreover, excellent organization and parliamentary experience. In their ranks were to be found professional men of all kinds, eminent jurists and savants. In the last Duma they headed the opposition to the Tsarist Government. It was natural that they should take the leading part in the formation and in the activities of the first Provisional Government. They called themselves a " non-class " party, their adherents and followers being found mostly among the intellectual workers and the town bourgeoisie. Their pre-revolutionary programme was based on was only from March they could start this, and from that time an immense number of adherents and sympathizers joined their ranks. Many joined up, not out of any particular conviction as to the efficacy of the various socialist programmes, but rather because they sympathized in general with their aims, and in any case they deemed it necessary at this juncture, when an active part should be taken in political life, to define somehow their own political position.

The socialist parties increased in numbers with extraordinary rapidity. They had, however, no experienced organizers, and their leading men were being more and more drawn away from the necessary work of organization by purely state and political problems. All this naturally reacted on the building-up of party organization, on the internal discipline and the solidarity that were so needful. From their confinement these parties brought forth to the surface every form and variety of opinion, view, programme and method of action, all sorts of clear-cut, uncompromising, theoretical reasonings, not to mention the old pre-revolutionary spirit of refractoriness and separate action. [1] Before the War this spirit was mostly to be observed in the realm of ideas and theories. The War introduced new differences of opinion, and brought to the forefront such questions as the defence of the country, the international campaign to secure peace, or the continuation of the War not as an " Imperialistic," but as a civil concern. (*Zimmerwald and Kienthal*).[2] The Revolution added yet more problems. What were the political and social aims of the Revolution ? What was to be the

[1] One of the oldest and cleverest of the Russian Social Democratic leaders (Axelrod) noted that " nowhere was intoxicating and befogging phraseology to be found in Social Democracy to such an extent as with us. Nowhere did phrases bereft of any real sense so darken the mind and hamper the development of the Social-Democratic party as with us." This observation applies just as fittingly to the other Socialist parties in Russia.

[2] The Zimmerwald Conference held in Switzerland in September of 1915 was the first Conference attended by socialists of the Allied and Central Powers after the outbreak of the War. Those present belonged to the left wing of the socialist movement. Another such conference took place in Kienthal in the year 1916. Both conferences aimed at formulating a common programme of action to end the War.

attitude of New Russia to the War? What was to be the
new form of State power? What was to be their part in it?
In the beginning of the Revolution there was a strong
tendency for unity among the rank and file of the Socialists
working in Russia. But soon the arrival of the leaders and
the professional party organizers from exile and abroad
accentuated once more party differences. The old courses
of many currents of opinion were rapidly altered. New
independent centres of action were created. The various
socialist parties were now manœuvring for position on the
political arena and for the strengthening of their influence.

Social Democrats.—The influence of the two Marxist socialistic movements (Social-Democratic Bolshevik and Social-
Democratic Menshevik) seemed bound to succeed mostly
among the town-working population. Generally speaking,
however, the economic conditions in Russia were hardly
favourable for the spread of Marxist doctrines.[1]

From the point of view of the pure Marxist conception of
history, the success of the social-democratic teachings in Russia,
where capitalistic industry had only just started to develop,
and where even the most elementary political freedom did not
exist, could not be extensive. The materialistic Marxist
interpretation of history, the theory of surplus value, the law
of concentration of capital, the principle of class struggle, the
conquest of power by the proletariat organized as a class
party, the socialization of means of production and distribution, the leaning to the collectivist theory of the supremacy
of the State—all these were cardinal principles common to
both wings of the social-democratic parties.

Already, however, in the first year of 1900 a serious difference

[1] For Bakunin and, later, the Bolshevik Communists, but not for
Marx, socialism and revolution had a more favourable field in " effete "
countries. Bakunin considered that the workmen of Europe had
become too *bourgeois* owing to good pay and opportunities of education.
The Russian workmen and peasants on the other hand are beggars
unspoiled by bourgeois traditions and customs and form excellent
material for socialist and revolutionary experiments. The Bolsheviks
now advance the same reason for the introduction of Communism into
tired Russia. They now look forward to the rapid realization of their
hopes in the effete countries of the east.

But soon opportunism took the upper hand. Urged on by an irrepressible desire for control of power and influence, and realizing how impossible it was by constitutional means to secure it in present conditions of the fullest democratic freedom, the Bolsheviks forgot their old reasonings and arguments. The conquest of power could only be attained by the demoralization of the army and by utterly discrediting democracy and its leaders. The theory by which they were guided in the course of action adopted by them in the Revolution, their programme of reorganizing Russia on the Soviet basis, and at the same time renouncing democratic rule on principle, were to be drawn up later when they could come out in the open as the Communist Party. For the present they exploited the dark instincts of blind natural forces by inflaming the passions of the multitude with shrieking demagogic appeals, anything to obtain power which they would eventually use for objects quite foreign to the wishes and will of the people.[1]

The tired-out soldiers and sailors, especially the soldiers of the rear, and extremists from the races and nationalities which had suffered under the oppressive regime of the Tsar (Jews, Finns, Letts, etc.) were formed into special cadres on which they (the Bolsheviks) based their hopes.

Mensheviks.—Very different was the Menshevik mentality. According to pure Marxian principles in all their political schemes and projects the Mensheviks based their calculations on the degree of development of the productive forces of the country, on the degree of ripeness of the industrial proletariat, in their eyes the only genuine upholders of the socialist ideal. They understood the backwardness of Russia in respect of capitalistic industrial development. In their opinion the transformation of a semi-feudalistic state like Tsarist Russia into a bourgeois-democratic republic should be the first stage. Only in this way could there be a wide outlet for the development of capitalism in Russia. Only in this way could the

---

[1] On the 4th April Lenin declared : " Our immediate aim is not the introduction of socialism but the immediate introduction of the control of national production and distribution by the Workers' Soviets."

ground be prepared for the advent of a socialistic change. Russia in this respect was sure to follow the general route of all other European states.

In the past the Mensheviks had already sharply differed from the Bolsheviks in the matter of tactics and in the methods of organization of the proletariat. They stood for organizing the proletariat openly, and some of their leaders maintained that this organization should have economic rather than political aims in view. The significance of the Menshevik party in the organization of Russian labour was very great. Of all the forcedly secret political parties it was indeed the least adapted for underground life and activity. The German labour movement had always been its model, the theories and tactics of the German orthodox Social Democrats its guiding principles. Its comprehension of the force and purpose of the German labour movement might almost be said to be greater than its realization of the actual conditions and needs of Russian life.

The War led to great divergence of opinion within the Menshevik party as everywhere among the socialists. Many prominent leaders like G. Plekhanov ranged themselves on the side of the defence of the country. But the majority of the party under Martov adopted a negative attitude on this question and endeavoured to follow the policy advocated by the international socialists of Zimmerwald. The Revolution did not find the organization of the Mensheviks so broken as that of other parties. They had known how to maintain their connections with the existing labour economic organizations such as medical relief societies, the Labour Group in the War Industrial Committee, Consumers' Co-operatives, etc. Their influence in the first period of the War among the labouring masses and especially among the great industrial centres, was immense. Their rôle in the Workmen's Soviets was a dominant one. The work and the policy of these Soviets were almost exclusively directed by them. And inasmuch as the head centres of industry played the most important part in the Revolution, the workers forming the chief force in those centres, so the general policy of New Russia and the fate of the Revolution depended in a considerable degree on the policy and tactics of the Menshevik party.

It must be acknowledged that on any really fundamental
questions they had no definite policy or clear line of action.
Of course, on some questions, such as war [1] it was extremely
difficult from their point of view to draw up a definite policy,
so complex was the whole situation, so dependent was it on
general international relations. Their incertitude and at times
their very duplicity brought about the most serious consequences. In other matters this lack of definite policy could
hardly be explained by the difficulties of circumstances. It
could indeed be ascribed to the defects of their system, to the
absence of leadership and statesmanship. To their mind the
Revolution now taking its course in Russia was a bourgeois-
democratic revolution, and meanwhile they gave no definite
approval to the principle of democracy and no real support to
democratic institutions. They could only accept the principle
of democracy very conditionally, guided by the doctrine of
Marx and Engels, the dictatorship of the proletariat,[2] a
doctrine which according to Karl Kautski " suffered, at the
very start, from the fact that it would be interpreted in so many
different senses." The principle of class struggle and its rôle
in politics made them look on the workers as an isolated class.
On no account whatever would they take part in any coalition
or compromise. They never aspired to power and avoided its
responsibilities. At the same time they would not give the
Provisional Government adequate support. In the conditions
holding in 1917 when the Mensheviks had a considerable

[1] In this question they did not show the necessary circumspection
and did not reckon with the fact that their varying declarations might
be very differently and even unfavourably interpreted by the Soldiers'
and Workmen's Deputies. Who could take seriously such plans for
finishing the War as this one : the stoppage of all military activity on
all frontiers at a certain hour on a certain day ; the decision by general
vote of the peoples in the border territories or the question as to which
of the countries at war they wished to belong to ; the creation of a
general fund of twenty-five milliard francs for the restoration of
devastated areas, etc., etc.

[2] In 1921 Kautski explained : " We have every reason to cease
using the expression ' Dictatorship of the Proletariat,' all the more so
that in the Communist manifesto dictatorship is never mentioned,
only the rule of the proletariat on the basis of democracy won by the
Revolution is spoken of."

influence in the powerful organization of the Workers' Soviet, such a policy of abstention was sure to weaken the authority of any government desirous of leaning on the sympathy and confidence of the people and not on military force.

Narodnichestvo.—Among the Russian Socialist parties the so-called Populist (*Narodniki*) parties occupied a peculiar position. The most powerful of these was the Social Revolutionary Party. The Labour or Toil party played no particular part in the Revolution. But in the Duma a group of this party strengthened by the adhesion of such men as Kerenski from the Social Revolutionaries was a formidable part of the opposition to the Government. The Narodnichestvo movement, which Herzen has called " Russian Socialism " was the inspiration of their philosophic and historical concepts. This movement, as we know, had started about the second half of the nineteenth century and up to the '90's of that century had an immense influence in Russia, especially in the literary, artistic and social movements. Its founders were A. Herzen, Ogarev and Chernyshevski. In its later development, P. Lavrov and K. Mikhailovski were among others prominently associated. An almost mystic faith in the calling of the Russian people, especially the peasantry, born and bred in the " communal " spirit of solidarity on the ground of social justice was its leading characteristic. " We call Russian socialism," wrote Herzen, " the socialism proceeding from the life and being of the peasantry—from their communal land system and the Mir, as also from those workers' associations (*Artels*) which are out for the economic justice which socialism everywhere is aiming at." [1]

Social Revolutionaries.—The Narodnichestvo traditions with their deep concern for the rôle of the peasantry in social and economic progress were followed up by the Social Revolutionary party. For the latter the complex process of social development could not be made to fit into the readily simplified scheme of things as interpreted by the materialistic philosophy of Marx. They attached a very real significance to ethical, spiritual, intellectual forces, to culture and to individuality in the process of social development. The Marxian conception

[1] *v.* pp. 89–92.

of socialism where the socialistic ideal is the exclusive property of the industrial proletariat for whom the rest of the people are a hostile, bourgeois mass, was quite foreign to the Social Revolutionaries. To this strange comprehension of confused ideas the Social Revolutionaries opposed the more reasonable conception and a higher ideal in the co-operation of physical and intellectual toilers of every condition, workmen, peasantry and intelligentsia taking part in the creation and development of all productive wealth.

The attitude of the Social Revolutionary party to " State Socialism " was very reserved. In its programme of January 2, 1906, it declared that such socialism was " partly a system of half-measures for putting the working classes to sleep, and partly another form of State capitalism concentrating different branches of production and trade in the hands of a ruling bureaucracy for fiscal and political interests." It tried to find some adjustment between the collectivist theory of the supremacy of the State and the syndicalist theory of the supremacy of the workers as producers. It paid particular attention to such forms and developments in the economic realities of Russian life as the Commune, the Artel, the Producers' and Consumers' Co-operatives, etc. Its agrarian policy was mostly based on the existing common law and on the prescriptive rights of the peasantry to the land. This explains the great influence of the Social Revolutionary party among the peasants.

The party was also much concerned with the problems associated with the question of nationalities and minority rights. Notable points in their programme were the decentralization of the administrative system, a large development of the principle of autonomy and the introduction of the federative system. Of all the Russian socialist parties it was the most consistent in its attitude to democracy and democratic institutions. Orthodox Marxism so influential in all countries at the beginning of this century found its reflection in the programme of this party. There you could find reference to temporary revolutionary dictatorship of the workers and to the class struggle. Although this dictatorship was only considered as a possible condition, not as the

domination of a minority over a majority, but as a strong
government endowed with special powers, and although the
tendency was to interpret the class struggle as a fact rather
than as a basic principle; during the Revolution, however, it
was quite inevitable that these doctrines should produce
sharp differences of opinion reacting on the policy and tactics
of the party. The party was also at a disadvantage in that,
while its influence was very strong among the peasantry, in
the organization of the latter innumerable obstacles were to
be met owing to the difficulties of communication with isolated
populations spread over vast territories. But even this is
hardly an explanation of the fact that the undoubtedly
considerable influence of the Social Revolutionary party at
the time of the Revolution did not arise and proceed from the
strength of its organization. Various groups of opinion badly
linked together by party discipline were to be found under
one standard—militant defenders of the interests of the
country, cautious pacifists, " defeatists," and extreme inter-
nationalists. The rebellious element nearer to Bolshevism
although numerically inconsiderable was enabled when
occasion demanded a vigorous and active policy to exercise a
baneful influence in counsels where decision and unity of
action were urgently needed.[1] In the time and the circumstances skilful leadership was essential. There was none.
The undaunted leaders of the old " underground " movement
were found unfitted for more exacting tasks of statesmanship.
And yet the party refused to change them. Hesitancy and
half-measures characterized its decisions not only in questions
of war and peace, but in such questions as participation in the
Government and the position of the Government as regarded
the Soviets.[2]

[1] The separation of this group from the party came too late, only in
August, 1917. It formed what was known as the Left Social
Revolutionary party. They joined with the Bolsheviks in the overthrow of the Provisional Government, but disassociated themselves
later from the Bolshevik policy.

[2] For instance, the entry of Kerenski into the Government was
approved of by the Social Revolutionary party. It insisted strongly
on his further participation in power, yet at the same time one of the
leaders of the party, V. Chernov, made several vehement declarations

became the decisive factor in the circumstances. This was especially to be observed in the capital where they formed an all too favourable, highly inflammable material in the hands of wily demagogues and propagandists. Yet in the very beginning of the Revolution it must be acknowledged that the moral of the army was much improved, and the process of dissolution for a while checked. The reason for this was obvious. The millions in the trenches and in the rear were lifted out of an abject submission and dumb despair. The Revolution had turned a helpless and downtrodden rabble into free citizens and warriors of a people's army. We have only to read the letters from the trenches, the resolutions of the various councils and committees at the front to understand this transformation. But the enthusiasm especially in the rear was transitory and unstable. That is why the process of dissolution was only temporarily stopped. The new-found fervour rapidly cooled. The masses only too readily responded to the catch-words and slogans of the agitators bent on the complete disruption of the army. Their instability determined the whole course of the Revolution, a factor with which the democratic leaders of the February Revolution seemed incapable of reckoning and which was exploited by the opposition. Such were the conditions in which the first revolutionary organization of the Soviet of Workers' and Soldiers' Deputies and the Provisional Government started to work. *The Soviets of the Workers' and Soldiers' Deputies* were of accidental formation and had been created under special circumstances. A very typical example is that of the formation of the Petrograd Soviet. On February 27, 1917, " the liberated political prisoners, among them representatives of the workers' group in the War Industrial Committee, party organizers, socialists, and public men and journalists who occasionally met in the Duma, started the organization of a Soviet of Workers' Deputies, forming a temporary executive committee of the same." [1] The form of representation and method of election were not drawn up. Mandates were not looked into. Already on the second day of its existence the Soviet had become a huge shouting assembly,

[1] *Chronicle of the February Revolution* (Zaslavski and Kantorovich, Petrograd, 1924).

more like a disorderly meeting. From March 2 it styled itself the Soviet of Workers' and Soldiers' Deputies. It soon became the centre of the Revolutionary movement in Petrograd. These Soviets were rather militant organizations designed to get the upper hand over the old regime. That was the object of their organization. The autocracy, however, collapsed almost without a show of resistance. In the provinces the Soviets were formed later and for a long time played no considerable part. They had neither the proper machinery nor organization. They lacked experienced leaders knowing well the local conditions and able to establish and maintain the necessary contact with head centres.

In Petrograd the Soviet not only displayed greater energy and activity at first than the provisional committee of the Duma, but rapidly acquired a powerful and decisive influence. Day by day its numbers increased. By March 9, it had already 2,800 members, 800 being workers, the rest soldiers. The looseness of its formation and organization, the absence of any executive apparatus—no regular minutes of orders of the day or of formal resolutions were kept—did not matter so much at first as long as the Soviet was busy giving information, creating its propaganda and concentrating the forces of Revolution. But when it came to deciding questions of State administration and organization the position was tragic. From the very start the Soviet unconsciously created that terrible confusion—government by double authority. On its first formation it made no declaration direct or indirect *re* the government power and had no pretensions to it. Without previous agreement or interchange of opinion all the most important functions and rights of government, its institutions and administration passed under the direct control of the newly created provisional committee of the Duma. At the same time it was clear to all that without the support and sanction of the Soviet no form of stable and authoritative government was possible. On March 2, the Soviet not only discussed the matter fully, but formally sanctioned a programme drawn up by mutual agreement, and decided the question of the participation of socialists in the Government. But if the Cadet party held firmly to the theory of a Constitutional Monarchy, was more disastrous. On this point the resolution was a contradiction in terms, merely instilling into the mind of the masses a prejudice against the Government and sowing the seeds of distrust and anxiety in public opinion. In the resolution we read (points 4, 5, 6) : " The assembly recognizes the necessity of a constant political control and pressure on the Provisional Government from the side of the revolutionary democracy. . . . The assembly calls on the democracy not to accept responsibility for all Government action in general. . . . It calls on the revolutionary democracy of Russia to organize and combine in the Soviets of Workers' and Soldiers' Deputies, and to be ready to oppose strenuously any attempt of the Government to evade the control of the democracy or to avoid fulfilling the obligations they have undertaken." After such a resolution the declaration of support to be given to the Provisional Government was naturally unconvincing. It was too conditional and bound no one. In this respect the first assembly of the Soviets forced the issue and predetermined in one way the whole course of the February Revolution. For the first time it put forward the question of State power in an All-Russian frame, and although it decided it formally in favour of the Provisional Government, it in fact pointed to the Soviet as the sole holder and guardian of this power.

The Soviet, the Proletariat and the Peasantry.—The decisions of the assembly on the fundamental problems of land and labour placed the Soviets in a perilous, indeed hopeless, position. We have already seen how critical this question was in the conditions of Russian life. In this connection the assembly's decision was very symptomatic. The labour question was to be solved by realizing in full the so-called " Minimum " programme of the socialist parties. Social legislation on a large scale was immediately decreed by the assembly—eight hours a day work, the fixing of a minimum wage, unlimited freedom of combination, the establishment of arbitration and conciliation boards and labour exchanges, workmen's insurance, grants for the unemployed, etc., etc. All this was carried through without consulting any other interest than that of labour. From the side of capital, no resistance was offered. The consequence of this was that it now lay on the Soviets to set limits to the appetites and ambitions of the proletariat, and to reckon the financial prospects of industry itself.

The land question was treated differently. It was proposed to start Land Committees all over the country, to settle all agrarian difficulties and especially to organize means for the proper tillage and sowing of lands left uncultivated. These committees were given the task of " opposing vigorously all attempts to solve the land question on the spot "—a solution which was to be left to the All-Russian Constituent Assembly. Thus in a pre-eminently agricultural country was to be observed the peculiar contradiction in policy of immediate surrender to every demand, put forward by an industrial proletariat minority, and of delay in the settlement of the land question so urgently needed by the overwhelming majority of peasants. The effect of this on the mind of the peasantry can be readily understood.

The Bolshevik Programme and Soviet Majority.—In the same assembly for the first time the Bolshevist programme was indicated with greater precision : " There is one means of creating the peace the whole world is striving for, and this is to turn the Russian National Revolution into the prologue of a rising of all peoples of all countries against the Moloch of imperialism, against the Moloch of war," declared one of its spokesmen. He further threw suspicion on the aims of the Provisional Government and praised the Soviets. He proclaimed the imminence of the civil war and of a " New International." Although the assembly was overwhelmingly opposed to this programme of the Bolsheviks, still the influence of the latter undoubtedly gained ground in the decisions of the assembly.

In this first stage of the Soviet activities we distinguish the chief factors which may be said to have determined the tendencies and the further course of the Soviet policy. The moderate socialist majority in the central executive committee of the Soviets soon began to realize a sense of their responsibilities, and showed genuine concern. Elemental forces seemed to be shaping to an all-destroying explosion. The majority could no longer remain inactive. Their knowledge of the real state of affairs in the country, of the problems of

the Provisional Government at home and abroad, was very
close. They now decided to formulate a more definite
programme of policy, and to modify their attitude to the
State power.

Tsereteli.—In the person of Tsereteli the Soviets had a
gifted leader, a man who knew how to bind together the
moderate socialist elements composing the majority in the
Soviet, and to maintain unity in their ranks up to the
" October days." Leader of the Georgian Social Democrats,
member of the second Duma, exiled to Siberia by the Tsarist
Government, he returned to Russia towards the end of March,
1917, and like most of the socialists inclined to " Zimmerwaldism." But he soon reacted to circumstances and created
the formula officially adopted by the Soviets, viz., the
continuation of the war for freedom side by side with the
contest for peace. His tall, clear-cut, ascetic figure, his deep-
set, burning eyes veiled with a certain melancholy, his straight-
forwardness and sincerity expressed with unusual warmth
of feeling and delicacy of manner, immediately arrested
attention and attracted general sympathy. A fiery orator,
winning all hearts by his persuasive talents, patient forbear-
ance, tireless energy and unconquerable spirit, in whose
composition the doctrinarianism of party was but little evident,
Tsereteli, with his large intellectual and political outlook,
seemed from the beginning marked out for a leading rôle in
the Soviet. His moral cast inspired the admiration of his
friends and compelled the respect of his foes. But in that
richly endowed nature one requisite indispensable for the
leader of a revolution was lacking, the strength of a single,
resolute purpose standing out clearly and dominantly against
the background of unreality where the shadow is too often
taken for the substance. The motive and the cue for passion
were there, and yet before the complex problems of the drama,
Tsereteli remained strangely " impregnant of his cause."
In this picture we may read the whole tragedy of the Russian
Intelligentsia with its overwrought speculation, its feverish
reflection, its exalted idealism, where simple faith refused to
be seduced by the lessons of plain reason and experience.
" I know," says Tsereteli, " that it is only in their blindness

that the peoples follow the route of an imperialistic bourgeoisie. I know that there also the same hour will strike
which has already struck in Russia . . . that these peoples
will compel their Governments to relinquish their aggressive
policies." By nature he was much inclined to compromise.
He stood firmly for coalition in the Government. His
compromise was not that of the trained politician. It was
rather a compromise between what he wished to believe and
the stern reality of facts. He unbosomed himself with words
to convince others of the truth of his ideals, but was impotent
to give them practical effect. When later the decisive struggle
between opposing forces came to a head, Tsereteli was
completely absorbed in devising means for reconciling
the discordant elements.

Moderate Majority of the Soviet.—By the end of April the
democratic majority in the Soviets decided on taking a more
active part in the Government, and six prominent socialists
took office. The executive Committee of the Soviets now
urged more frequently the need and necessity of active
support of the Provisional Government and its policy. But
the vast masses of the people, especially the soldiers in
the rear and the town workers, had been already so
effectively influenced by the attitude of distrust previously
referred to, that they looked to the Soviet as the guardian of
their interests, as the only power in the State to decide the
questions of war, land, etc., etc. Gradually the Soviets were
leavened by the anarchistic and improvident elements of
every sort among the masses of the population. These
elements opposed to discipline of any kind were later on to
prove of the greatest value in the hands of the Bolsheviks.

The All-Russian Assembly of the Peasants' Deputies which
met early in May, was in fact unable to exert any real influence on the course of events. The position taken up by
these deputies was definite, cautious and at the same time
statesmanlike. Yet the strong reserve forces of this assembly
were hardly broached. The Soviets of the Workers' and
Soldiers' Deputies took and held the lead everywhere.

Up to July the moderate socialist opinion dominated all
their counsels. It was only gradually that the elements in

opposition to the policy of moderation were united. The socialist majority succeeded for a time in preventing the complete collapse of the army, in averting the horrors of civil war, in putting off the explosion. They made every effort to restore the economic life of the country. The armed rising of the Petrograd Bolsheviks in July dealt a deadly blow to socialist hopes. The forces of reaction, of militant monarchism which had completely vanished in the first months of the Revolution, reappeared in the political arena. The Bolshevik revolt inspired the reactionary forces in Russia to bring about another *coup d'état*. At the same time the anarchistic elements were reinforced at the expense of moderate socialist influences. The August revolt of General Kornilov against the Provisional Government and Soviet was made possible after the July Bolshevik rising in Petrograd. The Kornilov revolt only strengthened the hand of the extremist elements, especially the Bolsheviks in the Soviets. Like a turbid flood, sweeping over the banks of a river the unsettled masses of the soldiers in the rear, who had drifted away from all discipline, the workers no longer held together by strong class cohesion, the peasants still awaiting the final decision of the land question from the Constituent Assembly, were carried away by the hope of immediately attaining the satisfaction of all their desires—land, wealth, the end of the War—through the Soviets. The Petrograd Soviet of Workers' and Soldiers' Deputies, backed up by the Kronstadt sailors, was gradually becoming the stronghold of Bolshevism. The October revolt was being more and more foreshown.

CHAPTER VII

THE PROVISIONAL GOVERNMENT

THE Provisional Government assumed the full control of power in accordance with strict legal procedure. On his abdication Nicholas II transferred the supreme power to his brother, the Grand Duke Michael. The latter in his manifesto formally handed this over to the Provisional Government " created on the initiative of the State Duma and fully empowered to act until the Constituent Assembly should be summoned." The Provisional Government hastened to record this assignment. On March 8, it published a decree to the effect that it had assumed the liabilities of the last Government with all its commitments. Its declaration on the War and on foreign obligations where the previous agreements with the Allies were re-affirmed was another proof that the question of the succession from the old to the new power was now definitely settled. But the endeavour of the first Provisional Government to establish law and order by right of due succession, while in principle well grounded, was yet inspired by a real misunderstanding of the causes and objects of the Revolution. The explanation that the Revolution had been effected by people whose sole aim was to prosecute the War to a victorious end, who had realized that the old regime blocked the way and that the Tsarist Government was impotent, created not only a false impression of the character and motive forces of the Revolution, but a short-sighted and obstinate official optimism among some members of the first Government. The task of liquidating the old system, of creating a new order and administration, of preserving the needful state machinery whose destruction might react adversely on the issue of the War, was a complicated and serious problem. The War brooded over all counsels. Every plan, every initiative yielded to its exigencies. Hence arose the first difficulties of the new Government. The War was the chief cause of the final collapse of democratic government in Russia.

The Government was in a position of tragic contradiction. It had to decide between concentrating all its energy on carrying on the War to a successful issue and giving immediate

Prince Lvov would have been an excellent Prime Minister in peace time for a free Russia. But as the Prime Minister of the first Revolutionary Government with all his great moral advantages, he was no leader. He had no political authority. In the Cabinet Prince Lvov not only acted as Premier but took on the Ministry for Home Affairs, which was the most difficult and responsible of offices during the Revolution, making the greatest demands on energy and decision. In this post his moderation was not so infirm of purpose as might be supposed. It found at least in his own deep democratic convictions a justification which counts for very little nowadays in the eyes of shrewd politicians, unquestioning faith in the self-restraint of the people, in the soundness of their considered judgment, in the triumph of their common sense.

Minister for Foreign Affairs, Miliukov.—Of another stamp was P. Miliukov, the leader of the Constitutional Democrats (Cadets) and the Minister for Foreign Affairs. An eminent historian, an authority on the past of Russia, a shrewd parliamentarian, well known outside his own country, he had long made problems of foreign policy and international relations his speciality. In the Duma his pronouncements on questions of foreign policy, especially in the Near East, marked him out as the right man for the post of foreign minister in a liberal Government. Quiet and methodical in manner and expression he never carried away his hearers by the eloquence of his appeal. Rather he arrested their attention by the clear analysis and logical development of his subject. The impression created was that of a professor lecturing to a rather backward and unenlightened audience. He was somewhat like Lenin in this respect. Miliukov's speeches were certainly richer in matter, more cultured and more varied in form and in interest than Lenin's, but in their methods of construction and exposition, in the superior attitude they adopted to their audience, in their didactic manner and in their immovable tenacity they were very much alike. Miliukov's strength lay in his remarkable talent for analysis, his weakness in the application of the soundest deductions to practice and policy. In the very thick of the political fray he stood out a strange contradiction of uncompromising combativeness and absolute detachment. His

intellectual disposition and mental attitude to life unfitted him
for the leadership of a political party in the existing conditions. He seemed incapable of feeling the pulse of reality
and bereft at times of all political foresight. The most convinced, sincere and resolute of democrats during the Revolution
he was to be democracy's evil genius on many occasions.

Foreign Policy.—It would be incorrect to divide public
opinion in Russia on the question of the War and foreign
policy, at this time, into two camps, national and Zimmer-
waldian (or internationalist). The vast majority inclined
neither to one nor the other of these extremes. Aggressive
nationalism had been too diligently fostered and nourished
by the Tsarist Government. In reality it had never found a
fertile soil in Russia. It was the general opinion that the
Revolution having at last succeeded in overthrowing the
autocracy, would now introduce principles of justice and fair
play in internal as well as external national relations.
Zimmerwaldism had not taken a great hold on the Russian
people. The democratic majority of Russia fully realized
the necessity of armed resistance to the enemy. Under
what name the War should be continued, what were its
ultimate aims, had these altered since the Revolution, or
were they the same as before—these questions now acquired
a special significance and gave occasion for grave conjectures.
It must also be noted that even if it did not pay much heed to
the actual state of affairs this majority yet felt that the War
could not be carried on indefinitely, and that its continuance
would lead to disaster. On the other hand Russian democracy,
particularly after the Revolution, was full of Utopian idealism.
It eagerly awaited miracles from the new order of things, the
renewal of a Golden Age, when the spirit of justice would
once more reign supreme over mortal counsels and solve all
knotty problems of international relations. The manifesto of
March 14 (*v.* p. 156) aroused great enthusiasm. It sounded
the advent as it were of the new era, the speedy termination
of the War. Such being the general state of mind, even the
convention of the Cadet Party found it difficult to come out
with a policy on the old aggressive lines. It merely confined
itself to cautious, non-committal expressions of conviction

such as "that the Provisional Government would steadily uphold the liberating aims of the War as enunciated by the Allied democracies, without violating the liberties of other nations, but at the same time not permitting any damage to the vital interests and rights of Russia."

In such circumstances the rôle of the Minister for Foreign Affairs in the Revolutionary Government became very important. At this time it is true that the socialist parties over-confidently founded greater hopes on a change of public opinion among the warring nations than on the possible success of traditional diplomacy. But all awaited from the Minister for Foreign Affairs some lead, some indication of a new and definite programme based on securing an early peace, on the renunciation of an aggressive policy, and on exerting due influence on the Allies to that end. It was quite natural to expect that the Allies should be kept correctly informed about the general situation and the prevailing opinion in Russia. Meanwhile, Miliukov either could not understand, or would not reckon with, these factors. He obstinately ignored the changes effected by the Revolution and continued the old aggressive policy. It seemed as if he was deliberately provoking internal conflicts.[1] On March 23, appeared an interview of his in the papers on the subject of President Wilson's message. In this interview Miliukov defined the special problems and aims of Russia point by point, and developed the old aggressive policy to the full. The interview revealed clearly the yawning gulf between foreign policy and public opinion in Russia. The extremists exploited the situation to the utmost, and although there were semi-official *démentis* to the effect that Miliukov had merely expressed his own opinion "which did not represent the views of the Provisional Government," the Government, under the pressure of public opinion, was eventually compelled to come

[1] The same line was followed in the matter of the old diplomatic corps. Unwillingness to change the old foreign office representation abroad led to " an undue toleration, as in some cases people who had sworn fealty to the Provisional Government most decidedly did not play the game," writes K. Nabokov, the Russian chargé d'affaires in London after the death of the Ambassador Count Benckendorf (*Ordeals of a Diplomat*).

out with a definite programme on the question of the War
and of foreign policy.

" *To the Citizens of Russia.*"—Its declaration of March 27,
" to the citizens of Russia," stated that the vital interests of
Russia demanded " the defence by all available means of our
national possession . . . . . Leaving it to the will of the people
in close union with our Allies, to decide all questions connected
with the World War and its termination, the Provisional
Government deems it right and necessary to declare that the
aim of free Russia is not dominion over other peoples, not to
deprive them of their national rights, not the seizure of other
territories, but the establishment of a sound peace based on
the principle of self-determination . . . . . The Russian people
do not aim at strengthening their authority abroad at the
expense of other peoples." The final words of the declaration
that " these principles would be at the base of the foreign
policy of the Provisional Government which, without flinching,
would give effect to the will of the people and defend the
rights of our country while fully observing all obligations to
our Allies," gave foundation to expect and believe that the
Ministry of Foreign Affairs would at length take the proper
steps with the Allied Governments. The declaration was so
understood and interpreted on every side. For instance, the
Republican Officers' Union recognized it as " the first step
towards abandonment of the aggressive policy of the old
regime." The entry of America into the War greatly
encouraged public opinion. Only one doubt arose to disturb
the general confidence. How could a minister, who had
uncompromisingly stood for a distinctly aggressive policy,
now sign a declaration so different in tone. The answer to
this question was soon given by the Minister for Foreign
Affairs. Its consequences were disastrous. On April 18, the
Minister for Foreign Affairs wired to the Russian Representatives accredited to the Allied Powers, instructing them to
hand in a note, which for individual interpretation of a
Government declaration by a minister in the position of
Miliukov, stands unique. In this note it was stated that the
united efforts of the Russian peoples to prosecute the World
War to decisive victory were now all the more strengthened

by the recognition of the common responsibility of each and all. It also made reference, though not so clearly as in previous notes, to guarantees and sanctions. Its purpose was to dissipate rising doubts and suspicions in the minds of the Allies suggested by the Manifesto to the Peoples of all the World and the latest declaration.

Critical Position of the Government.—This note of Miliukov's in the present conjuncture was like a trumpet call to battle. It cleared the ground for anti-Government hostilities. In the street manifestations two irreconcilable enemies could be seen coming to grips. The concord of the early days of the Revolution was ended. The line of demarcation between the opposing forces was now clearly drawn. A bitter social-political conflict ensued. The " April days " effected a complete break between the Provisional Government and the Soviet. In the streets of Petrograd the bodings of the coming storm grew more and more portentous. The Government had found itself forced to interpret Miliukov's note more in the spirit of its own declaration of March 27. The withdrawal of Miliukov from the Ministry of Foreign Affairs was imperative for the reconstitution of the Provisional Government.

The formation of a new cabinet now took place in very altered circumstances. It had to reckon with two opposing elements striving to gain the upper hand. One wanted a strong Government and a military dictatorship. The other sought to establish the dictatorship of a class, the proletariat. Each of these tendencies attracted inconsiderable yet very active followings for whom every means was permissible as long as the end was attained—*i.e.*, the control of supreme power. Already in the beginning of April General Krymov had planned a *coup d'état* to get rid of the Soviets. The monarchists also began to revive activities, placing their hopes on the Grand Duke Michael as " legal " claimant to the throne. In the beginning of May among adherents of the Cadet party, the bourgeoisie, officers and some sections of the town populations there was to be observed a growing movement in favour of a strong government independent of particular interests and influences. It aimed at military dictatorship. About this time were planned those measures which materialized so tragically in the unfortunate revolt of General Kornilov. The old ministry had been weakened by the interference of the Soviets. The newly-formed one could not rely on the full support of the bourgeoisie which had also endeavoured to weaken Government authority, thereby repeating the first mistake of the Soviets.

The Bolshevists now definitely concentrated their forces. At the end of April they already numbered 80,000. The active support of the unruly anarchistic elements in the masses strengthened their influence. They made a regular system of enlisting this support in their All-Russian Convention at the end of April. They held out for fraternization along the whole front, " the simplest manifestation of the solidarity of the oppressed " according to them. They urged the immediate seizure of landed property by the peasantry without awaiting formal solution of this problem by the Constituent Assembly. They insisted on immediately sweeping away the existing administration, on the introduction of the workers' control in factories, the raising of wages, etc., etc. They stood for " the right of self-determination even to the point of separation." They made a fearless and energetic propaganda for the forma- tion of Red Guards as an exclusively class military organization for the purpose of a class dictatorship. Absorbed by the single idea of seizing power they cleverly exploited the food difficulties, the protracted War, the delay in summoning the Constituent Assembly, for their own ends. The Provisional Government was blamed for all that went wrong. Class dictatorship—in reality the dictatorship of their own party—was the immediate goal. The Soviet was the means to this end.

Disorder and anarchy spread rapidly all over the country. Administration of law and order suffered in the provinces left to their own resources during the last two months. The alarming state of affairs at headquarters did not improve matters. The relations between the various nationalities in Russia became very critical. The Government in its declara- tion of April 26, just before its reorganization, clearly understood this : " Unfortunately and to the great danger of freedom the growth of the new social connections which should keep the country together is not making up for the process of disintegration which is the result of the collapse of the old state structure. . . . Elemental forces at work striving to realize the desires of individual sections of the population for separate action . . . are threatening to destroy the cohesion within the State and to create a favourable base for violent acts. . . . Before Russia stands the terrible shadow of civil war and anarchy which will bring on the destruction of liberty, . . . lies the road leading away from liberty through civil war and anarchy to reaction and the return to despotism." On April 29, Kerenski at a meeting of the delegates from the front in Petrograd declared that he no longer had " the previous confidence that there stood before us not slaves in revolt but citizens conscious of their rights creating a new state worthy of the Russian people. . . If we are such unworthy slaves that we will not create such a state, then our ideals will be crushed under the heel of might which will then be law." The moderate majority of the Soviets soon realized the tragic reality of the situation. A greater sense of their responsibilities was now evident. In their desperate efforts for a sound peace, for bringing an end to the sanguinary war which gave no hope for the reorganization of the Russian State, they were still buoyed up with the belief that the other peoples, especially the workers in the Allied countries, would strive for the ending of the War, would understand the tragedy of Russia. One has only to read the appeal of the Soviet to the soldiers concerning the proposed Stockholm conference, and compare it with the Manifesto to the Peoples of All the World in order to understand the changes that had taken place : " Only relying on you (the army) that you will not permit the military defeat of Russia, can the Soviet of Workers' and Soldiers' Deputies carry on its struggle for peace." The Soviets interpreted this as the ending of the War by common agreement between the Allies. The moderate majority in the Soviet felt it was no longer possible to continue the policy of irresponsible control over the Government. The old mentality of the underground, ever more disposed to prove the soundness of a theory than the practical advantages of its application, had now to yield to the force of circumstances. The socialists realized that they must now come to some decision. Three ways lay before them. To take power completely in their own hands was never their intention. Besides, the Soviets were unfitted to cope with the general situation and with administration. There was no use thinking of leaving power in the hands of the non-socialist groups—such a Government would not hold out a week. There remained the formation of a Coalition Government on a definite programme in which socialists would take a responsible share. The Soviets should give it full support.[1]

Coalition Government.—In this way was formed the Coalition Government, in which six prominent socialists and nine liberals and radicals took part. The circumstances of May were very different from those of February. Extremists on either side striving for dictatorship were already organizing their forces—on the right the old governing classes, the landed interests and the bourgeoisie, on the left the Bolsheviks and the closely allied anarchistic elements. The new Provisional Government, " resting on State power, not on arbitrary force, relying on the voluntary submission of free citizens to that power which they themselves have created," was to be amid the dangers threatening from anarchy, " restoration," and dictatorship the only power standing for democratic principles in Russia. But the heroic efforts of the healthier elements of the Russian people met with almost insurmountable obstacles, and not merely within Russia. The Government declaration which, " according to the wishes of the people, rejected any thought of separate peace," [2] but at the same time openly declared its aim to be the earliest possible attainment of general peace, a peace without annexations or

[1] " I was always an opponent of socialist participation in bourgeois governments," declared Tsereteli in defending the coalition. " It is all the more difficult for me to take my present stand. But I think that the Revolution has placed us before quite exceptional circumstances."

[2] The answer of the Petrograd Soviet (May 26) to the Hindenburg radio categorically rejected the offer therein as a proposition of separate peace which would bring on the defeat of the Allies. To Hindenburg's declaration that " the Central Powers since Easter had almost stopped all hostilities on the Eastern Front," the Soviet replied that he (Hindenburg) had forgotten " whither the German divisions and heavy batteries from our front had been removed . . . that the echoes of bloody battles on the Anglo-French Front were being carried back to Russia."

indemnities, on the basis of the self-determination of peoples, received the very coldest of receptions from the side of the Allies. The answers of the latter to the note of the Provisional Government were thus characterized by one of the more moderate Russian papers of that time : " With democratic Russia they (the Allies) speak as they never would have dared to speak with Tsarist Russia." The Allied Governments looked on the formulas of all these declarations as ambiguous catches and cleverly laid traps " not invented in Petrograd, but imported from abroad, their origin being clear." [1] They either did not see or did not want to see the widespread and unambiguous desire for peace, and that the State was quite incapable of continuing a war, whose prolongation would bring on the complete ruin of Russia.

In such an atmosphere it was not astonishing that the proposition which soon followed from the Coalition Government : " to summon a conference of representatives of the Allied Powers—for the revision of the agreement concerning the final objects of the War," was not given any attention by the Allies.[2] The Provisional Government and all political leaders knowing the chaotic state of affairs in Russia, had placed great hopes in this conference, especially in view of restoring the fighting power of the army. A new problem, but of old standing, was now to be added to the list of Russia's overwhelming difficulties, calling for urgent solution.

Problem of Nationalities.—We have already referred to the very complicated setting of the question of nationalities in Russia (*v.* pp. 81-4, 124). It looked as if the Revolution in the beginning had brought peace and mutual goodwill among the peoples of Russia. " Separatism " seemed to have died out during the War. The peoples of Poland, the Ukraine, etc., apparently preferred to link their destinies to a free Russia rather than to a victorious Germany. The circumstances were now changing. The Provisional Government could not,

---

[1] *v.* speech of Bonar Law in House of Commons, May 30, and of Ribot in Chamber of Deputies, May 18 and 24, 1917.

[2] The London Agreement of December 15, 1914, *re* non-conclusion of separate peace by any of the Allies was excluded from this proposed revision.

had not the right to, give definite decisions on any questions where the Constituent Assembly alone should decide. The inability of the Government to take definite action on the various problems of nationalities was soon intrepreted as intentional delay by the peoples in question. In Finland, the Ukraine, etc., German propaganda ably exploited this fertile field of trouble. Still, as far as it could, the Provisional Government satisfied all the more important demands of nationalities put forward under the Tsarist regime. It re-established the constitution of Finland, recognized the independence of Poland, the autonomy of Estonia, and in principle that of Latvia and the Ukraine, and granted local government to the Caucasus. Nationalist appetites only increased. · From all sides arose irreconcilable demands which the Government was not entitled to satisfy. The first Provisional Government might be reproached for paying but little heed to nationalist demands. This reproach can hardly be made to the Coalition Government. In the awful conditions prevailing as a result of the disastrous War, the Government acted with the greatest forethought in tackling these problems. Finland, meanwhile, took every advantage of Russia's difficulty. It evidently followed German leads. For Finland the fall of the monarchy liquidated all relations between Finland and Russia. These were now merely neighbouring states—their future relations with one another remained to be defined. The Provisional Government handed over to the Finnish Senate all matters previously in the prerogative of the Monarch. Still the Finnish extremists were unsatisfied.

In the Ukraine, separatist tendencies were also much in evidence. The Central Rada, a body of somewhat irregular formation, not elected by the Ukrainian people according to usual methods, now insisted on being formally recognized as the National Assembly of an independent state. The Lithuanian Seim, by a majority of conservatives and clericals against liberals, progressives and socialists, declared for immediate determination of the question of Lithuania's constitution. Again, the Coalition Government within the limits of its competence, leaving the final word to the All-Russian Constituent Assembly, tried to satisfy these demands and to compose misunderstandings by negotiations, conferences, etc. The centrifugal forces gathered speed day by day.

Economic Situation.—Meanwhile, the economic life of the country was in a lamentable state. In the two years immediately preceding the February Revolution its collapse had been very evident. Productivity fell steadily. Machinery deteriorated. To replace it was not easy. The proletariat was utterly exhausted. In these years it had completely changed in character as well as in its formation owing to the addition of casual elements attracted not only by the apparently high rate of wages, but by the freedom secured from military service. These elements were unaccustomed to factory discipline and lacked the proletarian mentality. The break-up of the railway system was one of the first effects of all this disorganization, the consequences of which were immediately felt in the supply of raw materials, fuel and especially food. The Revolution seemed to give a new impetus to this disorganization. A struggle began for higher wages which almost completely left out of account the realities of the economic situation. From the very beginning this struggle showed its one-sided character. Indeed, no serious resistance could be offered by organized industry—during the War the economic weapon of the lock-out could not be resorted to. The consequence was that eventually the State had to make up the difference on the concessions won from the industrialist, and in the final account it was the peasant who had to pay. On the one hand the bourgeoisie blamed the workers for all this. On the other the workers blamed the capitalists for being unable and unwilling to restore industry and develop productivity, for artificially controlling scarcity and unemployment, for holding back raw materials, for promoting "sabotage." And so from the economic struggle for a living wage the workers went on to the question of the organization of production, and of the workers' control over it.

The plan of handing over the factories to the workers, of nationalizing them began to gain ground. Industrial organization in respect of management had always been very weak in Russia. Even the wealthiest and best-equipped undertakings depended more on individual directors and on their

business acumen and foresight than on sound technical
organization and administrative system. In a sharp crisis
the strain told. Production suffered. The decrease in the
productivity of labour which had fallen by almost 30 per
cent in the early part of the Revolution, could not be ascribed
solely to the reduction of working hours. The general
disorganization, the lack of raw materials, fuel, food, the
growing difficulties of communication, must be taken into
account here. At the outbreak of the Revolution the peasant
willingly brought his corn to the market. As the War went
on, as industrial production diminished, as the general unrest
especially in the towns increased, the peasant grew more
cautious and withheld his corn. The slight improvement
in this respect which was to be observed in the beginning
of the Revolution was soon set back not only in the
capital, but all over the central and northern parts of the
country.

Food Policy.—These facts coupled with the prevalent
administrative disorganization could not help reacting on the
food problem. It was difficult to expect any betterment
of conditions for two reasons : (1) The food question was
closely linked up with that of the peasantry among whom
organized effort of any kind was rather slow. This class,
intensely preoccupied with the settlement of the land question,
had benefited least of all in the results of the Revolution. It
was now compelled by circumstances to await the solution
of what was for it a most vital question, and from old
experience it had reason to suspect that this solution would
not meet its wishes ; (2) The enormous increase of the army
and of its immediate needs made unparalleled demands on the
resources of the agricultural population. In 1914-15 the
Government had to purchase over 5,600,000 tons of corn and
grain for the army. In 1915-16 the quantity exceeded
8,300,000 tons. In 1916-17 the Government found that at
least 16,500,000 tons were required, *i.e.*, almost the whole of
the market supply in Russia. The food problem, already
difficult enough for any Government in normal conditions, was
especially difficult during the Revolution. In May of 1917,
the food reserves amounted to hardly more than one-half of

the requirements for the army, and the town populations during the period of one month.

From the very start the Provisional Government endeavoured to introduce system and efficiency in its method of dealing with the food problem. The fall of the Tsarist Government may be partly ascribed to its failure to cope with this task. The Provisional Government introduced the corn monopoly by law, March 25, 1917. A special Food Committee was formed to regulate and control all matters in question. Under the Coalition Government a Ministry of Food was created. While some real benefits resulted from this creation the solution of the problem was not achieved. A well-organized, efficient administrative machinery was necessary to enforce such a measure. This the Government had not. It strove to find the solution by providing the villages with all the manufactured articles they might need, by raising fixed prices for corn, by making use of the co-operatives and private enterprise for purchasing, etc., etc. But with an army of such huge dimensions the food difficulties increased from day to day. In existing conditions there were no hopes for a rapid solution of the problem.

Army.—As long as the War continued there could hardly be any question of reducing the army. The Revolution had wrought great changes in its moral. The authority of the officers had long been on the decline.[1] When the crash came the old cohesion was at an end. The old discipline, which had been based on blind, automatic obedience and the strictest formalism, gave way to openly displayed disaffection. The army regulations no longer held their former force when the Provisional Government came into power. The higher command seemed incapable of realizing the change and of reacting to the new conditions. It showed its helplessness from the very beginning. Some of its members, amazed and disgusted, looked

[1] " The break-up of the army was not merely a post-Revolutionary phenomenon. Unwillingness to fight, decline of discipline, distrust and suspicion of the officers, desertion in the rear—all these phenomena were already evident before the Revolution. They were the product of general exhaustion, of the wretched conditions of life, of insufficient nourishment . . . and of lack of authority on the part of the commanding officers." (*History of Second Russian Revolution*, P. N. Miliukov.)

on passively. Others did their best to save the situation by insisting on re-establishing strict discipline. Others, again, gave in and now outvied in revolutionary zeal the most advanced revolutionary leaders just as readily as they had previously backed up arbitrary absolutism when it was the vogue. All were convinced of the urgency of a thorough reorganization in order to restore the fighting capacity of the army. In no case, however, did the higher command produce a single man of outstanding personality able to deal with the situation, to maintain authority and to point the way to this reorganization. It would be a mistake to assume that the majority of the officers were counter-revolutionary or monarchist. Not only the greater part of these but a certain number of the Staff itself openly and frankly sided with the Revolution. The autocracy had no real support from the army. It was difficult, however, to alter at once the old principles at the base of army discipline, to put an end to the long-standing antagonism between officers and men. How to restore the authority of the officers was the question. The army which under the Tsarist Government had been kept strictly isolated from the rest of the population was now seen to be without proper equipment for the purpose for which it was to be made use of, without a proper organization to prevent it from breaking up. In no other country were the army conditions anything like those holding in Russia. In a war of " exhaustion " where all the latest improvements that destructive science could devise played a dominant rôle, Russia, almost as much cut off from the rest of the world as the Central Powers, but, unlike the latter, with a very weak industrial organization, without adequate technical support from the side of her Allies, could only give of her best available resources, her life force. The terrible conditions of trench life, the clear evidence of the technical superiority of the enemy during all these years, could not help reacting disastrously on the mentality of raw and ill-equipped forces, however patriotic and heroic their spirit. When the Revolution broke out the now brutalized, tired-out soldiery were thrown more or less on their own resources. They began to " dismiss " unpopular and unsuitable officers, to elect new commanders, to organize everywhere all kinds of committees with and without

Petrograd garrison." Its authors remain unknown. It certainly was not an individual act. It was published on March 1, in the name of the Petrograd Soviet of Workers' and Soldiers' Deputies. The executive committee of this Soviet only heard of it next day through the papers. It appeared on the day before the Provisional Government was formed. There was no word in it about officers being elected by the soldiers, or of the right of the latter to arrest their superiors in rank. It merely referred to the organization among the divisions and regiments of the Petrograd garrison of soldiers' committees subject to the control of the military committee of the Duma, the participation of the military in political activities without the approval of the Soviet was strongly deprecated ; the strictest discipline should be observed by soldiers in the execution of their military duties ; when not actually on duty, soldiers should enjoy all the civil and political rights of other citizens and need not stand at attention in saluting their officers, who in turn were warned to refrain from rough behaviour to the soldier and addressing him as " thou." It should be remembered that this order appeared in the very midst of the Petrograd revolt, when the struggle with the police was at its height, when the troops in Petrograd were without officers, when all authority seemed lost, when soldiers of every regiment were taking active part in the street fighting. Its aim was evidently to restore some order among wild armed bands, some discipline among the soldiers in revolt—120,000 odd—in Petrograd. Indeed, the necessity for this order may be understood when we remember the facts of the first days of the revolt in Petrograd. We can judge of the exceptional difficulty of the situation here from another order which was published before No. 1, not in the name of the Soviet, but in that of Col. Engelhart, a conservative member of the Duma, a staff officer appointed by the provisional committee of the Duma as Commander of the Petrograd Garrison. " In consequence of rumours," ran the order, " that officers of regiments are depriving soldiers of their arms, rumours which, on verification in the regiments were found to be false, the chief of the Petrograd garrison declares the most energetic measures will be taken to prohibit any such action on the part of officers, even to the extent of shooting the guilty." Such was the atmosphere of Petrograd at this moment, when even conservative politicians and military men of the highest standing, who sided with the Revolution, were compelled to insist on the application of drastic measures against officers who might be inclined to favour the restoration of the old regime. These sharp conflicts did not exist on the front. By agreement with the War Minister, Order No. 1 was withdrawn. In both these orders we can recognize the same background of chaotic upheaval. Something had to be done to bring back even a semblance of order in an almost desperate situation. The enemy was not slow in taking full advantage of it. The Russian army, thoroughly exhausted, was thirsting for peace. The Germans started " fraternizing " along this front. Military operations were held up. Pacifist propaganda was everywhere at work. The demoralization of the Russian army rapidly progressed. The Germans now staked all on transferring most of their divisions and guns to the western front before autumn, so as to strike the decisive blow before the arrival of the American forces. The need of keeping the German forces engaged somehow or other on the Russian front was vital for the Allied Powers who insisted on military action threatening " that otherwise all economic support would be withdrawn." [1] Strongly supported by public opinion, the Coalition Government at once set to work to restore the fighting capacity of the Russian army. In this Government the most responsible post, that of Minister of War and of the Navy, was given to Kerenski.

A. F. Kerenski.—As Minister of Justice in the first Provisional Government, Kerenski had not a post from which he could exert a decisive influence on general policy. It is true that from the very first days of the Revolution he had distinguished himself by his great organizing ability, by his energy and by his determination. On the outbreak of the revolt in Petrograd, Kerenski was one of the very few of the members of the Duma who did not lose their heads. He at once became a leading figure in the Revolutionary movement. " In those days," it was said of him, " his name meant more

[1] *v. World after the War.* (C. R. and D. F. Buxton.)

Hindenburg, in his Memoirs, says : " The Russian unwillingness
to fight (February-April, 1917) was particularly noticeable
in the northern front.¹ Towards the south it was less noticeable. The Rumanians were evidently quite unaffected by it.
From the beginning of May even on the northern front it was
becoming clear that the authorities once more had the reins
in hand. Friendly relations along the opposing trenches died
out gradually. Recourse was had to arms as of old. Soon
there was no doubt left that in the rear of the Russian front
the restoration of discipline was proceeding apace, and that
intense activity was being displayed. So the Russian army,
at least in part, was becoming not only capable of resisting,
but of advancing." Russia was now fulfilling her strategic
obligations, bringing back the enemy forces to her front and
holding them there so as to prevent a decisive German victory
elsewhere before the arrival of the American troops. In army
despatches from the Russian Headquarters in September, we
read : " More than six months have elapsed since the start of
the Revolution, yet our army continues to hold up the enemy
forces on the front as previously. Instead of decreasing,
these forces have now increased. On the day when our forces
began to advance in Galicia (June 18) the number of the
enemy divisions engaged on the Russo-German front was the
same as up to February 27. At the very height of the struggle
in Eastern Galicia and Bukovina the enemy forces had increased
by nine-and-a-half divisions of infantry . . . . . The increase
was from the German side, the Turkish and Austrian numbers
having diminished. The enemy artillery during this period
was strengthened by the addition of 640 guns of varying
calibre. The Caucasian front is not included here."

May-September, 1917.—Not only was the army moral slowly
yet perceptibly improving between the months of May and
September, but the authority of the Government was distinctly
strengthening. The Coalition Government was undoubtedly
stronger than the previous one. The leaders of most of the
political parties displayed a soberness of judgment and a realization of their responsibilities which had been almost entirely

¹ Because, perhaps, it was nearer to Petrograd where incurable
disease was working its course.

lacking before. All over the country order was rising out of chaos. The administrative machinery was once again at work and doing it effectively. The casually, hastily-formed revolutionary bodies and groups which had taken on the administration of law and order in the provinces gradually yielded to the authority of the new Commissars appointed by the Government and to properly elected local institutions. A new local Government system was established freeing the old local government institutions for towns and country from most of the needless Government restrictions, enlarging their scope and introducing general suffrage. The local government system was extended even to the smallest administrative units, the Volosts, whereby the peasantry were enabled to exert a considerable influence on, and take a full share in public life. Up to date we have but little reliable information, statistics and data regarding the real conditions of Russian provincial life during the Revolution. But from personal impressions and observations confirmed by more recent expressions of opinion by writers well qualified to judge of the facts, we think we are justified in saying that in the country and in the provinces, the re-establishment of order was effected without great difficulty, and that healthier conditions for the development of sound democratic institutions were in evidence. The new institutions began to root themselves in the life of the people. The rule of the Government was felt on the spot and justified the exercise it had made of its authority. The administrative apparatus was working fairly smoothly. The results of the elections for the Zemstvos and municipalities testified to the moderation and soberness of political opinion in the provinces. In the agricultural districts and the villages the majority voted for moderate Social Revolutionaries. In the towns the Liberals obtained considerable support, the moderate Social Revolutionaries and the Social-Democrat Mensheviks following up closely. The country, however, was still in a state of war, and the question of food supplies, transport and other economic problems were very urgent. The revival of normal conditions could not but be slow and subject to frequent relapses. The " new life " had started on an almost desert soil where the experience of democratic traditions had long been forcibly limited, where there were not many practical men to point out the way to progress. The future historian of the Russian Revolution in possession of all the material necessary for his task will undoubtedly pay a special attention to the unmistakable progress that was being marked in provincial life at this period.

A very different picture was to be seen in Petrograd where during all this time the Revolutionary fever never abated. Petrograd felt itself to be the " hero of the Revolution." The executive committees and head organizations of the various Revolutionary groups and parties were all concentrated in Petrograd. The atmosphere was tense with excitement which infected every soldier and every workman in the city. The soldiers and sailors of the garrison looked on themselves as the bulwark of the Revolution, as the guardians of its achievements. They refused to go to the front. The first duty was " to defend the Revolution in Petrograd." This feeling of superiority and the exaggerated estimate of their own importance were craftily made use of by the Bolsheviks in spreading broadcast the most disruptive propaganda. The Bolsheviks succeeded in transplanting the same sentiments among the workers who had already from the very first days of the Revolution, as we pointed out, arrogated to themselves the right of speaking for all the workers of Russia. In Moscow, industrially no less important than Petrograd, the mob did not immediately gain the upper hand. Until November the atmosphere was quite different. The Bolsheviks in Petrograd made direct appeals to the passions of the mob with such declarations as : " Arrest 50 or 100 of the biggest millionaires, publish the incomes of our master capitalists—else all phrases about peace without annexation or contribution are empty words ; " " declare that you (the Government) consider all capitalists as highway robbers " ; " immediate peace over the heads of Government "—all these slogans were specially designed to rouse mob feeling. Street manifestations were organized, culminating in an armed demonstration of June 17 quickly suppressed by the Coalition Government. A yet more serious rising occurred July 3–5, when the Cadet Ministers resigned office on the question of granting autonomy to the

Ukrainians before the meeting of the Constituent Assembly. The Ukrainian question was the immediate pretext made use of by the Bolsheviks for their rising. Kamenev now declared : " In view of the Government crisis we insist that the All-Russian Soviet of Soldiers', Workers' and Peasants' Deputies should take all power in their hands." As another prominent Bolshevik asserted later that all these risings " were managed and controlled by the military organization attached to the Central Committee of our party. It had exact details of the position of the military forces, and of armed workers in the various districts. In the hands of this organization were collected all data *re* intelligence, guards, etc. It issued military orders for the armed risings, for the sending of armed cars, of cruisers from Kronstadt, etc. It had marked on a map all the strategical points which were to be seized."

The July revolt was not, however, sufficiently well prepared. After two days of desultory fighting in the streets it was suppressed. In the country and in the army no sympathy was shown in this rising. For the Bolsheviks, however, the revolt was a trial of strength. The experiment proved that in the streets of Petrograd they could find real support. They knew how to attract the mob and fashion it to their own ends. They were now convinced that in a short time they would be able to overcome without difficulty the power of the Government, the Soviet and the army. The same hope emboldened the very opposite elements, those of the extreme Right, while the suppression of the July rising raised their spirits immensely. The example of the revolt as a means of attaining their own ends more readily was not lost on them. They felt justified in taking vigorous measures not only against the weak Government but against everything savouring of democracy.

New Government Crisis.—The Coalition Government in overcoming the July revolt did not reckon with the fact that its authority was already very much undermined. Its optimism was rudely upset by the refusal of the Cadets and other members of the Cabinet to forestall the decisions of the Constituent Assembly, not only on the question of the grant of autonomy to the Ukraine, but on that of the form of Government to be adopted by Russia, etc., etc., decisions which they declared to be only within the competence of the Constituent Assembly. The Prime Minister, Prince Lvov and a number of other Ministers resigned and Kerenski was invited to form a new Cabinet. After several ineffectual efforts to overcome difficulties among the chief political parties, Kerenski resigned, and then by special decision of these he was again requested to form a new Government. The Cabinet was completed on July 25, when all parties with the exception of the Bolsheviks and extreme Rights were represented. The prolonged crisis, however, very clearly indicated how fatal to the stability of any sort of government was the absence of authority deriving from a representative assembly of the whole nation. The new Provisional Government meanwhile was becoming more and more affected by the poisonous atmosphere of Petrograd. There was no hope of being able to summon the Constituent Assembly before the end of the year. The first Provisional Government had appointed a special commission to frame the best possible electoral law. To deprive the army of the right of voting was out of the question, and at the same time the difficulty of holding elections in the midst of war activities was evident. All these things combined to delay still further the date of elections for the Assembly which alone could bring Russia back to sanity and reason. The Government meanwhile acutely felt the need of the support of the country. It tried the temporary expedient of summoning in Moscow in the middle of August a State Council composed of representatives of the various political parties, municipal organizations, economic interests, etc. A month later it summoned a similar Council in Petrograd, and even formed from this a permanent consultative organ—a " fore-Parliament " as it was designated. But none of these substitutes could hope to replace even temporarily a regularly elected assembly of the whole nation's choice.

Kornilov Revolt.—We have seen that the July rising of the Bolsheviks had revived the extremist activities on the right as well as on the left. Both sides were aiming at dictatorship. The position of the centre parties weakened. After the July rising the activities of the right groups were especially noticeable. Every pressure was put on the Government. Secret conspiracies were organized to overthrow it, to get rid of

" revolutionary " institutions and committees, to establish a military dictatorship. Meanwhile the Bolsheviks having completely in hand the vast masses of casual, disaffected war workers and utterly demoralized soldiers of the rear, were just as methodical in carrying out their own plans for a general rising. The partisans of military dictatorship had not behind them the numerical advantage of and the well-organized and vigorous forces of revolution. Moreover, they were not inclined to carry out their object by riding on the crest of the revolutionary wave, by direct appeal to the more moderate elements of the country. They now concentrated all their efforts on the organization of plots for a *coup d'état*. Different groups urged on by different motives were drawn into these activities. Among them were to be found sincere and earnest patriots like General Kornilov, unscrupulous politicians like Savinkov, and many more for whom the Revolution spelled personal disaster. On the military side there would seem to be no doubt that the leaders of the conspiracy were well-meaning. During the Revolution they had steadfastly held to their posts at the front and borne unflinchingly all the horrors of the trench warfare. The army was breaking up. They could yet save it and Russia from impending disaster. They could yet bring back to Russia her old might. At Army Headquarters plans were carefully laid and means devised to bring about a military *coup d'état*. The moving spirit was none other than the Commander-in-Chief, Alexeiev. General Kornilov was the willing instrument of this able man. Even now it is difficult to get at all the facts of the Kornilov revolt towards the end of August.[1] But the more one studies the evidence at hand the more one is convinced that from this period dates the beginning of the civil war in Russia which gave the death blow to the army at the front and opened the way for the Bolshevik regime. The country had to choose between three solutions: (1) a military dictatorship; (2) a Bolshevik dictatorship; (3) the rule of the Coalition Government which had arisen from the Revolution, and rested on the support of the nation. In the existing condition of affairs in Russia at this time the

[1] General Kornilov was appointed Commander-in-Chief, July 24, replacing General Brussilov who had succeeded General Alexeiev.

The Bolshevik position in Petrograd was now very strong. In the beginning of September they had already succeeded in getting a majority in the Petrograd Soviet. Their influence spread rapidly in the army, in the front as in the rear. So serious was this influence as shown by the mass desertion, indiscipline, etc., etc., that the authorities were forced to reconsider the question of the continuation of the War. A last effort was made by the Government to save the situation by demobilizing the more infected divisions and regiments in order to re-form the remainder into a smaller but more efficient fighting force. At the same time it took steps to urge on the Allies the necessity of calling an immediate conference for the discussion of the terms of a general peace. It was, however, too late meanwhile to think of restoring discipline in the army. The possibility of immediate help from the Allies, and the hopes of an early conclusion of peace were vain. The idea of separate peace could not be entertained in view of many obligations. There seemed to be no exit for Russia out of this blind alley. The second effort of the Russian people to establish a democratic system was stifled in the very War which had given birth to it. The exhausted masses thirsted for peace. The land hunger of the peasantry was as unappeased as ever. The yearning for more settled conditions was general. The Bolsheviks now came to the front as harbingers of peace. " We want immediate peace. All land must be handed over to the workers. Help to the poor. . . . Put the homeless in the houses of the rich. . . . Supply milk to the children of the poor. . . . Hand over factories and banks to the control of the workers. . . . The victory to the workers of the whole world," these were the promises held out by Lenin to capture the minds of the people. Trotski on October 9, in the Petrograd Soviet came out with the declaration : " Let all be ready for the fight to seize power." About October 20, the Bolsheviks formed a special military Revolutionary Committee at the Headquarters for organizing the *coup d'état*, the date for which, October 25, was indicated. This day had also been fixed for the General Assembly of the All-Russian Soviets in Petrograd. As the Bolsheviks were not quite sure of having a majority in the Assembly, they started their rising on the eve of October 25 and issued a proclamation : " The Provisional Government is deposed. The powers of the State had passed into the hands of the organ of the Petrograd Soviet of the Workers' and Soldiers' Deputies, the military Revolutionary committee standing at the head of the Petrograd proletariat and garrison." The seizure of the principal Government institutions and offices was immediately taken in hand. On October 26 a new Government was declared, the " Soviet of the People's Commissars," at the head of which was Lenin. Lenin had at length gained his first object. The formula now was : " War against war. Let us transform the imperialist war into a civil war."

reasonable elements to influence the masses, to control unbridled forces and guide them into certain directions ended in failure, whereas the efforts of those men who were the morbid product of the War and of the demoralizing conditions of secret propaganda during the Tsarist regime were crowned with success. It was not to be wondered at that the ignorant masses, thrown on their own resources or else urged on by adventurers exploiting them from interested motives for ulterior aims, gave the fullest licence to their destructive propensities.

All the political parties in Russia during the summer of 1917 had foreseen that an outbreak of violence was inevitable. But each party looked upon this possibility from quite a different angle, and from these points of view arose the differences in method and action to be observed among the various Russian political parties in 1917. Some among the Liberals and Conservatives had not accurately gauged the real significance of the disruptive forces at work ; others, the Radicals and Moderate Socialists, made desperate efforts to deal with the serious evidence of facts and to cope with the situation ; while the Bolsheviks in the interests of an idea quite foreign to Russian aspirations staked their all on an immediate outbreak, come what might. The Bolsheviks had divined the secret of how to sway the masses by urging them on at first to the worst excesses and then exacting unconditional obedience to further orders for more methodical destruction. By such incitements the vast unorganized masses could be easily led and eventually brought under some sort of control. The lavish promises of the Bolsheviks gradually won over the land-hungry peasants, the workmen and the soldiers. The Bolshevik leaders, however, realized the comparative insignificance of their forces as a party organization. The municipal elections in May and August, as also the November elections in 1917, for the Constituent Assembly, had given considerable majorities all over the country to the democratic and moderate Social Revolutionary parties. On the very eve of the Bolshevik *coup d'état* of October, 1917, Lenin had put the question : " Will the Bolsheviks be able to retain power ? " His answer was : " The State is an organ or machine for the domination of one class over the others. One hundred and thirty thousand landlords have been able to rule over Russia. Cannot 240,000 members of the Bolshevik Party now do the same ? " What they wanted at first, he argued, was the support of some sections of the population, the passive attitude of others and the indecision of the great majority. The discontented elements could and should be forcibly suppressed. The Bolsheviks should put into practice the counsel of the greatest master of Revolutionary tactics, Danton, *re* audacity. They should go for the enemy, while his forces were scattered and take him unawares. With these objects in view, the Bolsheviks drew up their plan of campaign before they seized power and during the early period of their rule from 1917 to 1918. The people were already weary of the War and thirsting for peace. The Bolsheviks immediately held out the promise of peace, though they well knew that they had much less chance of bringing about a general peace than the Provisional Government, that separate peace would mean the humiliation of Russia, the ascendancy of Germany and the beginning of civil war within the country. To satisfy the land hunger of the peasants the Bolsheviks advised the immediate seizure of estates. They were indeed quite aware that this seizure would not solve the agrarian problem, that an out-and-out " black " redistribution would result in futile destruction of valuable property, in immense economic losses. The peasantry was not a reliable element from the Bolshevik point of view. However, by giving it this immediate satisfaction the Bolsheviks hoped to secure at least its friendly neutrality. In order to win over the peasantry to their side at once they dropped their own land programme and gave effect to that of the Social Revolutionaries. Meanwhile the national minorities were striving vigorously for the realization of their national independence. To win their support the Bolsheviks had not only promised them autonomy, but had even incited them to press for complete separation from Russia (*v.* p. 171). At the same time Lenin asserted, " as soon as the State becomes proletarian and can be made into an instrument of repression and violence against the bourgeoisie, we shall then stand unhesitatingly for centralization and strong authority." The summoning of the Constituent Assembly was eagerly awaited by all. Before seizing power the Bolsheviks had constantly accused the Provisional Government of deliberately postponing the date of its meeting. Over and over again they had declared that as soon as ever they came into power the Assembly would be immediately summoned. One of the very first acts, however, of the Communists, when they at length succeeded in overthrowing the Provisional Government, was to proclaim and disperse the Constituent Assembly (January 18, 1918), which was now an obstacle in their way.

The System of Terror.—From the very first days of the Soviet rule, Lenin's oft-repeated formula, " The State is the tyranny of a minority over a majority," was put to the practical test by the Bolsheviks. In order to safeguard the power so hazardously won, terror was now organized into a regular system. At first the ignorant masses were goaded on to every excess of lawlessness and violence in order to destroy completely the existing bourgeois order of things.

In comparing the two periods of the Russian Revolution, that under the Provisional Government from February to October and that under the Soviet rule after the Bolshevik *coup d'état* of October, 1917, one cannot help being struck by the remarkable difference not only between the methods of government of the two regimes, but in the application of these methods in civil and private or personal relations. The Provisional Government cannot be accused of having at any time endeavoured to maintain its power by the forceful methods of the Bolshevik leaders. Indeed, one might say of it, it preferred being exterminated to exterminating others. On the other hand, the Bolsheviks long before the Yaroslav and the Cheko-Slovak " rising," long before the assassination of the Communist Commissar, Uritski in Petrograd, and the attempt on Lenin's life in Moscow, by an edict of the Soviet of the People's Commissars (Sovnarkom), February 8, 1918, decreed " the shooting on the spot (*i.e.*, execution without examination or trial) of counter-revolutionary agitators—men and women of the bourgeois class refusing to carry out orders for the digging of trenches." We have the unchallenged evidence of I. Steinberg, who was then the People's Commissar for Justice, that in March, 1918, the Executive Committee of the Soviet seriously considered the proposal of one local Soviet to shoot down wholesale all the leaders of the Mensheviks and right-wing Social Revolutionaries. The merciless system of terror put into practice by the Bolsheviks as soon as they assumed power was as unjustifiable as it was unreasonable. At first individual Communists declaring themselves to be members of a body called the Military-Revolutionary Committee, fearful of the odds against them, took the law into their own hands and indulged in all sorts of arbitrary acts with the object of terrorizing the easy-going citizen. By December, 1917, Dzerzinski, one of the master-minds of the Russian Terror system, had put an end to this irresponsible procedure by establishing the " Supreme Extraordinary Commission to Combat Counter-Revolution and Speculation " (Cheka) whose punitive apparatus now became the chief arm of the Bolshevik power. Henceforth terror was the central dogma of the Bolshevik creed. One of its leading exponents, Bukharin, declared : " Proletarian compulsion in every shape and form beginning with shooting is one of the means for producing the Communist man out of the material of the capitalist era." This was no mere clever aphorism of a young man aping for effect. It revealed the basic principle of Bolshevism, a principle resolutely put into practice from the very first days of Lenin's dictatorship. That the utterly ruthless application of this theory in Russia did not immediately provoke the outraged conscience of humanity in the rest of Europe to a more vehement and vigorous expression of its moral indignation, and has so far failed to do so, can only be explained by the general decline of moral sense and authority as the result of a merciless war of extermination.[1]

---

[1] It is interesting to note that Professor Aulard maintains, not convincingly in our opinion, that throughout the whole period of the French Revolution terror was never organized as a system. The Revolutionary rule was cruel at times, but its cruelties were provoked solely by the opposition of its enemies. They were, in his opinion, inevitable reprisals, indeed the only means of self-defence. The Bolsheviks have advanced the same arguments in justification of their own cruelty. Professor Aulard rightly does not admit this reasoning for what was essentially an organized system of terror. On the contrary the wholesale murder system adopted by Lenin and his followers arouses the Professor's vehement indignation.

To seek the explanation of the undoubted horrors of the Bolshevik Revolution in the innate barbarism and cruelty of the Russian himself, an argument often advanced by the Communist, is a preposterous argument for the intelligent observer who has had opportunities of closer contact with Russian life and thought. The explanation must be sought elsewhere. It is quite true that the vast majority of the Russian people had become almost indifferent to suffering after centuries of serfdom and arbitrary rule, during which they developed a capacity for endurance under oppression for which no other nation can offer a parallel. At times, however, a fierce and ungovernable resentment betrayed itself. But it was seldom shown, and never of long duration. The argument of the innate cruelty of the Russian is certainly not borne out by the evidence of competent observers on the spot as far as the villages are concerned. Many reliable witnesses for whom the Russian Revolution was an unspeakable disaster from many points of view, testify to the exceptionally calm and peaceful nature of its course on the countryside. " It is by no means necessary to be an idealist and a lover of the people," writes a landlord referring to the earlier stages of the Revolution, " to affirm that no social revolution was ever carried out so peacefully and bloodlessly as the Russian one where property was the sole issue, not the person." The brutal treatment and murder of landed proprietors were quite exceptional occurrences. " Nine-tenths of the victims of the really bloody Revolution (*i.e.*, the Terror) fell at a time when the peasantry was no longer a creative force in it, but rather its object (of attack)." It was not in the country but in the towns that the Terror started. The towns were, in the first place, more accessible and manageable from the point of view of Communist control. They at the same time were extremely dangerous centres attracting all kinds of organizing talent which might be used for hatching counter-plots. There was every reason for starting the Cheka Terror in the towns and then extending it from there to the villages.

Systematic terror was looked on by Lenin not only as the logical consequence and embodiment of the idea of the dictatorship of a minority over a majority, but as a great educational force for the creation of a new type of man. As long as the Communist party remains in power in Russia, it is hopeless to expect that this weapon will be laid aside. As long as this Party considers itself to be above the State, the army to be a Party and not a State force, the State interests to be a Party concern, so long will terror be absolutely necessary in order to maintain this Party in power. We saw how democratic principles within the Bolshevik organization had had to yield to the absolute authority and strict orders of a Central Committee of the Party long before the Bolsheviks declared war against democracy as a form of State structure. As long, however, as the State power was in other hands, unfettered democracy was the rallying slogan of Bolshevist oratory. But when at last the State power was completely in their control, they started to reconstruct it on the bases on which their own Party was built.

In order to arrive at a proper estimate of the existing regime in Russia we must take into account the peculiar mentality of the Communist Party, the principles of its organization, and more especially the dominating character of its foremost spokesman, Lenin, the creator of the proletarian dictatorship. As already pointed out (pp. 144-6), this party was from the very start a party of conspirators, of professional revolutionaries formed on the autocratic principle of blind submission of rank and file to a central authority controlled by Lenin. The failure of Lenin to establish the supremacy of his group within the Social Democratic Party had led to the splitting up of this party into Mensheviks and Bolsheviks, the latter unweariedly striving to gain the upper hand over all political movements in Russia and claiming the sole right to speak in the name of the Russian working classes. To attain its object the Bolshevik group made use of men of the lowest reputation and even of well-known provocateurs. They resorted to every means to raise funds for their organization—armed attacks on banks and wealthy individuals (so-called "expropriations"), blackmail and extortion under the threat of immediate exposure, the issue of false money etc.[1] In 1907, J. Martov, one

[1] *v.* the interesting correspondence between two leaders of the Social-Democratic Party, P. Axelrod and J. Martov from 1901 to 1916 in

of the leaders of the Social-Democratic Party wrote: "I confess I am more and more of opinion that even a nominal participation in the policy of this band of highwaymen is a mistake." Such a peculiar political organization could only have arisen in the abnormal conditions under the Tsarist system, where the open exercise of healthy political activities was sternly repressed; where the subject masses had no possibility of acquiring political experience. Its success is in a great part to be attributed to the immense strength of will and the almost maniacal obstinacy of its creator and organizer, Vladimir Ilich Ulianov Lenin, a man of whom it might well be said, *le parti c'est moi*.

Lenin.—Vladimir Ilich Ulianov, born in Simbirsk in 1870, was the son of a district inspector of schools. The family sprang from a stock of impoverished nobles. Like the majority of the Russian youth frequenting the University, Lenin, as he was afterwards to be known, early took part in political activities, more particularly during his residence at the Petersburg University. The execution of his elder brother, Nicholas, who had been associated with the People's Will party for his share in the attempted assassination of the Tsar Alexander III in 1887, threw Lenin into the revolutionary movement. He joined the ranks of the Russian Marxists and was soon sentenced to a small term of exile in Siberia for propagating revolutionary ideas among the working classes of Petersburg. During his exile he wrote his first work, *The Development of Capitalism in Russia*, in which he attempted to prove that the land reforms of Alexander II after the abolition of serfdom had brought about the "proletarianization" of the Russian peasant. On settling down abroad after his term of exile was at an end, he became what was known in Russia as a professional revolutionary, devoting himself exclusively to the work of revolutionary organization and secret propaganda. In the underground *milieus* frequented by fellow-conspirators and workers he soon won recognition for his indefatigable energy. While never coming up to the high intellectual level of his mentor Plekhanov or of Martov, Lenin soon dominated the counsels of these *milieus*. He had a remarkable talent for getting at the facts he wanted, for reducing the most complex problems to a plausible simplicity. The immediate purpose was clearly visualized. To attain this no obstacle was allowed to stand in the way. The end justified any and every means. Lenin was but little concerned with the moral qualities of his adherents and followers. Indeed, it might be said that such qualities were serious handicaps in his eyes, unfitting men to be the obedient servitors and executors of his will. Simple and unaffected in his own mode of life, he was among his immediate associates considered good company. Perhaps this characteristic was not so much the effect of good nature and kindliness on his part as of imperturbable good humour resulting from the satisfaction of feeling his own superiority, a good humour combined with a strong dose of contempt for human nature in general. This contempt was at times just as freely expressed for friend as for foe, and could be gauged by the cynical jibes and coarse sophistries with which he brushed aside intellectual doubt and speculation. By holding the masses at a distance he was enabled to strengthen the prestige of his authority. Even when he found it necessary to make a complete change of policy or of method he never lost for a moment his supreme self-confidence. In the most unexpected turn of events he could speak of himself thus : " I don't yet know where I am going to, but I am going there resolutely." As an orator he lacked the fire of Kerenski, the erudition of Miliukov, the all-redeeming sincerity of Tsereteli, the flashing brilliance of Trotski. Lenin's oratory was specially distinguished by the almost irresistible power of suggestion of his masterful mind. His speeches were always direct and to the point, as he saw it, and generally very simple in form even if crude in matter. Lenin at no time showed any desire to argue with opponents or to bring them to his own views. He preferred to cut off all communication, and this he did most effectively by flinging the coarsest catchwords, taunts and jeers at their heads, and covering them with contempt and ridicule. With such phrases as " If you don't understand this, you under-stand nothing," Lenin would sweep away opposition to his views. His speeches had always a definite purpose. With different variations he would repeat the main thesis with an almost monotonous iteration, and hammer it as it were into the heads of his hearers.

Lenin's immense strength of will and boundless energy rendered him eminently fitted to be a leader in the underground revolutionary activity into which he threw himself. He soon gathered round him a great number of willing executors of all his schemes. Among his adherents few men of principle were to be found. They were all men of action. Few perhaps agreed with him, but they all believed in him. Lenin had created his organization on the basis of unquestioning obedience to a central authority where he was the supreme dictator. At first it formed only a small group within the rather loosely knit ranks of the Social-Democratic Party. It was, however, a strongly disciplined force of resolute men out for a definite purpose, viz., the complete overthrow of any form of government showing a tendency to compromise with the " bourgeois system," and the substitution therefor of the " dictatorship of the proletariat."

Lenin has been acclaimed by his followers as the Mahomet of the Marxian gospel. His orthodoxy, however, is distinctly open to question. According to Marx, in existing economic conditions the transformation of society on socialistic bases can only be achieved through a gradual and natural evolution of capitalism culminating in the concentration of industry in the State. Theories of gradual development, of the natural evolution of economic laws and forces gathering increased strength from their very suppression under the industrialist regime, asserting their authority and righting old wrong in the fullness of time, cannot be said to have much preoccupied at any time the impatient mind of the out-and-out empiricist that was Lenin, except in so far as they might serve to bait the Bolshevist hook. Lenin, who was no economist in the Marxian or any other sense, could never reach beyond the conception of a state of society where physical force consciously and vigorously applied was the first as well as the last word of the argument. In every circumstance he believed in taking time by the forelock, giving scarce a thought to the consequences that generally follow the miscarriages of premature birth.

He saw that in a state no power can enforce its authority without the means of compulsion. Only in this way are minorities enabled to establish their rule over majorities. How to seize this power was the vital question, the prime consideration for Lenin. Success he knew well was often as much the result of mere chance as of conscious effort and careful preparation. That the working classes should be awakened to a full realization of what was in their own best interest was by no means essential. All that was needed was the formation of a group of determined men, however insignificant they might be in numbers, knowing what was for the best of these classes, what were the quickest means of seizing power and ready to exploit every occasion and situation to this end. Russia with her 80 per cent of an agricultural population, with her very limited and almost unorganized labour element, was the very last country Marx would have chosen for putting his theories of the proletarian revolution and dictatorship to the test. Lenin, on the other hand, had no hesitation in taking advantage of the War to precipitate this revolution in Russia; and he over and over again declared that the Marxian teachings were bound to triumph immediately in such countries as Asia, India and China, by reason of the growth not of industrial development, but of conditions making for racial and national unrest. Lenin evidently shared the opinion of Bakunin that the working classes of western Europe had become too bourgeois owing to good wages and education of a sort, that they were only to be distinguished from the real bourgeois by position rather than direction. The Marxian light should be brought to them from the east whence the Russian Communist Party was to extend its dictatorship over Labour movements all the world over.

The persistent energy and dogged obstinacy displayed by Lenin in the pursuit of his object were astounding. In the counsels of the Communist Party his will was supreme, his word was law. When the War was declared, " he from the first moment came out as a so-called defeatist, *i.e.*, affirmed his belief that it would be to the greater advantage of the

Russian proletariat that Tsarist Russia should suffer defeat "
(*Zinoviev*). He was but little concerned with considerations of
what the triumph of Germany over her enemies might mean
for the Russian people. Absolutely unperturbed by the defec-
tion of most of his adherents on the War issue, he stolidly
stuck to the opinion that the defeat of Russia would inevitably
and rapidly bring about the outbreak of the proletarian
revolution within the Empire, whence it would spread all
over Europe and the rest of the world. When in the spring of
1917 the Russian Revolution did actually break out (the
Bolsheviks played no rôle here) Lenin, before he was quite
aware of what was happening in Russia, declared it to be a
bourgeois revolt, and the Provisional Government to be the
" servant of the capitalists." He at once decided on exploiting
the situation to the utmost. The German authorities gave him
every facility for expediting his journey, a most risky undertaking, from Switzerland *via* Germany and Sweden into
Russia. He was well aware that the German Government
reckoned that it would be to its great advantage if " these
Bolsheviks " cropped up just now in Russia to add to the
worries of the Provisional Government. Lenin accepted this
help with the same alacrity with which later on in Russia he
accepted the monetary and other services of persons having
nothing in common with the socialist parties, but undoubtedly
in contact with the German Headquarters.

At the very time when Lenin was straining every energy to
make the Soviets seize power, whereupon he would immediately
take the upper hand over them, when he was urging every
argument for giving immediate effect to this " regular conspiracy," he encountered serious opposition from such
prominent men of his own party as Zinoviev, Kamenev,
Rykov, etc. At this very time Trotski characterized Lenin
in the jargon of the period as the professional exploiter of
every backwardness in the Russian Labour movement. Yet
in face of all this opposition Lenin resolutely followed his line
of policy, relying now on the less discriminating support of
the man in the street. Even after the seizure of power by the
Bolsheviks the same leaders, Zinoviev, Kamenev, etc., for-
warded an ultimatum in November, 1917, demanding the

creation of a coalition government formed from all the parties represented by the Soviet. They believed that in no other way could they avoid the establishment of a government based on political terror pure and simple. But Lenin had his way.

The seizure of power in Petrograd was not recognized in Moscow, where the Bolshevik rising encountered strong opposition from all sections of the community. The army was immediately put into movement by Lenin and the bombardment of the city and the old Kremlin began. This measure called forth indignant protests from even such convinced members of the Bolshevik party as Lunacharski and Gorki. Lenin was no wise deterred. He foresaw that if he won the day these men would be the very first to justify his so-called " barbarity." What right had they, he said, to call this a great Revolution if they allowed the White Guard " sabotagists " to escape their punishment? Peters, one of the chiefs of the Cheka, frankly admits that Lenin's closest adherents were at first very unwilling to join this organization and to take part in its work. It was only by the strongest pressure that Lenin eventually succeeded in inducing them to realize the necessity of adopting " exceptionally severe measures to save the Revolution." There could be no war, he said, without victims (*v.* Peters, *Proletarian Revolution*, No. 10, Moscow, 1924).

After the successful *coup de force* of October they were now faced by the problem of how to maintain power. Lenin's previsions had turned out to be correct. He had calculated, as we have pointed out, on the support of a few sections of the Soviets, the passive attitude of others and the indecision of the great majority. He was quite aware of the fact that the peasantry was not on his side. Its sole concern was to acquire the land. It had no other interest in the Revolution. Lenin lost no time in securing the passive acquiescence of the peasantry by putting forward such a programme of land reform as would answer to its immediate requirements, a programme in direct contradiction to Marxian doctrines and the land programme he had himself previously drawn up. The new programme, however, was carried out after serious objections from the more orthodox members of the Communist Party, " root and branch " men opposed to any measure savouring of makeshift or compromise.

The Brest-Litovsk Peace Treaty supplies another illustration of Lenin's almost unlimited influence. Up to the October *coup d'état* the Bolsheviks had fed the soldiers with promises of " immediate peace." As soon as ever the Bolsheviks were in power, said Lenin, " the German proletariat would compel the Kaiser to agree to start negotiations for peace," and the same thing would happen in all the other Allied countries. This would be followed by the immediate overthrow of the capitalist system all over Europe. The time had now come for the translation of words into action. Promises had to be redeemed. The story of the Brest-Litovsk Peace Treaty is one long tragedy of piteous disillusion for the Russian people. The Bolshevik efforts on November 20, 1917, to start direct negotiations with the German General Headquarters for an immediate truce brought no response from the German side, and only resulted in the murder of General Dukhonin, the Russian Commander-in-Chief, " for refusal to fulfil Government orders." On November 24, Trotski, who was then Commissar for Foreign Affairs, addressed a note to the representatives of the Allied Powers in Petrograd proposing " the immediate calling of a truce on all fronts to start negotiations for peace." This note was also addressed to the Governments of the Central Powers. The Allies answered by protesting against a conclusion of separate peace which would be a breach of the Inter-Allied Agreement of 1914. No answer having been vouchsafed by Germany, orders were accordingly dispatched to the soldiers on the front to start fraternizing and opening up peace negotiations on the spot. The Russian army was thus brought to a state of complete collapse and was now incapable of any further resistance. It was only on November 28 that the Central Powers informed the Bolsheviks that they were willing to entertain peace proposals. It was now no longer a question of concluding peace with the workers and communists of Germany, but with the Kaiser and on conditions dictated by him. The Bolsheviks at once agreed to the preliminary condition of stopping all propagandist activities on the front and in Germany and Austria. The Central Governments turned down every proposal of a political nature. " It is doubtful what would have happened to our Revolution," writes Zinoviev, " if Comrade Lenin had not been present in those bitter moments and stirring days." It was indeed Lenin, as Trotski testifies, who insisted on the immediate conclusion of peace with Germany in the face of strong opposition from many of his own adherents. He preferred to have the party split up than to see the complete wreck of his hopes. Meanwhile Trotski was making desperate efforts through the French Captain Sadoul, who subsequently went over to the Bolsheviks, to induce the Allies to intervene. He even indicated the terms on which such intervention would be accepted : (1) It should be an intervention of all the Allies, not of Japan alone ; (2) it should not be made use of to overthrow the Soviet Government ; (3) Japan should specify the terms on which it was ready to intervene ; (4) France should give immediate military and financial assistance (*v.* Capitaine Jean Sadoul, *Notes sur la Révolution Bolchévique*, Henri Barbusse, Paris, 1924). Lenin, however, realized that the Allies would never be able or willing to give full support to the Soviet power, whereas the Germans were quite ready to do so, but at a price. He insisted so strongly on the acceptance of the German conditions as " the only means of saving our Revolution " that he had his way. The conditions were terrible. Soviet Russia agreed to clear out of Finland, Poland, Latvia, Lithuania, Estonia, the Ukraine and the south-eastern districts of Ardakhan, Kars and Batum, and to pay 6,000,000,000 gold marks as compensation for losses sustained by Germans through Russian military measures. The iron ring of the Allied blockade was at length broken.

Vast food and mineral resources were now at Germany's disposal. She was free to withdraw her forces from the eastern front and hurl them against the Allies in the west, and Lenin had no reason to regret his policy. Germany gave every support to the Soviet Government not only by supplying efficient instructors for the Red Army, but in the suppression of the insurrectionary movements that followed the humiliating treaty. The Allied forces still to be found on Russian territory took a very active part in many of these movements. " Our moreover, an old personal friend of Lenin and his financial adviser. He felt that he could at one and the same time give loyal service to capital and honourable tribute to Communism. When in the summer of 1917 the Bolsheviks were carrying on a fierce propaganda for higher wages, for direct action and for the seizure of factories by the workers, Krasin, in the interests of " big industry," urged the Provisional Government to take strong secret action against the workers in order to restore discipline. Among the Bolsheviks of to-day he is undoubtedly the greatest authority on the financial side of industrial economics, and the best qualified man for carrying on nego-tiations with foreign capitalists. After the Bolshevik *coup d'état* of October, 1917, Krasin was appointed controller of the nationalized industries, and later, when the time came to establish commercial relations with capitalistic Europe, he became the Commissar for Foreign Trade. Lenin soon found that Krasin was the most suitable man for starting nego-tiations of any kind abroad. That Krasin is a convinced Communist few believe. Indeed, his influence in the Communist councils is quite insignificant. His position in the Soviet Government is solely to be ascribed to Lenin's strong personal esteem for the engineer who in his opinion was best qualified to bridge the chasm between Soviet Russia and capitalistic Europe.

The Polish Jew, Radek (Sobelson) and the Bulgarian Rakovski, typical representatives of live " intelligence " and journalism ; and the æsthete Lunacharski, the Commissar for Education, are also interesting by-products of Communism having one trait in common. They devote all their energies to applying the Communist rule and method to others, but for themselves they prefer the full enjoyment of the advantages, nay, the luxuries, of bourgeois life in all its expressions. They send their own children to the bourgeois schools and universities abroad while insisting on educating the children of others at home in the pure gospel of Communism. They have two standards of right and justice. This particular group has naturally attracted many ardent converts to Communism.

In an entirely different category are such men as Dzerzinski, Stalin (Djugashvili) and Bukharin. In this group of what may be called sincere Communists there are few leaders of men.

It is recruited mostly from simple souls for whom the word of the teacher is gospel, and his orders are law. Intensely dissatisfied with the existing order of things these men fell readily under the dominating influence of Lenin with his dogmatic insistence on immediate, direct action for the reorganization of society. Their obedience was unquestioning. During 1906–9, for instance, Lenin required funds for his organization. Without any hesitation, as if merely performing his bounden duty, Stalin carried out a series of armed attacks on banks to raise the money. Again, when in November, 1917, Lenin inaugurated the systematic terror, Dzerzinski undertook to organize the redoubtable Cheka and to control its working. In Bukharin, Lenin found one of the most ardent, and at the same time useful, missioners of his ideas. Bukharin may be called the evangelist of Bolshevism. From the words of his master he created the gospel of Communism.

As we see, Lenin had succeeded in gathering around him extremely energetic and capable men, essentially sincere idealists on the one side, and ambitious or disappointed opportunists on the other. His policy drew both sides to him irresistibly. His strength of will banished all moral scruple in the minds of devoted, even fanatic followers. The realization of Lenin's immediate purpose seemed to be their sole principle of action, for Lenin at least knew what he wanted—contributions from any and every source for the cause. He alone could make the dictatorship of the proletariat attractive and advantageous for ambitious individuals. There was every reason for the interested and the disinterested alike among his followers to hail the idea of a dictatorship under Lenin's leadership. The Dictatorship of the Proletariat, as it was called, was in reality an autocracy more absolute than Russia has ever known in the past. After Lenin's death this dictatorship continued as the oligarchy we now behold, no less absolute than its immediate predecessor.

Civil War and its Consequences.—Before examining more closely the Bolshevik policy and system of government some reference should be made to what is usually called the " period of the civil war and blockade." From its very start the Bolshevik *coup d'état* had provoked fierce opposition. But the own aspirations. He was now only entering the political arena. He could not yet put forward a spokesman of his own, capable of defending and advancing his interests. It would, however, be a mistake—a mistake which is constantly being made—to consider the peasantry as an almost blind, unconscious force that could easily be taken in hand and moulded by others. The Revolution made it clear that the Russian peasant was a very real, live and conscious force. The mujik left to his own guidance after 1917, without anyone to stand up for him before the powers that be, almost groping in the darkness that had been created around him, proved this. When the attempt was made to restore the land seized from the landlords, the peasant, who had no sort of sympathy with the Bolshevik dictatorship, who had fought against it stubbornly, had no hesitation in giving his support to the Soviet power as soon as he realized the danger of a restoration of the old regime. He deliberately chose the lesser of two evils.[1] The conduct of the peasant determined the course of the civil war. The triumph of the Soviet power was now assured. Control was gradually gained over the scattered bands of marauders and plunderers. A regular army under iron discipline, incorporating such alien elements as Chinese and Lettish battalions, was now formed by Trotski. Born in conditions of civil war, it was created not as a national army for national defence, but as a weapon for political purposes at home. It was wholly under the control of the Communist Party. In 1920 it numbered 5,300,000. The Red Army soldier was from the first a privileged individual. Specially privileged battalions of so-called pure Communists and of well paid foreign hirelings—Chinese, Lettish, etc.—formed crack regiments of ultra-loyalists. The triumph of the Soviet power was further secured by the creation of the Cheka organization, the elaborate police system to which we have referred.

[1] Later we shall see how the mujik showed the same shrewd, deliberate common sense when the Soviet Government eventually tried to give effect to its anti-peasant policy. He countered the Red taxation directed against him by reducing the area of his sowing, and all the punitive expeditions of the Soviet rulers were powerless to make him alter his decision. With the same grim determination he cleared his village of Communism, and preserved his church from all aggression.

The blockade of Russia inaugurated by the Allies towards the end of 1918 yielded results very different from what was calculated. Public opinion in Europe was cut off from closer acquaintance with the actual condition of things in Soviet Russia. This gave rise at times to very false impressions and exaggerated hopes. On the other hand, Russia isolated from contact with the western world now became the well-appointed testing field for trying out Communist experiments. Another result of the blockade, which was of very immediate advantage to the Soviet power, was that the poorest, almost famine-stricken elements of the population, absorbed in the struggle for mere subsistence, could now be readily and most effectively exploited for political purposes. Here was a weapon to be kept well in hand. When later on opportunities arose of opening up economic and cultural relations with western Europe, the greatest obstacles came from the Soviet power afraid of losing its grip over this most useful instrument of policy.

The blame for the catastrophic economic situation culminating in the famine of 1920 cannot be wholly ascribed to the effects of the civil war and the blockade. No doubt the national economy, already rudely shaken by the War, suffered severely from these effects. The blame must to a great extent be placed to the account of the Soviet Government itself. As we shall see, the whole policy of the Government was bound to lead to the collapse of the national economy and the impoverishment and enslavement of the Russian people. An examination of the chief features of the Soviet State system and of the economic policy of the Government will make this clearer.

tentative were our first efforts in connection with the workers' control of industry. It (then) seemed the very simplest thing to us. In practice it led to showing the necessity of construction, yet we were quite at a loss to answer the question of how to construct." Later, in the Ninth Assembly, 1920, he again pointed out : " The Soviet system in which we followed the lessons of 1905, and which was elaborated by our own experience, proved to be an universal, historical phenomenon. . . . It is true that we did plenty of foolish things in the Smolna [1] period and about that time. There was nothing disgraceful in that. Where were we to find reason and common sense when we first set to the new work ? We tried this way and that. We followed the current because it was impossible to distinguish the elements of what was better or worse. Time was needed for that."

There were several reasons for the extraordinary activity displayed by the Communist rulers in respect of decrees, orders and regulations. (1) First of all it was necessary to make some attempt to redeem the promises they had scattered with such a liberal hand before coming into power. (2) Moreover, the Communist Party, as we have seen, had no definite programme of construction. Its ideology had no distinctive originality— it was a crude combination of the dogmatic teachings of Marx and of the anarchical theories of Bakunin. In its application to problems of government it aimed at : (*a*) the regulation under one single control and from one centre of all production and distribution ; (*b*) the creation of a dictatorship " limited in no ways whatever, by no laws, by absolutely no regulations, a power unfettered and directly based on force." (3) By its organization the Communist Party more nearly resembled a religious sect or order than a political party. Now that it was in power its methods were not very different from those of the old days when it worked underground as a well-organized body of conspirators under a strong central control. (4) It must also be borne in mind that quite apart from the question of lavish promises to the proletariat, the Communists had a

[1] The Smolna Institute in Petrograd for the daughters of nobles became the stronghold of the Soviets in 1917 and the first seat of their government.

still more difficult problem to deal with in the matter of concessions and compromises forced on them by the circumstances of the moment when power had to be held at any price.

Three stages in the life of the Soviet State have been distinguished. The first is that of Pure Communism, the period of Communistic experiment, 1918–20. The second is that of State Socialism, 1921–2, " merging into that of Industrial State Capitalism commingling with waning private trading enterprise and individualistic agricultural industry— the New Economic Policy (N.E.P.)." These are the distinctions usually drawn by the Communist leaders themselves. High sounding terms apart, this division is convenient for present purposes. The first stage was characterized by the nationalization of all branches of the national economy so unsystematic and anarchistic in the means adopted, as to lead to almost complete economic and administrative chaos, and to the social disorders which gave rise to the policy of a more general militarization of the State. The second period is characterized by the stubborn and determined efforts of the Government to centralize control over all activities in the State by the creation of a colossal bureaucratic system. The third period is characterized by concessions forced from the Government of greater economic freedom for peasant agriculture, co-operatives and private trading, and by efforts to establish more regular forms of juridical procedure. The experiments of the first two periods ended in complete failure. The symptoms and signs of failure are very evident in the present period.

The Soviet State and State Power.—In the preamble of the Constitution of the Union of Socialist Soviet Republics promulgated 6th July, 1923, we read : " Since the formation of the Soviet Republics, the States of the world have divided into two camps : that of Capitalism and that of Socialism. In the camp of Capitalism we see national enmity and inequality, colonial slavery and chauvinism, national oppression and pogroms, imperialist brutalities and wars. In the camp of socialism we see mutual confidence and peace, national freedom and equality dwelling together in peaceable and brotherly collaboration of peoples."

Sweeping statements of this kind are very characteristic of

the rapid enactment of laws as for their rapid abrogation, if necessary. The living issue, not the dead letter, prevails with us." Not only did the Soviet power deny the principle of formal inviolability of law as established by the state ; it went even further by putting into practice the favourite principle of the Oriental despot, viz., the retrospective force of its own laws and decrees. In this way it created that extraordinary contradiction designated by Lassalle as : " absolute injustice abolishing in general the very idea of law and right."

Just as unconventional is the Soviet point of view on the question of the territory of a state. " The Union of Socialist Soviet Republics," says a Soviet leader, " is not necessarily limited to a particular portion of the world. It is larger than mere divisions of the world. The Union is meant to cover the whole of the earth's surface." In protecting its territory the constitutional state is *ipso facto* protecting the private individual rights of its nationals. According to the Soviet theory the state is the sole proprietor on its territory. According to the constitution of the Russian Socialist Federal Soviet Republic the state is empowered to fix and alter the limits of the Russian territory, and even to alienate any parts of it or certain rights in these parts. The population, in the eyes of the Soviet state, is nothing more than a tenantry, having no rights of property secured to them, and liable to be evicted from their holdings at any time. Indeed, in this connection the foreigner in Russia, if " sound," stands in a more privileged position to-day than the native Russian. The decree of the Soviet of the People's Commissars in 1920, *re* concessions, where unusual special privileges are fixed for foreigners, while at the same time the rights of natives are considerably curtailed, is an interesting illustration of this.

The Soviet state's conception of citizenship is also peculiar. In the Soviet state power is theoretically in the hands of one class, the proletariat. It is in fact in the hands of one political party, the Communist Party, which claims to be the brain of the proletarian body. The Party is above the State. It demands sacrifices not for the country, but for party. It insists on the unquestioning loyalty of all. Class solidarity

is the test of loyalty. In Article 20 of the Russian Socialist
Federation of Soviet Republics it was laid down that on the
basis of the solidarity of the workers of all nations full political
rights of Russian citizenship could be granted to foreign
workers living in Russia, and even local Soviets were empowered
to grant these privileges of citizenship.

Federalism or Centralism ?—The Soviet State calls itself a
Federation or, after the agreement of December 30, 1922,[1]
a Union of Socialist Soviet Republics. That the federative
principle in the usual sense of that term is irreconcilable with
the despotic character of the Soviet State system is very
evident. Centralism is the keynote of Communism. The
Marxists, said Lenin, in 1913, are naturally hostile to federation
and decentralization. The Bolshevik Party should bear in
mind the precept of Engels : " The interests of the proletariat
can only be satisfied by a republic one and indivisible." How
deeply rooted in the minds of the Communist leaders was this
principle of centralism may be judged by a characteristic
comment of Lenin in March, 1919 : " Why all these self-
determinations when there is this splendid Central Committee
in Moscow." And yet in contradiction with all this the Soviet
State holds to the designations: Russian Socialist Federation
of Soviet Republics and Union of Socialist Soviet Republics !
The contradiction, however, is not without its advantage to
the Bolsheviks. These designations are in fact very useful
window-dressing devices. They provoke attention and attract
custom. The slogans of national freedom and self-determination were invaluable as means to an end, viz., the destruction
of the imperialistic, bourgeois state. Lenin had no hesitation
in exploiting them for his own ends. For him the positive
aim was centralization, pure and simple. We have already
seen how the Bolsheviks before and during the first period of
the Revolution had made the most of the slogan of " self-
determination even to complete independence," in order to
gain the support of the minor nationalities. After the
successful *coup d'état* of October, the Bolsheviks altered their
tone, as witness the various declarations of the Communist
Party on this point. In January, 1918, at the All-Russian

[1] Promulgated as a law 6th July, 1923.

communications by water, road, railway, post and telegraph, and the organization of labour, are among the matters where the central power shares control with the local executives. Again, Article 49 gives to the All-Russian Central Executive Committee in Moscow a general control over all home policy, as also the right of legislating for the whole of the Federation as well as of altering civil or criminal law. Article 50 goes still further by giving the central power control over all matters whatsoever in the Federation which the Moscow Central Executive considers to be within its competence! In actual practice the Central Executive can overrule all local opposition, the autonomous People's Commissariats being held responsible before the All-Russian Central Executive Committee for their every act and for the due fulfilment of decrees and orders from the central authority. When we also bear in mind that according to the R.S.F.S.R. constitution the central power alone is entitled to fix frontiers and limits of authority within the Federation and to issue decrees of general state interest ; when we also remember that the Soviet system of government and administration—in a word, the Communist Party rule—is everywhere established in the Federation, we are bound to recognize that the term R.S.F.S.R. is not exactly what it seems.

U.S.S.R.—The Russian Socialist Federal Soviet Republic, with the addition of the Soviet republics of the Ukraine, White Russia, the Transcaucasian Federation, form what is now officially called the Union of Socialist Soviet Republics. To these must be added the nominally independent Republics of Bokhara and Khorezm in Central Asia, which are bound by definite treaties with the Union. The Transcaucasian Republic is a federation of three units : Armenia, Azerbaijan and Georgia. Most of these republics passed through a stage of complete political independence during the post-revolutionary civil war, holding quite aloof from pro- or anti-Soviet activities. In course of time, however, the Moscow Soviet power succeeded in extending its authority over them either directly by force of arms or through well-organized Communist risings. Up to 1923 the relations of the aforementioned republics with the Moscow centre were not clearly defined. It was only in July, 1923, that the new constitution, that of the Union of Socialist Soviet Republics, was drawn up, defining these relations more closely. It was ratified in a general assembly (held in January, 1924) of Soviet delegates representing the component elements of the Union. This constitution is simply an extension of the R.S.F.S.R. constitution. A representative assembly of the Soviets of the Union elects a Central Executive Committee, a Praesidium for the same and a Soviet of People's Commissars. Each individual republic is ruled by its own General Assembly of Soviets, Executive Committee, Praesidium and Commissariat. Besides these Commissariats, so called " unified " (joint) Commissariats are established. The constitution, moreover, establishes for the whole of the Union, a Supreme Court of Appeal and a joint Political Control (the O.G.P.U.), replacing the Cheka. In the new Union a return to " bourgeois " constitutional practice is noticeable. Efforts have been made to establish a regular procedure for the enactment of legislation, and to extend the authority of the central power as far as possible, in spheres of activity supposed to be within the sole competence of the local authority. The new constitution is decidedly better calculated to increase the authority of the central power than that of the R.S.F.S.R. One citizenship is established for all members and individuals of the U.S.S.R. alike—that of the Union. According to Article 19 : "All decrees, regulations and orders of the Central Executive Committee are binding and must be immediately put into force throughout the whole territory of the Union of Socialist Soviet Republics." Legislation for land and agriculture, for forest, water and mineral resources ; for labour ; for education ; for the people's health ; for emigration ; for the organization of statistical information, etc., etc., is no longer a matter of purely local competence. To such an extent, indeed, has that competence been restricted and narrowed that hardly any freedom of initiative in administrative as in legislative matters is now left to the individual republics in the Union. The authority of the central power is now supreme in every part of the Union, and in almost every field of its members' activities.

constitution this organ has legislative and executive powers which enable it to enforce Government measures and instructions without awaiting the formal approval of the houses of the Central Executive Committee. As before pointed out, these houses only sit periodically, whereas the Praesidium is a permanent institution.

Many Soviet apologists explain the functions of the Praesidium as being in general those of the President of a Republic. This is not exact, however. In reality the Praesidium is one of the supreme organs of State replacing at need and even superseding on occasion the Assembly of the Soviets of the Union and its Central Executive Committee. The powers of the President in other Republics never over-ride those of the Chamber and Senate.

In the whole course of the Communist rule the fourth supreme organ of power, the Soviet of the People's Commissars, has played a very prominent rôle. This Soviet forms the only real Government in the Soviet State, and shapes its policy. Under the R.S.F.S.R. constitution it was the supreme organ controlling the administration of all the departments of State affairs. Under the U.S.S.R. constitution it has in addition become the executive organ of the Central Executive Committee of the Union, issuing decrees and edicts which have legal force in every part of the Union (Article 38). Among the "administrators" should be noted the Commissars for Foreign Affairs, Army and Navy, Foreign Trade, Ways and Communications, Post and Telegraph, Finance, Food Supplies, Labour, Workmen's and Peasants' Inspection, as also the President of the Supreme Council of National Economy. At the head of this Soviet is a President appointed by the Central Executive Committee, a post at present held by Rykov.

The extraordinary dexterity displayed by the Communist Party in the handling and management of the puppet show called the supreme organs of the Soviet Government, is at times quite beyond the comprehension of the occidental mind. The Soviet system presupposes the elimination of all political opposition as a necessary condition for its own existence. The dictatorship of the Communist Party must be supreme.

Herein lies the only assurance that its orders and decrees as voiced by its mouthpieces, the docile supreme organs of the Unions, will not be subject to revision or, even worse, to annulment, by an opposition majority. The real Government behind the Soviet Government with its supreme organs is the Communist Party which never comes out in the open. It rules all the more effectively by cloaking its activities under the legal forms and methods referred to.

The Communist Party in the State.—The Communist Party, with its powerful well-organized Central Committee controlling Communist activities in every part of the world, is now supreme all over the territory of the U.S.S.R. Without its instructions or approval no initiative, legislative, administrative or executive, can be taken. According to Zinoviev, it " realizes " the dictatorship of the proletariat, and for that reason it remains the only party in the Union. It has crushed all other political parties. For itself alone it monopolizes the liberty of the press and freedom of political action. Consequently, says Zinoviev, there is only one means of coming out in the " political and even economic arena of the U.S.S.R. at present, and that is joining *our Party* in one way or another." The Communist Party having succeeded in transforming the Soviets into pliable instruments of its policy, identifies itself more openly with the Soviet Government, " our Government," whose apparatus is now nothing more than the executive organ of this Party. For example, when a new organ of control over transport was created the Assembly of the Communist Party described it as " a provisional organ of the Communist Party and of the Soviet Government." Moreover, this assembly, much concerned over the composition of the Central Executive Committee of the Soviets, decided that the members of this committee should be recruited chiefly from competent local men (*i.e.*, Communists). Zinoviev, at the Thirteenth Assembly of the Russian Communist Party, 1923, openly declared that his Party's Central Committee had during the year been able to put through a number of highly significant appointments, *e.g.*, that of the President of the Soviet of People's Commissars, that of the President of the State Planning Commission. " We also had the advantage of higher education. Among the rest very few persons of the working classes are to be found. The posts are generally well paid, and under the new economic policy, holders can add to their fixed salaries by commission. Necessity has driven a considerable number of individuals from the old bourgeois classes to offer their services to the Soviet authorities under the Economic Council.

In 1923, there were 38,179 members of the Communist Party in the Red Army and Navy. Almost every one of them occupied a position of importance. Among these were 13,500 former officers of the Tsarist forces. Stalin notes that 96 per cent of the Communists in the Red Army and Navy joined the Party after the Bolshevist *coup d'état* of October, 1917, mostly after 1919. The Party ticket naturally gives the *entrée* to the highest posts. If not every commander in the Red Army and Navy is a Communist, at least every Communist there is a commander in one form or other.

The Communist Youth (*Comsomol*), an organization of over 40,000 members, has a very privileged position in the U.S.S.R. They have immediate access to all schools and universities from which all non-Communists may be dismissed at a moment's notice. They are supported and educated at Government expense. Yet, with all the advantages offered them, they remain a comparatively insignificant portion of the young generation.

The Party holds a yearly assembly of its delegates, electing a Central Committee of 19 members. According to Lenin : "Without instructions from the Central Committee of our Party, not one State institution in our Republic can decide a single question of importance as regards matters of policy and organization." From 1919, all power in the Party was centred in a smaller committee, the Politburo. After Lenin's death the Politburo (Kamenev, Stalin, Zinoviev) exercised the right of dictatorship.

Pure Communists have been much perturbed over the system of privilege necessarily associated with all this Communist activity. In their opinion it must inevitably lead back to the old bourgeois practices. " We fear," it is said in a recent manifesto of the Communist workers' opposition, "that the Soviet power is now showing signs of transforming itself into a capitalistic oligarchy." How does this Party maintain its influence?

O.G.P.U. (*The United State Political Department*).—One of its chief instruments which has an enormous significance in Russian Communist activities is what is commonly known as the O.G.P.U. It is the new designation of the old Cheka, the executive organ of the Red Terror. According to Peters, who succeeded Dzerzinski as president of the Cheka, the Cheka was the organ created for exterminating political opposition. Its first steps were very tentative, many Communists not having realized that they were faced by tremendous opposition. They preferred dreaming of the coming earthly paradise to destroying the " bourgeois enemy." It is true, as points out Peters, that the bourgeoisie was quite disorganized. No anti-Soviet conspiracies were being hatched. Opposition was open. It had not yet been driven underground. When the Cheka raised its awful head in January of 1918, all sentimental dreams and open opposition faded away. It was not only a court of preliminary investigation and a court of " justice." It was " a military organization fighting on the home front in civil war. It did not try the enemy. It went out to exterminate him. It showed no mercy. To kill everyone on the other side of the barricade was its business." In his instructions Peters laid down : " We are bent on destroying the bourgeois class . . . . Don't search for evidence and proof that the accused has acted by word or deed against the Soviet power. The first question you must ask him is, what class he belongs to. Find out his profession, education and upbringing. Such questions ought to determine his fate. This is what we should understand by the Red Terror." [1] Soon all Russia was covered by the Cheka net. There was hardly a town or village that had not its branch of the terrible organization which was now the mainspring of the Government administration. In 1920, more than 1,000 offshoots were to

---

[1] Robespierre said : " In order to execute the enemies of the country it is enough to establish their identity. Their destruction, not their punishment, is needed."

be found in all the Governments of the R.S.F.S.R. Their power was almost unlimited. It is very difficult to estimate approximately the number of victims of the Red Terror. Peters affirms that in the first year of the Cheka Terror the number of people shot could not be more than 600. Yet, while speaking of the first months of Cheka activities, he states : " During this period many curious things happened. It is enough to remember that we did not shoot Purishkevich (the well-known Monarchist deputy in the last Duma) and the notable provocator Schneur, not to mention other minor figures. We had not the experience we gained after a few months of work." Another prominent Chekist, Latzis, has said, that during the second half of 1918, the number of " executions " in central Russia was about 4,500. The *Izvestia*, of October 17, 1918, declared that during the preceding month of September, there were 1,206 executions, when 3 were shot for spying, 185 for treachery, 14 for not executing military orders, 65 for insurrection, 59 for counter-Revolution, 467 for desertion, 20 for drunkenness and bad conduct, 181 for official corruption, 160 for highway robbery, and 23 for concealing fire-arms. We see that little distinction was here made between the proletariat and the bourgeoisie. The Cheka was supposed to be under the control of the Soviet of People's Commissars. In reality it always remained under the direct control of the Central Committee of the Communist Party. This dependence was clearly recognized by Peters. " The Cheka," said he, " and the Central Committee of our Party were right when they followed a strong line of policy in maintaining the Cheka as an organ of avenging justice."

In order, however, to create a more favourable impression abroad, the Soviet power which had been long desirous of establishing diplomatic and commercial relations with the rest of Europe, decided on the policy of giving a greater semblance of legality to its rule. In pursuance of this policy, in 1922 the " abolition " of the infamous Cheka was loudly proclaimed. In its place was created a new institution under the control of the Home Commissariat. It was called the State Political Department, usually called after the initial letters of the Russian words for this, the G.P.U. The change, however, was merely nominal. Indeed, according to Zinoviev, the only real change was that of the letters. When the U.S.S.R. was formed, however, the dependence of the G.P.U. on the Commissariat for Home Affairs ceased. The constitution of the U.S.S.R. re-established it as an independent supreme organ of the Union, its president being *ex officio* a member of the Union Soviet of People's Commissars. It was now called the United State Political Department, commonly known as the O.G.P.U. Like the Cheka, the O.G.P.U. is under the direct control of the Central Committee of the Communist Party. It has its own special armed force with a special staff quite independent of the regular army control. In the composition of this force of " Red Gendarmerie " are to be found infantry, cavalry, artillery, machine-gun and armoured car detachments, etc., etc. It has the advantage over the Red Army of better upkeep, clothing and pay. Moreover, it can always rely at need on the special armed forces of the local committees of the Communist Party. In addition to regular allocations from the State budget the O.G.P.U. receives considerable subsidies from the secret funds, and all the Soviet institutions as also co-operative societies must contribute in some form or other to the support of the different activities of this powerful department.

In the administration of the O.G.P.U. we have an almost perfect model of centralized organization. Its activities may be summed up under six headings : (1) The foreign section looks after the vast net of foreign agencies and keeps in close contact with the military intelligence staff and the Comintern (*i.e.*, the Communist International). The forged passports and visas for the latter are specially prepared in this section, which has its representatives on most of the Soviet missions abroad. (2) The economic section is mostly occupied in dealing with what it calls economic counter-revolution and economic espionage, crimes which have not yet been clearly defined by the Soviet laws. (3) The transport section looks after the protection of the railways and of the railway services. (4) The special or military section deals with counter-revolution in the Red army, and is responsible for the organization of the intelligence service. (5) The so-called operative section is responsible for the working out of a general policy to be followed in all the sections of the O.G.P.U. (6) Last, but not least, comes the secret section, which keeps a watchful eye over every movement of any political significance in the Union. Its agents, whose appointment is almost exclusively in the hands of the Central Committee of the Communist Party, are to be found in every part of the Union. It is the duty of all good Communists to support them in every way.

Under the Soviet constitution the O.G.P.U. is allowed a very wide range of action. We have already referred to the Tsarist measures of martial law and reinforced protection (*v.* p. 60) whereby under conditions of menacing disorder the ordinary administration of the law in certain governments or districts was transferred to specially appointed higher officials and to the police, whose power was absolute. The same system has been followed by the Soviet rulers. We see the revival of the Imperial Ukazes, of August 14, 1881, and July 18, 1892, in the Soviet decree of March 8, 1923, instituting "extraordinary measures for the maintenance of revolutionary order." These measures can be applied at any time the Government finds need for them. Any pretext, real or imaginary, will serve to put them into force. There is no sort of security against the abuse of this power. All administrative and executive functions of government are transferred to specially appointed organs which can at once create new executive committees according to their own image and likeness. The O.G.P.U.'s power in these conditions is absolute.

The Electoral System.—To maintain the Party in power a special electoral system was put into force. Before the *coup d'état* the Bolsheviks had insistently demanded that all the members of an administration should be properly and regularly elected. As soon, however, as they came into power they changed their tone completely. They now realized that citizens should only be allowed the exercise of very conditional electoral rights and this only in so far as it could help the work of the administration. If this support were not forthcoming, said the Soviet leaders, they would not hesitate to ignore the electorate and appoint their nominees directly to office. The Soviet electoral law, according to Reissner, a Communist authority, aims " at the selection of the best working team for the Soviet organization," *i.e.*, of useful servants. All the efforts of a powerful administration are directed towards this end. This is the purpose of the Soviet electoral law.

There is no universal suffrage in the Soviet State. In its place the constitution has established a class electoral system where a whole mass of " non-workers " is disenfranchised. This disability only affects about 8 per cent of the electorate in the villages. In the towns this percentage is much higher. Among the " non-workers " are included people mostly of non-proletarian origin. For more effective control the curial system has been introduced in the towns, *i.e.*, there are electoral colleges for factory workers, artisans, employees in various institutions, the professional classes, etc., etc. Women have equal electoral rights with men.

In the Union direct voting only exists for the election of members of the town and village soviets. For the district, government and the central soviets of the autonomous republics the voting is indirect. For example, the village voters elect their own soviet, which then elects its representatives for the volost soviet. The latter elects members to the district soviet. This soviet then returns members for the government assembly of soviets. The latter in its turn elects its representatives for the Union assembly of soviets. The " equal vote " does not hold in the Soviet electoral law. This is especially to the disadvantage of the peasantry. In the district soviet elections the peasant representation is one per 2,000 electors, the town is one per 200. In the government soviet the peasant representation is one per 10,000, the town is one per 2,000. In the Union assembly of Soviets the figures are one per 125,000 and one per 25,000 respectively. The same inequality holds in the town electoral colleges. The workers have one deputy per 50 electors, clerks, etc., one per 200. The peasant representation on the Soviets, as we see, is out of all proportion to the figures. The diminishing ratio is clear reorganization of local self government was carried through with the object of turning the Soviets in question into useful instruments under the control of the Central power. This was effected : (1) by the electoral system just referred to, whereby Government nominees were sure of their election ; (2) by giving all executive power to executive committees under more direct control of the central administration ; and finally (3) by making these committees dependent on " instructions from above."

The local Soviets and their assemblies were in this way gradually transformed into mere instruments for Communist propaganda and agitation. The government Soviets were supposed according to the constitution to meet four times yearly. Soon these assemblies became less and less regular. In 1919 they were only summoned twice. In 1921 it was decreed that they should meet only once a year. Thus all local administration gradually began to be concentrated in the hands of small executive committees. These executive committees now became the regular organs of local administration fully empowered to alter, modify and even cancel all the decisions of the ordinary assemblies. Moreover, in order to make sure of having more subservient organs on the spot the Government began to reduce the representation of members on these committees. But even this measure was found not to be comprehensive enough. The executive committees were gradually replaced by (1) the Præsidium in the districts and governments, and (2) by the President of the Soviet in the villages and volosts. In this way the local administration fell completely under Communist control. As we have shown, the Communist representation on the volost Soviets in 1921 was only 11·7 per cent. On the executive committees of these Soviets it was 40·1 per cent. The president of the village and volost Soviets was of course a Communist. Again on the district Soviets the Communist representation was 54·4 per cent. On the executive committee of these Soviets it was 81·9 per cent. On the government executive committee it was 85 per cent. The Præsidium of these Soviets was of course purely Communist. By a decision of the All-Russian assembly of Soviets in 1919 the executive Committees, præsidiums and presidents of all local Soviets were made responsible for carrying out the instructions and orders of the next higher executive organ. By these means the central government secured complete control over local affairs.

Apologists of the Communist rule are fond of exercising their imagination by drawing plausible analogies between the Soviet system of local government and that of England and the United States of America. The similarities, however, are very superficial and very deceptive. We must go back to the pre-revolutionary Zemstvo and municipal organizations (*v*. p. 48) for sounder analogies. These organs of local administration had distinctly mapped out fields of independent activity assigned to them and had a very clearly defined competence. The Soviets have no such local competence. The local government we know in America and England does not now exist in Russia. The so-called self government there is a mere pretence. The peasants, as we have shown, understand this thoroughly. More recently the Soviet Government has been greatly perturbed at the growing discontent of the popular masses with the unsatisfactory state of affairs in this connection. By a decree of October 16, 1924, a " reform " was introduced in local administration with the object of reinforcing the somewhat waning influence of the local Soviets so as to secure a more effective control from the side of the central authority. A number of smaller volosts were formed into single administrative units having " volost executive committees " controlling all Soviet organs and institutions within their limits of administration. For the first time these new volosts were given the right to strike their own budget and thus develop from their own resources some forms of cultural and economic activity. In these new organizations the Government is now trying to secure the support and co-operation of non-party peasants. Instructions to this effect were sent out to all local party organizations before the last election in 1924. It was, however, of little avail.

From the official figures of that election we learn that in many volosts considerably less than 10 per cent of the electors recorded their votes. The peasants till continue to maintain their attitude of hardly disguised hostility towards all these pre-occupation was to redeem some of the promises lavishly given to the workers. Its whole future depended on the support of the latter. The Marxian precept of the " expropriation of expropriators " was immediately put into rough-and-ready practice. Everywhere the workers were instructed to seize factories and remove the directors. This was carried out in a most disorderly manner. By decree of November 14, 1917, the Workers' Control was established over industrial production and distribution and over the finances of all industrial and trade undertakings, banks, companies, etc., etc. Soviets of Workers' Control were organized on all sides. About the same time was created the Supreme Economic Council. Besides this a number of commissariats formed their own departments controlling particular fields of commercial activity quite independently. The workers looked on any factory they seized as their own property. For them, according to a Communist critic, the industries transferred into the hands of the proletariat were like an inexhaustible sea whence unlimited wealth could be withdrawn. Were there not also more immediate riches and stores at hand to be shared out ? The result of all this was the complete collapse of industry—the Communists describe it as the destruction of the old capitalistic economic system. The knock-out blow to the " old system " was dealt by the decree of January 28th, 1918, nationalizing all industrial, bank and trading organizations. In this decree no principle or plan was laid down for transforming private into state ownership. By November, 1920, 4,547 industrial undertakings had been nationalized, *i.e.*, about 65 per cent of the whole number. The same month the nationalization of all industrial undertakings employing more than five workers was decreed. The complete centralization of nationalized industry was now started. " We started," says Trotski, " our economic policy by a definite and irrevocable break with the bourgeois past. Before, there was a market—it was abolished. There was free trade—it was abolished. Competition and commercial speculation were abolished. What took the place of all these ? The centralized, supreme, most sacred Economic Council which orders and organizes and supervises everything, sees to the procuring of raw materials, machinery, etc., and to the disposing of manufactured goods. From one centre this council through its various dependent organs decides everything." Through the nationalization of industry, trade and banking the Communists aimed at dispensing with the slow process of the economic laws of supply and demand. Commercial competition and speculation should have no place in a scheme of national economy where scientific foresight guided by practical experience could accurately gauge a situation and anticipate results years ahead ! If we bear in mind that in Communist parlance science means theory, and experience means experiment, the real meaning of this and many similar Communist affirmations will be abundantly clear.

Marxists have always attached great importance to the process of concentration of industry. In the formation and development of the American trust they recognize a stage of capitalistic evolution leading to the nationalization of industry. It is not surprising, therefore, that the Communists applying the lesson of the American model are now rearing on the ruins of Russian industry a series of " head-quarters " for various branches of industry which they quite frankly designate Soviet trusts. The Workers' State, they declare, has nationalized the capitalistic trusts (as a matter of fact such trusts were almost unknown in Russia); has incorporated in them a number of hitherto independent undertakings within their range of activities. In this way, they claim, industry is gradually developing into a number of powerful "vertical trusts" isolated one from the other and linked together only on the top by the Supreme Council of National Economy. What so far has been the result of the work of this Council ? Every one of its experiments on Communistic lines has been a failure. Many more organs since created for the purpose of stimulating production in special fields such as the Soviet of Labour and Defence under Trotski, and the Central Department of Vertical Trusts have had no better fortune. At the end of the third year of Soviet rule the Bolsheviks had to acknowledge that none of their aims had been achieved. The various State Departments and organizations are still busy trying out new schemes for pulling the national economy out of the ruts into which it has fallen. In 1918 a trade unionist described the situation in piquant fashion : " We have raised a Bohemia on this ruin. At first a tailor was placed at the head of a huge metallurgical factory. Then an artist was put at the head of the textile industry. . . . To think that with such an administrative apparatus we can do anything, nationalize, etc., can only be left to the imagination of those who people Bohemia." Needless to say that the growth of bureaucracy and of crowds of useless officials developed enormously. From Soviet statistics we learn that out of the 3,135,000 industrial workers in 1920 there were 2,000,000 officials. On all sides were to be seen stillborn institutions and organs ceaselessly rising one above the other, full of officials, " doing nothing and having nothing to do because there was nothing to do." According to Rykov after the *coup d'état* industry merely subsisted on what was left over from the bourgeois regime. These resources were soon exhausted. As industry decreased it was natural that the material position of the worker grew from bad to worse. In 1920 the wages of the ordinary worker according to index fell as low as 18 per cent of pre-war rates. The immediate result of this was an enormous flow of workers back to their villages. In January, 1918, there were about 2,400,000 workers engaged in the basic industries. For 1919 the figure was 1,200,000. For 1920 the nominal figure was 750,000—of actual workers there were only 400,000. The workers' own productivity meanwhile diminished considerably. Again from official figures we find that in 1920 it had fallen to 24·3 per cent of the pre-war rate, and in 1921 on the railways it had fallen as low as 18·6 per cent. To tackle this problem Trotski initiated the policy of the militarization of labour. He had come to the conclusion that " even in serfdom there were distinct conditions making for progress and for increased productivity of labour." But what was good for the Red Army was not suitable for the national economy. The stalwarts of nationalization had to confess their complete failure in 1920. Official figures of the Central Statistical Department show that in that year the output of industry was only 13·8 per cent of pre-war production. Many of the more important branches suffered particularly. The corresponding figures for the metallurgical and textile industries were respectively 6·7 per cent and 5·6 per cent. Mining was almost at a standstill with the figure 2·3 per cent. The home industries (*kustarny* industry), which were more independent of State control fared better, the figure being 26 per cent of pre-war rate. Other resources of the national economy such as the timber exploitation yielded still better results, the explanation of which is obvious. The natural wealth in question could only be " mined " properly by private enterprise, and this enterprise in its own interest the State found itself forced to encourage. Contractors took up timber concessions and succeeded in creating such a strong position for themselves that the State eventually reversed its policy. In every respect the nationalization of industry and the State control over production and distribution turned out a failure. Especially was this so with regard to trade. In the first period of the Communist rule private trading was prohibited. The severest penalties, even death, could not, however, make it disappear. In 1920 the Government itself had to acknowledge that " the speculative market [*sic*] is at present an important source of supplies for the Republic." Contraband trade and smuggling especially in the necessities of life became quite general. " The worst elements of the outworn capitalist classes forming a new bourgeoisie " observes a Communist, " have created a complicated yet clever apparatus to be used by speculative capital in its attack on the Soviet system, and on this front they are waging a fairly successful war." As a matter of fact the Soviet State began to realize that it was just as impotent in dealing with the problem of distribution as with that of production. The people had to live and to find the means. The State could not supply the means. An abnormal situation was thus created, exploited as much by the State as by the people. Private trade was now every one's occupation. The peasantry was just as much drawn into it as any other class.

Agriculture.—The first measures of the Soviet Government in respect of agriculture and the peasantry were guided exclusively by tactical considerations. The Communists were not blind to the fact that no active support could be expected from the peasants. For the moment, however, all that was needed was a passive attitude on their part. This could be won by giving an immediate satisfaction to the land-hunger of the mujik. Accordingly the day following their entry into power the Bolsehviks issued a decree handing over the possession of all landowners', State and Church lands and everything thereon to local land committees and soviets. In the decree no forms or methods for carrying out this measure were defined. The peasants' hunger was appeased temporarily and the Government preferred to take no further action for the time being. The village was left alone. It is true that the fundamental law of February 19, 1918, *re* the socialization of land declared that ownership of any land (including the peasant's) with its forest, mineral and other resources was abolished for ever in the territory of the R.S.S.R. and the first aim of the State was " a just redistribution of arable land in equal shares among the working agricultural population." But even this measure did no more than sanction what was already being done on all sides. From October, 1917, to the end of summer, 1918, the Government, very inadequately equipped from the administrative point of view, had as much as it could do to strengthen its hold on the towns. The villages were left to themselves in carrying out this distribution. They concentrated solely on this work, showing no kind of interest in what was taking place elsewhere.

The most remarkable feature of this distribution was the calm and peaceful manner in which, without any intervention from the State, it was carried out by the peasants. Now that the secular claim for " land justice " was in way of being satisfactorily settled, that the last survival of an odious past, landlordism, was definitely swept away, the ancient grudge of the peasant died a natural death. The living issue for him was no longer the wiping off of old scores with the " usurper " of his rights to the land. He was now only concerned with the question of its fair and just repartition. In his Mir organization the Russian peasant once more found the best means for this purpose. We have already referred to the evidence of those who suffered most from the abolition of their privileges, showing how mistaken is the generally-accepted opinion that the changes brought about were accompanied by grave disorders and excesses and by brutal reprisals against the old landowning class. " Thrown solely on their own resources the peasants carried out the land partition quite after their own fashion, quite peaceably and as fairly as could be expected. In this way a land redistribution on a scale unheard of in the past was effected by the people themselves, without land surveyors. The peasant had behind him the full strength of long experience gained in the Mir." Another thing to bear in mind is that in this redistribution every effort was made by the peasantry to correct the abuses surviving from the 1861 reform, when in the land allotments which the landlords were compelled to make to the peasantry many unfair advantages had been taken over the latter (*v.* pp. 47-8, 79-81, 107-110). The Stolypin reform of 1908 had also given occasion for much dissatisfaction. Generally speaking the landowners' properties were not divided up among all the peasants of the village or volost but among the descendants of the former serfs of these landowners. In addition the land acquired by individual farmers under the Stolypin reform was included in the redistribution.

With the disappearance of the old landed nobility, which for over 300 years had played the leading rôle in what was known to the outside world as Russian life, the last relics of serfdom vanished. The peasant was freed from the heavy burdens in the form of rent which he had been forced to bear since the Abolition. The obstacles which had been created in order to make him rent more and more land were removed at last. There was no longer a landless peasantry. Small farming, hitherto hopelessly handicapped could now hold its own successfully. The official figures for small farming in the U.S.S.R. up to date (1925) show the following percentages :

Small farms of 11 to 32 acres .. = 49·5 per cent.
  „   „   less than 11 acres = 31·3   „
  „   „   more than 32 acres = 19·2   „

The redistribution carried out in this manner was not distinguished by the uniformity which might have been expected from a maturely-considered land reform carried out by a State. A distinct type of peasant economy had not yet been evolved. In some parts of U.S.S.R. we can observe an undoubted revival of the old communal system. In other parts of the U.S.S.R. a predilection is shown for individual farming.

The extra land acquired by the peasantry in the re-distribution did not probably exceed 25 per cent of the pre-war holdings. In this connection we should remember that many peasants who had long ago left their villages to take up work in the towns and industrial centres had to be included in the sharing out when they returned to the country. There were at least 8,000,000 of these to be considered.

The immunity from State interference in the village did not last long. Towards the end of the summer of 1918, the Soviet Government decided to deal with the situation. Two motives were at work here. First of all the Government needed food. For this it was dependent on the peasant. Secondly, it realized the danger to its own authority of leaving the peasant to develop on his own lines. Without further delay the Communistic theories and experiments should be tried in the village. Was not the peasant a "small bourgeois," in his heart quite opposed to Communism, quite indifferent to interests beyond his immediate advantage ? The Soviet Government decided that the quickest way to gain a footing in the village was to import " class warfare " from the towns. In every village the Communists started to form " Committees of the Poor," chiefly composed of the worst elements on the spot, shiftless idlers and ne'er-do-wells, many of them, newly returned from the towns whence they brought back nothing good—the so-called proletariat and semi-proletariat of the village. A peasant has thus described them : " They were drawn from the lowest types, cow-herds, etc., and beggars just returned from the towns. They completely plundered the peasants and hardly left them enough seed for sowing." These committees, although of small membership, had con-siderable powers assigned to them, and had the right of being armed. It was especially on their help for extorting food supplies from the unwilling peasantry that the Government placed their hopes. Lenin described them as strong bulwarks whence they could proceed to a more rapid transformation of agriculture on Communistic principles. But these hopes were vain. The committees certainly did succeed in sowing trouble and dissension among the peasants. But they reaped no advantage at least for the Government. When they were able to extort corn they kept it for themselves. At the same time the peasantry showed such an obstinate and determined hostility to the committees that the Government found it useless to insist. At the end of 1918, these committees were deprived of their powers (in the Ukraine they still exist). The Government, however, cherished the hope of transforming agriculture on Communistic principles. In a decree of February 14, 1919, it defined its aims thus : " For the organization of agriculture on the basis of Socialism it is necessary to bring into being a single system of productive culture which will supply the Soviet Republic with the maximum amount of agricultural products." The methods to be adopted should be the organization of so-called Soviet Communes and of Soviet Farms. Special Government loans were advanced for the planting of these communes which began to be organized by soldiers returned from the front and by workers from the towns. Even in 1921 it was recognized that " the number of these communes was very small, that they were for the most part situated on lands of the former landowners, that the peasants showed no desire to yield any of their own land to these communes, and that all hopes based on drawing the peasantry into socialistic farming should be abandoned." The real object of the Soviet farm was to place the town and industrial populations in a position to be independent of the peasantry as regarded food. It was an attempt to create " State organization of latifundias, of huge State agricultural properties." It was intended that the management of these farms should be in the hands of the town and industrial workers, but that the actual work should be carried out by the compulsory labour of the local peasants. Already in 1920, it was quite evident to the Government that these Soviet farms could not manage their own affairs. In 1921, the Government was anxious to liquidate them and even offered them on concession bases to foreign contractors. From official data we learn that in 1922 only 2·1 per cent of all arable land was in the hands of the Soviet " farmers," and only 0·2 per cent in the hands of the Soviet communes. In reality their significance in agricultural production hardly counted. Ninety-nine per cent of agricultural production

was now in the peasants' hands. A cautious policy as regards
peasant agriculture was clearly called for. The food policy,
however, of the Government, as we shall see, led to the almost
complete destruction of the peasant economy.

Food Policy.—We have already pointed out the great
difficulties encountered by the Provisional Government in
securing adequate and regular food supplies for the army,
towns and industrial centres even on payment in the form
of manufactured goods delivered on the spot. In the autumn
of 1917, monthly deliveries of 3,800 waggons were not sufficient
to meet Government requirements. When the Bolsheviks
came into power they continued the old policy of fair exchange,
but at the same time they tried to organize this exchange on
Communistic principles by insisting that the manufactured
goods and machinery delivered by the State should be
evenly distributed among all the peasants. In this way,
they considered, the poorer peasants would have an interest
in compelling the others to send in supplies. But soon the
Government, owing to the industrial collapse was not in a
position to satisfy its creditors. During 1920, in the Ukraine,
it could only supply 5 per cent of the peasant requirements in manufactured products, agricultural machinery, etc.
Consequently, in autumn 1918, the Government could not
obtain more than 700 waggons of food stuffs monthly.
Meanwhile, the masses of the people, owing to the prohibition
of private trading, were unable to satisfy their own requirements in the open market. At the same time the nationalization of industry and trade had given rise to an enormous
bureaucracy. In 1919 the State had to provide for the
support of no less than 23,000,000 people. In 1920, this
figure rose to 35,000,000. The Government in the face of all
these difficulties, was still determined to continue the Communistic experiment. The food dictatorship was established
by the decree of May 13, 1918. The measures for enforcing
it remind one of the comprehensive and thorough-going
methods of the Tartar Khans. All surplus agricultural
products, beyond what was needed for individual consumption
and for sowing were to be immediately handed over to the
State. A new department of State connected with the

People's Food Commissariat, that of the " Chief Commissar and Military Director of Food Detachments," was created, later reorganized under the name of the " Department of the Food Army." The force was chiefly composed of town workers and soldiers forming detachments of seventy-five men. Each detachment had three machine guns. As they marched on the villages all sorts of excesses were committed. In many cases the peasant was fleeced not only of his own minimum of food requirements, but of his seed for the next year's harvest. It is true that the Government made strenuous attempts to assess these " contributions " according to statistical data for the various governments and districts. But such data were very incomplete. It was beyond the wit of the man on the spot, much less the official in Moscow, to estimate readily " surplus " figures needed. As, however, food must be had immediately and regularly, the Government did not interfere too much in the Food Army campaign.

The answer of the village to this challenge was no uncertain one. Peasant risings spread rapidly. In some governments the food commissars were simply exterminated. But the peasant had a still more effective means of reprisal by reducing his sowing area. He limited his cultivation to the utmost merely growing what was sufficient for his own needs. He almost completely gave up cultivating flax, hemp, cotton, etc. The sowing area, as compared with that of 1916, diminished by 45 per cent, and even in some places 60 per cent. Productivity per acre fell very considerably. The Government was now getting frightened. A scheme of general electrification for agriculture was put forward—as a cure for all these ills ! In December, 1920, Lenin declared : " Our chief task now is to know how to raise agricultural productivity by enforcing State compulsion." The Eighth Assembly of All-Russian Soviets decided that henceforth the State should define the area of yearly sowing and the peasant should be compelled to sow according to plan. But this measure was never put into force. The Government had to give up Communistic experiments the results of which were so tragic for the national economy.

Results of the Communist Economic Policy.—In consequence

been definitely expressed. We must reckon with this. We are sufficiently sober politicians to be able to speak our mind. Let us reconsider our policy *vis-à-vis* the peasantry. Essentially the position is this. We must either satisfy the "middle" peasant economically and allow freedom of exchange, or else maintain the power of the proletariat (*i.e.*, the Communist Party) in Russia, which is impossible by reason of the delay of the International Revolution. Economically we can't do this." The New Economic Policy (N.E.P.) was the immediate result of this reconsideration.

New Economic Policy (*N.E.P.*).—Lenin clearly realized that the crisis just referred to was of a definitely political character and menaced the very existence of the Communist power. Everything now seemed to point to a complete change of government policy. The Communists, however, were determined not to give way on what was for them a fundamental principle : the maintenance of the economic as well as the political dictatorship of their Party. In the preceding chapter, we have seen that no real change so far had taken place in their political programme. The only modifications that could be entertained lay in the direction of concessions of a very limited kind in the economic field. "We must strengthen our power and make no political concessions," said Bukharin, "but, on the contrary, we must make as many economic concessions as possible. Opportunists have formed the opinion that at first we make economic concessions and then political. As a matter of fact we make economic concessions in order not to be forced to political concessions. We cannot allow equality of rights between the peasants and the workers (*i.e.*, of towns)." But concessions on the economic ground did not mean that the Communists were yielding on the question of the control of the national economy. "The proletariat state (*i.e.*, the Communists)" said Rykov, "cannot consistently allow freedom of trade and the development of capitalism. At most, it can only allow these things to a very limited extent, and even then, only on condition of state regulation of private trade and private capitalistic initiative."

As regards nationalized industry the policy of the Government was to reorganize it on such an economic basis that every undertaking should bring profit to the State. As regards agriculture the policy should be " to release the economic initiative of the hard-working peasantry," and especially to replace the present food policy by a system of food taxes. The Communists were pleased to call this " State capitalism." It did not imply for them any surrender of principle. " Our hopes for the development of socialism in this country," said Trotski, " are based on (1) the political power of the Party ; (2) on the nationalization of the means of production, and (3) on the monopoly of foreign trade. If one or other of these elements is wanting our whole structure falls to the ground." We must add a fourth element, the most indispensable of all, to which Trotski, for the best of reasons, makes no reference here, viz., that of the Communist International, whose ceaseless, tireless activity abroad, especially during this period, failed to convert the world to Communism. We shall deal with this matter in the next chapter.

How has the economic development of the country fared under the N.E.P. ? In the first place, there has been an unmistakable revival of economic life and a partial improvement in the national economy. In the second place, it must be noted that the credit for this revival and improvement is not the Government's. In the third place, the conclusion is forced on us that the new economic policy far from helping the development of national economy is still seriously handicapping it. The Government at present is in a position of the greatest difficulty, and can find no issue. That the final decision of this problem cannot be much longer delayed is becoming every day more evident.

Revival of Trade.—One of the first effects of the economic revival which was brought about by the N.E.P., was the rapid development of private trade. The number of trade undertakings officially registered during the earlier part of the 1923-4 fiscal year was about 444,000. Of these 87·6 per cent were private, 8·3 per cent co-operative, and 4·1 per cent State. The trade turnover during this period was 55 per cent of the pre-war total. The trade revival was especially noticeable in such big industrial centres as Moscow, but not in dying Petrograd. The Government now began to give personal profit. They were placed at the head of the various Government trusts. These were not trusts in the American sense. They endeavoured to develop an independence in commercial activities which would relieve them from being in the position of mere Government monopolies. They were usually aggregates of smaller factories and workshops working independently, yet all producing goods which in one way or another came under a special grouping of output. Often on the other hand they were combines of all and sundry factories in a particular district. For instance from official records of 1922 we learn of trusts in which were combined such unrelated undertakings as timber-sawing mills, sweet, leather and brick factories, locksmiths' workshops, dairies, etc.[1] These trusts to the number of about 430 now replace the system of one single State control in the economic field. Legally they are State monopolies. In fact they are private organizations in so far as their whole success depends on private initiative. They have the right to carry on business dealings not only among themselves, but with people outside. Their whole aim is to free themselves from the deadening control of the State, and to broaden the field of their commercial activities. What have been the results so far? They have not been entirely disappointing. Factory management has been restored to its proper place in industry. Directors are enabled to direct. The number of workmen and employés has been reduced to reasonable limits and greater care is given to their selection. The number of working days has been increased, and piece work is encouraged in every way. In consequence the productivity of labour has considerably improved. In 1924 it was 67 per cent of the pre-war rate. In 1922 the production of the rubber industry was three-and-a-half times that of 1920, the electrical two, the textile three, and sugar even four. For the same period coal production only showed an increase of 27 per cent and oil of 18 per cent. In 1924 the total production of industry for the U.S.S.R. area was about 50 per cent of the pre-war figure, showing a distinct advance on the road to improvement. We should not, however, exaggerate the significance of these

[1] *v. Russian Industry in* 1922 (Supreme Council of National Economy Moscow).

figures. Distinct progress was undoubtedly being made by the trusts, but this was only to be ascribed to initiative freed from the paralysing control of the State. The grip of the State, however, was still very strong. This was especially noticeable on the financial side. The trusts had very little capital to work with beyond that granted by the State. The State grants for industry over the period 1922–3 were 178,000,000 roubles. But as, about the same time, the State decided to raise its revenue budget on a basis of taxation it began to experience great difficulties. It was in a very ambiguous position. For 1923–4 the State assigned only 112,000,000 roubles to industry. For 1924–5 it has marked out 78,000,000 roubles for this purpose. But as industry could not carry on without sufficient working capital some way out of the difficulty had to be found. In consequence of the gradual withdrawal of State support the indebtedness of the trusts to the various Soviet banking institutions naturally increased. Manufactured goods had to be realized at once and at a considerable commercial profit in order not only to settle outstanding liabilities but to raise badly needed working funds. Prices soared. On the other hand the Government in 1922–3 decided on fixing the selling prices of agricultural products within the State. By reducing these prices it was in a position to increase its own considerable profits on the export of corn abroad. The peasant, however, thus docked of his means was not in position to buy all the manufactured goods he needed. He was still less in position to do so when confronted with the high prices for these. The inevitable market crisis arose. The peasant refused to buy dear goods. Industry found itself practically boycotted. The State could no longer support it. To shut down the factories seemed to be the only thing left to do. The hitherto well-remunerated workers [1] gradually swelled the ranks of the unemployed. According to official data in fifty-two government towns during 1922 there were 68,000 unemployed workers. In 1923 this figure had increased to 283,000, and in 1924 to 610,000. The figure for the whole of the U.S.S.R. in 1924 was just over 1,300,000. We

[1] In 1922 wages were 24 per cent of pre-war rates, in 1923 52 per cent, in 1924 65 per cent.

over the disaster. The Government was forced to give up its Communistic experiment in the village and to alter its food policy. In place of enforced contributions it now tried taxation in kind. Three principles of agricultural policy were laid down : (1) the peasants were to be free to choose between communal and individual methods of farming ; (2) existing conditions of land ownership should be stabilized ; (3) everything should be done to stimulate agricultural productivity.

The " Land Codex " of 1922 was a distinct advance in the restoration of agricultural economy. In the first place all land *de facto* in possession of volosts, villages and other agricultural communities was declared to be henceforth theirs *de jure*. Technically all land in the State was State property. But now the peasants' inalienable right to the property of their land was definitely recognized. One of the very first results of this reformation was to be seen in the extension of the sowing area. Official figures for the U.S.S.R. (excluding the Far East, Turkestan and Transcaucasia) show :

		Sowing Area *in thousands of acres.*	*Percentages* *(comparison with* 1916).
1916..	..	222,402	100
1922..	...	150,262	63
1923..	..	166,612	75
1924..	..	172,714	78

(*The sowing area of* 1916 *was* 8 *per cent below that of* 1914.)

Cattle-breeding, which ranks next in importance to agriculture, suffered severely during the period 1916–22 and only very gradually recovered. The following are the official figures for the territory as above:

		In millions.			
		Horses.	*Cattle.*	*Sheep.*	*Pigs.*
1916 ..	..	31·3	50·3	79·9	19·3
1922 ..	..	20·1	35·0	52·5	8·6
1923 ..	..	20·0	38·6	55·2	9·1

From 1923 to 1924 the number of horses increased from 20,000,000 to 21,000,000, and of cattle from 38,600,000 to 42,900,000.

A considerable revival was also to be noticed in the cultivation of crops for manufacturing purposes, such as flax, cotton, beetroot, tobacco, etc. In the period of pure Communism this culture had almost ceased to exist. The cotton sowing area of 1924 was almost seven times that of 1922. And even then it was only half that of 1916. The increase of the flax sowing area in the same period was about 30 per cent.

Agricultural co-operative organization also showed signs of reviving, but it was very much hindered by the constant interference of the Government, jealous of its own trust organizations, and especially of its monopoly of export trade. In general, however, agricultural economy was looking up. Its revival would have been much more rapid but for the obstacles still put in its way by the N.E.P. As we have seen, the self-supporting village was tending to cut away from the industrial town. The town, on the other hand, was helpless without the village.

Finance and the Budget.—It is very difficult to ascertain the exact figures of the Soviet State budget during the period of pure Communism. The Government, during that time, made the most of what was left by the previous Government, and added very considerably to its means by requisitions in kind, expropriations of valuables of every variety, by confiscations, and more especially by the issue of paper money. From 1919, this paper issue assumed enormous dimensions. Its face value rapidly and steadily depreciated. At that time this did not trouble the Government much, as one of the chief aims of the Communists was to abolish money which, according to their doctrines, was a useless element in operations of exchange or distribution. When the changes brought about by the N.E.P. rendered the continuation of this means of raising money impossible—for money they must have as long as others were not ripe for Communism—the Government was forced to draw up its budget on a basis of regular taxation. The State Bank was re-established, which, from November, 1922,

started a new bank-note issue, the Chervonetz, equal to ten
gold roubles. These notes were guaranteed partly by gold,
platinum and foreign bank-notes, and partly by good short-
term securities and bills of exchange. About the same
time the exchange value of a new issue of paper money,
the Sovznak, was fixed. The Sovznak rouble of 1922 was
declared equal to 10,000 roubles of all previous issues.
In 1923 it was already equal to 1,000,000 roubles of all
previous issues. By the law of March 7, 1924, the deprecia-
tion of the Sovznak rouble from pre-war rouble value was
declared to be $\frac{1}{50,000,000,000}$th.

Soon a number of other banks were opened, among these
the Trade and Industrial Bank, the Bank of Foreign and
Domestic Commerce, the Vseko (Co-operative) Bank, and a
number of Mutual Credit Banks. All these so-called banks
were in reality State financial institutions serving as
reservoirs for the collection of State funds, and entrusted
with their distribution within the particular sphere allotted
to each one. The operations of these banks are not
considerable. Private capital plays a rôle only in Mutual
Credit Banks.

In 1923-4, the budget for the whole of the U.S.S.R. was
made out on the gold rouble basis for the first time.
Taxes, customs and duties were estimated in addition to the
compulsory lottery loan at 900,000,000 roubles. Direct taxes
accounted for 404,000,000 roubles, of which the agricultural
tax was to yield 340,000,000 roubles. In expenditure the
largest item was for the army and navy, and equalled
380,000,000 roubles, *i.e.*, 24,000,000 roubles more than the
previous year. This figure does not include financing of war
industries. Drastic reductions and cancellations in the
appropriations for educational work, re-equipment of industrial
plant, etc., etc., were made. Exports for the year valued at
pre-war prices amounted to 340,000,000 roubles against
133,000,000 roubles in 1922-3, and imports to 199,000,000
roubles as against 148,000,000 roubles. The policy of the
utmost restriction of imports was continued. Foreign
trade, as we know, was a State monopoly, organized by
a department called the Vneshtorg. But like home trade

it could not get on without the help of private enterprise. The majority of business deals abroad, effected by the representatives of the Vneshtorg (trade delegations, etc., etc.), went through the hands of many commission traders, mostly Russian traders knowing the foreign markets thoroughly and in a position to give and to get credits. For this reason and also owing to the great cost of maintaining a huge bureaucratic apparatus the running expenses were very high and were a heavy burden on foreign trade.

The N.E.P. Crisis.—The New Economic Policy was based on the calculation that private capitalistic enterprise should be in part released, and that the State should retain its hold on the " commanding heights " of the national economy in order to meet the competition of private initiative. The Government cherished the hope of creating in Russia an offset to the outworn capitalism of western Europe, a higher form called State capitalism, which would give some justification for its dictatorship. The partial release of private enterprise undoubtedly gave good results for the development of the national economy. But this development never followed the lines of the Communist economists. The political hopes based on it were never realized. In Russia industrialization was yielding to " peasantization." We know that before the War the national income from agriculture was a little more than twice that from industry (*v.* p. 66). In 1924, it was more than four times that. On the other hand the " commanding heights " of the national economy lost their commanding significance and were heading rapidly for bankruptcy. The crisis of over-production in industry in 1922-3 was brought about by the bad management of the State. Dear goods could find no buyers in the village. In the following table we see the extent to which the needs of the village for manufactured goods were satisfied since 1921. The figures show how the peasant, unable to pay exorbitant prices for these goods, had to stint himself. Even before the War the peasant had been suffering from the lack of prime necessities.

Consumption of Prime Necessities per head of the Population.

	Iron (*lb.*).	Cotton goods (*yards*).	Sugar (*lb.*).	Matches (*boxes*).
1913	65·0	19·1	18·0	25·0
1921–2 .. •• ..	2·9	2·9	2·2	6·7
1922–3 .. •• ••	4·5	4·2	3·7	11·6
1923–4 ••	12·5	7·4	6·8	14·0
Consumption of 1923-4 as compared with that of 1913	21·0 per cent	39·0 per cent	36·0 per cent	56·0 per cent

The Government now began to feel very perturbed over the future of industry and of foreign trade. Trotski expressed the fear that if Soviet industry continued to sell goods to the village at exorbitant prices, and at the same time continued to cover the losses of the State out of the peasant's pocket—the peasant would eventually say : Open the frontier ; away with the monopoly of foreign trade ! In other words he would begin to realize that for him the continuation of the State monopoly was in fact an economic blockade which he would take every means to counter. Indeed, in 1923–4 the counter-attack began in earnest. The peasant retaliated by greatly increasing the prices for his own products and for his raw and other materials, such as flax, etc. The crop failure of 1924, covering thirteen governments with a population of about 7,600,000, contributed to a certain extent in confirming the peasant in his resistance. He put no more grain on the market than was necessary in order to pay the State taxes. For the year August, 1923–August, 1924, the average prices for all grain cereals in the U.S.S.R. doubled. On the other hand in consequence of the crisis of over-production, prices of manufactured goods rapidly fell. For August, 1924, the index figure for these goods was 25·7 per cent below that of August, 1923. Meanwhile the cost of production per manufactured unit rose partly owing to increase of wages in consequence of increased food prices. The State was now compelled to sell goods below the actual cost of production, *i.e.*, to squander its stock capital. Confronted with these problems the Government decided to limit its exports of grain. It even started buying grain in Canada " to bring down prices to an average level." At the same time it was well aware that " if we find ourselves unable after all to export grain (by reason of the prevalent high prices in the Union), then we shall be compelled to shut down our textile mills, stop imports of cotton, of agricultural machinery, etc., etc." (*Kamenev*). Dzerzinski, the newly-appointed President of the Supreme Council of National Economy could only cast the blame for all this on the low productivity of the workers. But it was useless to blame the workers for what was in fact the direct consequence of bad management on the part of the State itself. The following official figures indicate the number of workmen required in 1923–4 *to turn out the quantity of goods which in* 1913 *had been turned out by* 100 *workmen in each instance :*

In coal mining	214
In petroleum production	179
In the cement industry	212
In the match industry	249
In shoe manufacturing	235
In tobacco manufacturing	318

Kamenev tried to frighten the workers by reducing wages. " Under the present level of productivity of labour so far from there being any question of further increases in wages there is to be faced the alternative danger of either our continuing indefinitely to ride on the back of the peasantry or else ' going up the flue ' economically." But to reduce wages was not so easy for a dictatorship calling itself that of the proletariat, in a State where this proletariat is a privileged class. Moreover the index of wages was still very much below the pre-war rate. The various palaces and princely houses handed over to the workers as residences during the period of pure Communism had long been abandoned by them. The State could not pay for their upkeep and the workers could not afford it. Meanwhile the workers' requirements had naturally increased.

The N.E.P. at the same time had brought about a new crisis in the relations between the village and the town. Now that the peasant was feeling somewhat better off he began to realize his own significance in the national economy. The Government could no longer ride rough-shod over him and ignore him. His demands became more and more urgent. He now began to insist on a share in the Government. On the other hand the Government was confronted with the demands of the " new bourgeoisie " of N.E.P. contractors and business men who were also beginning to feel their strength. This is the position of affairs as we write. All these questions are to be raised in the General Assembly of the U.S.S.R. Soviets which meets in May of this year at Moscow. One can hardly expect that this particular Assembly can solve the problems satisfactorily. The only possible way to restore the shattered health of the national economy in the U.S.S.R. is to bring Russia back to normal conditions of political life, to drop all further experiments with foreign nostrums and remedies which have only brought about greater suffering—to give the unhappy patient a much-needed rest-cure at home. The necessary peace and tranquility in the country can only be secured by the re-establishment of a democratic system of Government and administration where the rulers act on the principle of " trust in the people qualified by prudence." The Communist Party, however, cannot admit of such a course. This strong ruling caste is determined not to let the power it has gained slip from its hands. It will stick to it by every possible means, howsoever dear it may cost Russia. Rather than lose its grip on power it will even sacrifice some of its Communistic principles. That the Government feels no qualms on this score is evident even now. At present the Soviet Government is already looking for support in the village to the *kulak*, the strong farmer and clever business man, the " fist." The poorest are now quite forgotten. Private traders are being given special privileges in export and import trading, and private capital is protected in certain new private banking undertakings. There is even question of inaugurating a Newer Economic Policy on lines which are not yet clear to the minds of the Communist leaders themselves. One thing, however, is very clear and that is that the Soviet Government is afraid to draw the only conclusion that can be drawn by an unbiassed observer : its New Economic Policy is a complete and tragic failure.

CHAPTER XI

Two questions naturally arise to the mind of the reader who has acquainted himself more closely with the social, economic and political problems of the Russian people, and with the way they have been handled by them or, rather, for them : (1) How could the Communists ever think that it would be possible to establish the Communistic State or even the Dictatorship of the Proletariat in such a country as Russia ? (2) How could the Communists ever think that it would be possible for their dictatorship to hold its own for any lengthened period in a country like Russia so very backward economically and culturally, if the rest of the world refused to change its state, social and economic system of organization ? We must not run to the conclusion that these questions were left unconsidered by the Communist leaders, and from what we know of their way of thinking, of the character of their organization and of their principles it is not difficult to guess how they would answer them. Lenin was not in the least put out by the criticism of H. G. Wells : " It is not only the material organization of society you have to build. It is the mentality of the whole people. . . . Their very souls must be remoulded if this new world is to be achieved." Lenin and his fellow-workers knew quite well that Communism in power in Russia was a mere accident only to be explained by the very peculiar conditions of the country, by a conjuncture of special circumstances and more particularly by the forceful tactics of the Communist Party. The *fait accompli* was in direct contradiction with the Marxian theory according to which the social revolution should have taken place " first of all in a country with the oldest and most highly developed industrialism, with a large, definite, mainly property-less, mainly wage-earning, working class (*i.e.*, proletariat)." It was not, however, in contradiction with the Bolshevist theory of social revolution. As we have seen the first thing for the Bolsheviks was to create an active, well-organized, and well-disciplined minority, which would be able to stand up to the majority, and would know how to subordinate it. Accordingly, we cannot be mistaken about their answer to these two questions. Yes, they would say, it is mere accident, mere luck if you will, that Communism is a power in Russia. But that gives us an opportunity of creating in Russia a bulwark of Communism, a centre from which it can be spread abroad, a stronghold for the organization and support of active minorities in other countries. It is quite true that we have to rebuild not only the material organization of society in Russia but also the mentality of the whole people. To do this, however, all we have got to do is to destroy the bourgeois press, bourgeois science, art and education, and the bourgeois traditions of family and religion, and put in their place the Communist press, science, art, and especially education, based on Communistic principles. Under our dictatorship this is no more difficult, just as easy, perhaps, as the transformation of the national economy.

To the second question they would answer : Yes, the prolonged existence of Communism in Russia alone is impossible. To make it a success the western world must join in. Lenin had no doubt that the crisis of capitalism in western Europe was at hand, that throughout the whole world the forces of revolution were growing. They were, however, unable to take advantage of the existing crisis. They lacked " decisiveness, consciousness and organization." All these factors could now be supplied from Russia by the Communist Party, an international force, with experience, money, and all those other assets resulting from possession of power in a great State. The international revolution was now much more within range of possibility through the activities of the various Communist organizations abroad because of the existence of the Moscow centre. In order to be in a better position to form a judgment of the real state of affairs in the U.S.S.R., and also to be able to draw inferences from what lies in store for the future, one should give particular attention to the significance of these activities at home and abroad.

Foreign Policy and the Third International.—In the beginning the Communists made no secret that their whole policy was based on the hope that the social revolution would rapidly spread over the rest of the world, and first of all in the belligerent countries, that the Communists of the latter would soon seize

working class. Like the Soviet Government it follows the
instructions of the Communist Party and its executive organs.
It is subsidized exclusively from funds supplied by the Soviet
Government. The aim of one and the other of these is to
extend the rule of the Communist Party in every country.
A special task, however, is laid on the Comintern, and that is
to wrench the leadership of all labour and socialist movements
from hands of the present holders and to take it into its own
hands. In order to increase the efficiency of the Comintern
in the field of propaganda there have been established a press
organization where all languages are made use of ; a training
institution for propagandists where particular attention is given
to the study of languages, local conditions and customs,
especially in the East, and military revolutionary colleges
preparing young men for the career of leaders in insurrectionary
movements abroad.

Great things, as we pointed out, had been expected by the
Bolsheviks when they came into power from revolutionary
activities in the belligerent countries. Zinoviev whose reticence
is perhaps his least defect, is particularly outspoken on this
point : " In 1918 we all looked forward to the triumph of the
proletarian revolution in Germany, and in some other
countries, in the course of a few months and even of weeks."
The methods adopted by the Soviet Government with regard
to these activities abroad were copied almost exactly from those
which had served the Communist Party so well in Russia, viz.,
pacifist propaganda, the organization of revolts among the war-
tired soldiers and sailors, and strike movements among the
workers. The prisoners of war were thoroughly canvassed for
this purpose. In this way the Communists organized revolutions in Hungary, Germany and Finland. But the resulting
failures soon made it quite clear that by such methods they
would never succeed in " conquering " Europe. After the conclusion of the Versailles Peace the impetus given to the revival
of national feeling not only in Europe, but in Asia, prompted
a change of policy and tactics. National self-determination
was now exploited to the utmost. " Petrograd and Moscow
are becoming the Mecca and Medina of Mahometans " (*Pravda*,
Petrograd, December 7, 1919). Was ever irony more ironic ?

It is in the Communist activities in the East that perhaps the most convincing evidence of the very close connection between the work of the Commissariat of Foreign Affairs and that of the Comintern is to be found. The declaration of Eliava, the director of Soviet propaganda in the East, at a Congress in Bremen (December, 1920), throws a flood of light on this question : " Of course Moscow (*i.e.*, the Soviet Government) and we (*i.e.*, the Comintern) understand that the Mahometans of Turkestan are not yet ripe for socialism. But we thought and we knew that, however casually they might be linked up with Bolshevism they would yet serve as a bridge over which the Soviet power would forge ahead into the neighbouring eastern countries, and thus create difficulties for the Entente, and especially for England. . . . We should thank England for having driven the Turkish nationalists into our arms, although we knew and know that the Turkish politicants have leagued with us only from tactical considerations." In the same way the Soviet Treaties, agreements and concessions of this period had only tactical aims, viz., to corrupt and seduce bourgeois innocence everywhere. Up to 1921 the Soviet Government looked on itself as the General Staff for the forces of the revolutionary proletariat the world over. The Red Army formed the vanguard of these forces. The successes of the Soviet Government were the successes of the world proletariat on the road to victory. The Comintern according to Kamenev was a Headquarters for the world army of the advanced proletariat of Europe and Asia, which had already begun to move and is now marching to victory. The attitude of the Comintern at that time towards labour and socialistic movements was aggressive and dictatorial. In the well known " 21 Theses and Status " approved by the second congress of the Comintern, July, 1920, the terms on which labour and socialistic organizations could be admitted into the all-powerful and triumphant Third International were drawn up. Fundamental conditions were complete acceptance of the policy and tactics of this organization and unquestioning submission to its orders and instructions. But even in 1920 it became evident that the autocratic methods of the Comintern were far from being to the liking of many of its new members. Complaints arose that Moscow dictated certain policies for various centres which were quite unsuited for local conditions, and that in fact the Comintern was more concerned with the foreign policy of the Soviet Government than with other interests, that Communist organizations on the spot, as in Germany, were being needlessly and constantly interfered with by Comintern agents from Moscow, and finally that the funds were being made use of without proper discrimination.

The crash of the home economic policy in 1921 only made the failure of the Soviet Government's foreign policy and of the Comintern activities all the more evident. The expectations based on the immediate outbreak of the social revolution in the rest of Europe and in Asia had not been realized. Lenin now began to prophesy that the cultivation of at least ten to twelve years of good relations with the peasantry would be necessary " in order to secure the victory on a world scale." Indeed, so critical was the position at home at this time that all the efforts of the Bolsheviks should now be concentrated on saving the Soviet power within Russia itself.

The N.E.P. not only brought about those changes to which we have referred in the economic field at home. It also led to a change in foreign policy. In order to restore the economic forces of the State as quickly as possible the Government now decided to come to an agreement on certain grounds with bourgeois countries and to offer concessions to foreign capital. The Soviet State thus entered the Trade Agreement period of its existence.[1] One fundamental condition was stipulated by all the contracting countries in drawing up those agreements : the cessation of Soviet propaganda in their respective states. The Soviet Government from now on protested that the Comintern was a separate organization having nothing to do with the Soviet Government. The protest, however, means nothing. The fact remains that under two different firms one and the same business is being carried on, the first firm the

[1] The Anglo-Russian Trade Agreement, 16th March, 1921 ; then followed the German and Austrian Agreements. In 1922 came the French, Swedish and Cheko-Slovakian Agreements. 1924 brought *de jure* recognition from Great Britain, Italy, Norway, Austria and France, etc. In 1921 Treaties had been concluded with Turkey and some other eastern countries.

Sovnarkom, *i.e.*, the Government, concentrating more on the home Communist market ; the second firm, the Comintern, on developing new Communist markets abroad. The control over the business of both firms is in the hands of the Communist Party. But every effort was made to conceal this identity. It is not, however, difficult to show that the upkeep of the Third International is defrayed by the Soviet Government. We can even arrive at a rough calculation of the expenses incurred in its widespread propaganda. The budget of 1923-4 was estimated at about 1,800,000,000 roubles. According to the Commissar for Finance, Sokolnikov, this estimate did not include an expenditure in gold abroad of 200,000,000 roubles. From the report of the Commissar for Finance for the immediately preceding fiscal year we get the explanation of this : the expenditure of gold abroad comes under a " special category " not shown in the budget and is known only to the Government. This means that the Soviet Government disposes of a " secret fund " to the amount of something like 200,000,000 roubles yearly. The inference can be easily drawn.

A recent decision of the high courts of justice in Germany (April, 1925) *re* the so-called " German Cheka," and the attempted *coup d'état* of the Communists in 1923, makes it clear that the diplomatic representative of the U.S.S.R. in Berlin took an active part in organizing this plot. The revolutionary committee, organized in Berlin in 1923, was supported not only by the central committee of the Communist Party of Germany, but by the Comintern. Joint meetings were held in the house of the Russian Trade Delegation in Berlin. Ernest Bese, a deputy of the Anhalt legislature, former editor of a Communist paper who had just left the German Communist Party, referring to this attempt which was to have started in Saxony and Thuringia and to have prepared the ground for outbreaks all over Germany, says that the Soviet Government supplied officers in considerable numbers from the Soviet Headquarters to direct the military operations, as also money which could be drawn to any amount from a special fund of dollars.[1]

From 1921 the Comintern became the centre of the new

[1] *At the Grave of Communism*, Berlin, 1925.

revolutionary activities abroad. Besides financing it heavily the Soviet Government put all sorts of facilities at its disposition. This, after the inauguration of the Trade Agreements policy, was no longer done directly through the Commissariat for Foreign Affairs, but through the O.G.P.U. whose agents, as we pointed out, are now attached to every Soviet delegation and institution abroad.

Zinoviev in his " Theses " (published April, 1925) has mapped out the programme of the Comintern for the future. The change in the international situation gives him reason to suppose that the centres of the revolutionary movement in the immediate future are to be England, the Far East, the Balkans and south-eastern Europe. The task of the Russian Communist Party must now be to give *real, solid* support to the Comintern. Its policy should be on the one hand to give cheap manufactured goods to the Russian peasant, and on the other, " to give direct support to revolutionary movements in other countries."

Communists are now compelled to acknowledge that their frontal attack on the trade unions and socialist organizations of Europe has failed. They recognize that the workers of western Europe trust their own leaders and hold strongly to their own organizations. This being so, the Comintern now recommends the Communists abroad to alter their tactics. They must change from frontal attacks to flank movements. They must gain admittance into these Trade Unions in order to conquer them from within by wrenching the leadership from the hands of the present holders. How the Soviet Government at present can reconcile this policy to its own interests it is difficult to see. One partner in the firm would now insist on trying to establish good relations, political as well as commercial, with the other nations of Europe, while the other partner insists not only on exploiting any trouble that may arise abroad, but even on provoking it. So far the new policy has been as poor in Communistic results as the old one. To a certain extent labour organization abroad has weakened, it is true. A wedge has been driven into trade unionism, but the great objective has not been realized—the world revolution has failed to materialize.

Religion, Morality, Family.—It is unquestionable that the Soviet Government had more opportunities at home of remoulding the soul and the mind of the Russian people on Communistic lines. The Tsarist Government never had such an absolute power in this respect, and would never have dreamt of exercising it even if it had. From the point of view of the Communists the most serious obstacles in the way of re-creating the mentality of the Russian people were to be found in the existing " conventions " of morality, religion and family. In the new morality the conception of the family should be completely excluded. Religion, according to the inscription emblazoned on the front of the Chapel of the Iberian Mother of God in Moscow, an object of the deepest veneration to all Orthodox Russians, was " opium for the people." The Government, however, soon found that it was quite impossible to put into force against morality and religion the methods of blood and iron which had been so successful in crushing political opposition. The Communists had profited by the lessons of the French Revolution and were fully aware that such methods would arouse the fiercest fanaticism, even among the most indifferent. This, however, did not prevent them from trying, as far as circumstances permitted, to put into force the severest measures, especially against religion. The tragic tale of religious persecution in Russia under the Bolshevik regime will not be recounted here—the long martyrdom of the lately deceased Patriarch of the Orthodox Church, Tikhon ; [1] the more summary one of the Roman Catholic prelate Monsignor Budkevich; the no less terrible sufferings of thousands of their faithful adherents, priests and people, the desecration of sacred relics, the confiscation of church treasures, etc., etc. This persecution, whose worst period was between the spring of 1922 and the autumn of 1923, was not, however, carried out in the regular systematic fashion adopted by the Cheka in dealing with political opposition. Its more violent forms were soon found to be ineffectual. Other means were

[1] The Holy Synod had been abolished by the Provisional Government. The Orthodox Church recovered its independence. After a break of over 200 years a general Church Council was summoned in 1917, and Tikhon was elected Patriarch to the Russian Orthodox Church.

tried to deal with the religious obstacle. The institution of the Church as a form of union of believers was abolished and the dissemination of all religious knowledge and instruction was prohibited. On the other hand, the Government organized and subsidized a vast anti-religious campaign and a militant propaganda of " pure materialism." By decree of January 23, 1918, churches and religious bodies had no legal standing. Only distinct and separate religious groups of citizens were recognized. These groups were subject to the State regulations for associations, and as in Soviet Russia no association could own property, so all the property of these religious groups could be seized at any time. In this way the State was enabled to close very many of the churches and to make use of them for non and even anti-religious purposes, as also to enrich itself by wholesale confiscations of Church valuables. The Government went further : (1) It prohibited the setting up of religious emblems anywhere except in churches, the public celebration of any religious ceremonies, the formation of any kind of religious institutions such as monasteries, convents, etc. ; (2) the strictest regulations were drawn up as regards religious instruction. The decree of January, 1918, had not gone beyond prohibiting religious instruction in State, public and private schools. By the decree of July 13, 1921, the teaching of religion to persons under eighteen years of age was forbidden. The official explanation of this measure is worth noting : " Religious instruction only leads to the obscuring of the child's mind. The Soviet Government, which is responsible for the education and instruction of the children, should safeguard their minds from being filled with religious prejudices " ; (3) special checks were put on the activities of the clergy. They were deprived of all electoral rights. They were relegated to the lowest classes of the " non-workers," and even in this class they formed the last group. They were not allowed to occupy any posts in schools or under the education, justice, agricultural and food departments. In other departments they were only allowed to do the meanest kind of work.

Besides all these restrictive measures directed almost exclusively against the Christian religion, and more especially against the faith of the vast majority of the people, the Soviet Government made use of the very effective weapon of anti-religious propaganda. It not only distributed millions of copies of anti-religious books and leaflets, but also excluded from public libraries, reading-rooms and bookstores works of a religious character, even Tolstoy's. Its employees were forbidden such " anti-Communist practices " as attendance at church ceremonies and the observance of religious customs. Atheistic processions in the streets and festivals and dances in churches and other sacred places were specially organized. The consequences of this policy as they affected the Communists themselves and the rest of the people were soon evident. Perhaps the best criticism of these results is to be found in the words of prominent men and women of the Communist movement to be read in the current Communist press. In the organ of the executive committee of the Communist Party the *Pravda* of March 24, 1925, there is an article by Mrs. S. Smido-vich, a well-known Communist, on morals and conduct in Communist *milieus*, especially in the Comsomol, *i.e.*, the Communist Youth. It is a heart-rending revelation of the new morality in the U.S.S.R. Undoubtedly the materialistic and anti-religious convictions of some of the Communist leaders were very deep and their private life was above reproach, but the Communist rank and file obviously formed very different conceptions of Communist morality. The formula, *everything is allowed*, was a rule of conduct for many. " The Communist Youth evidently believes that the most primitive approach to questions of sexual passion is really a Communistic one. Everything which does not enter a frame which may be quite good enough for Hottentots or even still more primitive races is qualified as being bourgeois." Even a beardless boy con-siders it not only right but perfectly in accordance with Communistic ethics to give his sexual instincts full play. Any Communist girl who will not accept his advances is in danger of being denounced as a bourgeoise, as unworthy to be called a Communist. Mrs. Smidovich gives us some terrible pictures from life in these conditions. We get, however, still more appalling impressions from letters in the *Pravda* which have been elicited by this article and printed in extract in the number of

May 7. Here is one from a young girl : " I was ill, yet one of the Communist Youth told me straight that if I did not go with him, then I could not be one of theirs, I could not call myself a Comsomolka—a Communist girl. This produced an awful impression on me. As a candidate (for the Comsomol) I began to fear all sorts of intrigues." In another letter Mrs. Smidovich is warmly thanked : " With your help I have been able to understand much and to save my youth [*sic*]." At the same time we find many letters here in defence of " Hottentot " morality, a defence based on the materialistic teachings of the Communist Catechism, and finding its justification in examples of conduct provided by well-known Communist leaders. " What is our system ? Is it not one of methodical destruction of property ? Everything depends on this. As regards the family it means the systematic destruction of the conception of family." From another letter we read : " Among us we have not yet anything like proper Communistic relations between young fellows and girls," and further on the " young fellow " in this instance declares that it would be a very great mistake to forget the revolutionary rôle of so-called dissoluteness. " In the first years of the revolution it was necessary not merely to fight against bourgeois morality, but to trample it under foot. It was necessary to put one's self in contradiction with the old in every way, to do everything the opposite way, often without considering how this might not accord with ideals of the future." From these letters we get an insight into the real meaning of Bolshevism. We see the Communist youth translating into conduct and morality the principles and practices of his elders. In these letters the older generation of Communists and the leaders themselves of the Communist Party are directly taken to task for encouraging Hottentot morality by their own scandalous behaviour. A young girl writes : " You may observe this to a great extent among the old Party men." Yet another : " You referred only to the young Communists. But even elderly members of the Party are doing the same thing." A " Group of Women " points to the " too free and easy attitude in this connection of old stagers occupying most responsible posts." Such, sad to say, are some of the direct results of the Bolshevist efforts to remould the mind of the rising hope of the Communist Party—the Comsomol. This lamentable condition of things in the towns in the eighth year of the Soviet regime is now causing considerable anxiety to a large number of sincere Communists in the U.S.S.R.

The state of things in this respect as regards non-Communist Russia, especially in the village, is very different. In the last few years some serious contributions to the study of conditions of life in the village have been made by the Communists themselves. The village, they have to acknowledge, has not only preserved its family life, its customs and its church; guided by its historical traditions it follows its own route and has not yielded to the influences of Communism. The peasantry, as we have shown, solved the land problem in its own way, and is now organizing self-government after its own fashion. In the teeth of Government interference and legislation it still holds firmly to the right of property and of inheritance. As before, the church is the centre of village life where marriage, christening and burial services are regularly carried out. All children receive religious instruction. "If we look at the village," says the Communist Yakovlev (*The Village As It Is*, Moscow, 1924), "from the point of view of statistics, we get this picture. They can provide for eight persons looking after the church yet they cannot support one teacher [the explanation of this is very simple, as we shall see later]. The clergy are well off. Their houses are distinguishable by their good appearance." "The pope [the Orthodox priest] has studied. You cannot throw him over," says the peasant when questioned on this subject. "In the village," continues Yakovlev, "even Communists become religious, and notwithstanding all prohibitions, go to church and 'practise.'" The ex-Red Army Communist on returning to his village refuses to join the local Communist cell. "If you join the Party," he says, "you are forbidden to have your children christened. But how can you live in the village after that?" The above observations were made in a particular district towards the end of 1923. The following are more general observations made by a prominent member of the Præsidium of the Central Executive Committee of the U.S.S.R., Mr. P. Smidovich. "The religious movement in Russia is now becoming a sort of epidemic which has already seized all the small bourgeois elements and is now devastating the workers and the peasants. Since autumn (1923) last all the roads to monasteries and all the old routes followed by pilgrims are covered by long lines of people wandering to the holy places." It would seem, he continues, as if the peasants had entirely ignored anti-religious propaganda. Indeed, so much have earnest Party workers been impressed by all this that " they absolutely refuse henceforth to come out as anti-religious agitators."

Not having achieved all it expected from its campaign against religion and the Orthodox Church, the Soviet Government now tried to turn the Church into an instrument of its power. Every encouragement and assistance was given to the renegade clergy ready to conform to Government requirements and willing to proclaim Communism as a blessing of God. In direct contradiction to the spirit of its own legislation the Government pursued this policy by subsidizing a bishop, Antonin, and a priest, Krasnitski, to summon a Red Church Council, the foundation stone of a new Soviet Church, the so-called Living Church. It restored something very like the old system of the Synod and the Procurator. In every way the Living Church is now helped on by the Government in its work of dismemberment of the Church in Russia. Its efforts, however, to break the Orthodox unity have had no real success. The people still remain true to the old faith and refuse to acknowledge the " heretics." As Yakovlev, to whose work we have already referred, says : " The village has unanimously declared : ' We don't want the new religion.' "

Education.—The Soviet Government at the very start devoted much attention to education. But it was more concerned with inculcating Communistic doctrine than with spreading general education. Religious instruction was prohibited in elementary and secondary schools. All such subjects as history and literature were brought into line with Communistic theory. There were hardly any Communistic teachers. Children were bidden to see to the good behaviour of their teachers. Great changes were introduced into higher University education. The faculties of law, history and literature were almost everywhere abolished and their places taken by such obligatory courses as the history of materialism, the history of socialism and the history of the Communist Party. New faculties were specially formed called workers' faculties (*Rabfaks*) where admission was gained not by reason of working qualifications, but by favour of the Communist Party on the ground of proletarian origin. Perhaps in no other sphere of Communistic activities were such contradictions between plausible theories and real facts to be observed as in that of education. The school now became an experimental laboratory. At a moment's notice startling innovations might be introduced and made obligatory for the whole state without considering the fitness of person, things or conditions. About twice a year school programmes and methods would be quite altered. Orders might suddenly be given to start lessons of dancing, sculpture and Esperanto in a village school. In the same school a few months later the teachers would be ordered to appoint " a week for the abolition of illiteracy " when a round-up of the *babas* (older women) and men of the village would be organized to the scandal of local public opinion. Again orders would come from the centre to start a school in such and such a village, hardly any requisites being supplied. A woman teacher thus writes of one such school : " In 1919 each pupil received only one pencil and two nibs. During three years we never received any text-books. We could only teach geography through old periodicals and magazines we found at hand." It was impossible to buy the most necessary things. Books and paper were nationalized.

Under the old regime in Russia besides the State schools, primary, real, gymnasia, etc., there were a large number of municipal, Zemstvo and private schools. They were generally well-equipped. Now under the Soviet Government there are only State schools of different categories, viz., kindergarten, first-grade, second-grade, technical, and higher or university.

Below we give a few tables which enable the reader to

compare statistical data *re* education before and during the Soviet regime :—

Public Instruction.
Elementary Schools (First-Grade).

	1913	1917	1918–19	1919–20	1920–21	1922–23
No. of Schools	64,298	71,900	42,681	51,768	57,123	49,000
No. of Pupils	4,078,711	4,600,000	3,489,456	3,903,669	4,976,115	3,700,000 (about)
No. of Teachers	133,000	148,000	104,667	125,173	146,731	120,000

Secondary Schools (Second-Grade).

	1913	1917	1918–19	1919–20	1920–21	1922–23
No. of Schools	1,063	2,138	2,555	2,825	3,719	2,028 (about)
No. of Pupils	300,557	276,590	276,371	329,886	407,601	240,000

The figures for 1913 do not include higher primary schools, more than 1,000. These, however, were turned into second-grade schools by the Soviet Government and included in their statistics. On the other hand, the figures for pupils in 1913 include those lower classes (I, II, III) which are now included in the first-grade statistics.

Technical Institutions.

	1913	1918–19	1919–20	1920–21	
No. of Institutions	1,500	475	1,443	1,888	(Figures since last period reduced by 50 per cent)
No. of Students ..	170,000	33,259	92,376	106,484	

Workers' Faculties (Rabfaks).

	1913	1919	1920	1921	1922	1924
No. of Faculties	—	9	45	92	63	87
No. of Students ..	—	2,149	14,827	40,224	29,000	35,000

Children's Homes and Refuges.

	1913	1921	1923–24
No. of these	587	8,000	4,328
No. of Children ..	29,660	380,000	(not calculated)

Kindergartens.

	1913	1921	1923–24
No. of these	377	4,000	715
No. of Children ..	(not calculated)	213,000	4,000

The number of village (cottage) reading rooms in 1921 was 33,012 ; in 1924, 7,347.

(N.B.—The above figures are from data of the Imperial Statistical Bureau (1913) and of the Soviet Statistical Bureau (1918–22), and from particulars in the reports of Lunacharski, the Commissar for Education).

These figures show an increase in the number of schools and pupils towards 1920–1. But many schools were included which had merely nominal existence, having no teachers, scholastic equipment, etc., etc. From 1921 when the Soviet Government started framing a budget, a considerable reduction in the number of schools of every kind with a corresponding decrease of pupils was to be observed. The significance of these figures may be gauged to a certain extent by the comments of well-known Communists. We refer again to Yakovlev's *The Village As It Is*. He notes that in a certain district visited by a Government Commission at the head of which he was, not one Government school was open. The school buildings were dilapidated and roofless. To the question why the peasants could not maintain these if they were able to support the clergy well, their answer was : " Where can we get the straw [for thatching] from ? If the authorities don't bother about their schools, what can be expected from us who have nothing to do with them ? " These schools indeed were not the peasants'. They had no use for them. And yet they fully realized the need for education. They were quite ready to support schools which would satisfy their requirements. Yakovlev brings forward many facts showing how great was the thirst for knowledge in the village. In one village where the Communist school was closed, the priest's wife taught many of the children and received good remuneration such as the regular teacher would never expect to have. From the *Pravda* we learn that " in a place N. in the Kharkov government a well-equipped illegal (prohibited) school has been found which was carried on by a former director of a gymnasium (secondary school), the programme being adjusted to the requirements of the parents. The director Panov has been sent to trial." Zinoviev writing October, 1924, in the *Bednota* says : " On the railway journey you hear practically one uninterrupted voice crying: 'Papers, papers !' . . . From all sides we hear the unanimous demand of the peasants for education." Meanwhile in the village, only Communist publications and leaflets are allowed to be read, often written in a pseudo-scientific jargon which is quite unintelligible even to educated persons. The libraries of neighbouring great houses were in general unsuited for the peasant's reading—they were mostly composed of foreign books. Many of the best known works of Russian authors are now excluded from public libraries. Tolstoy is too religious, Gogol is too anti-Semitic !

The material position of the Communist teachers, especially in the village, is a miserable one. In 1924 the monthly salary of town teachers was 14·5 roubles, of village teachers 10·13 roubles, *i.e.*, three times less than the very low pre-war rate.

But even this salary is not paid regularly. The social position of the teacher is unenviable. He is compelled to do propaganda work of every kind for Communism, to collect statistics and even taxes. The Government efforts to control education in the villages through its teachers have signally failed. " These teachers," says P. Smidovich, " sent out to the village after going through special anti-religious propaganda and similar courses were promptly boycotted." Things were made so unpleasant for them that in many cases after holding the fort for two or three weeks they found there was nothing left for them to do but return to the town. It is quite evident that the position of education is not likely to improve in the near future. Recent cuts in the budget estimates for education and a policy of leaving the financing of it almost entirely to local budgets, without at the same time loosening central control over this, give us reason to draw this deduction.

The following comment by the sincere and earnest Communist, Smidovich, strikes a plaintive note. May we not say in concluding these remarks on the Russian village of to-day that it will have a very different significance for earnest and sincere anti-Communists :

" The village at present (end of 1923) has a greater significance, is more finished, more whole and closely-knit than it was before. The village is now more welded together. It is ruled by its own customary laws, to overthrow which is beyond the strength of the authority of instructors and of zealous workers for the Communist cause. . . . Many seem to think that the cohesion of village and town (*i.e.*, Government) is getting firmer ; but those who have a nearer knowledge of the peasants must confess that under present conditions this cohesion does not exist, and is impossible."

Literature, Art, Science.—What is the position to-day in the U.S.S.R. as regards the creative forces in science, art and literature ? We have already pointed out how rich and spontaneous was the growth of culture in Russia. Russian literature may almost be said to have been brought forth into the world by Pushkin, Russian music by Glinka, and Russian science by Lomonosov. By the end of the nineteenth century the contributions of Russia in these and other fields of creative energy were not the least prized possessions of the richly stored treasury of European culture. The teeming wealth of Russian talent was not exhausted after the giant figures of Dostoevski, Tolstoy, Chaikovski, Rimski-Korsakov and Musorgski left the scene. They were quickly followed by Chekhov, Gorki, Bunin, Andreev, Rakhmaninov, Glazunov and Scriabin, not to mention many others of a younger generation. Up to the very eve of the devastating disaster which swept away the Russian Intelligentsia, too confident in its spirit of self-sacrifice for an ideal of right and justice, the world wondered at the inexhaustible sources from which the Russian mind drew its inspirations. When the new era was proclaimed by Lenin it seemed at first to many as if the dreams of the more advanced thinkers of the Russian Intelligentsia were about to come true; as if the evil forces released by the great upheaval would soon exhaust their strength; as if the reign of right and reason were now at hand. For none was the awakening more tragic than for the dreamers themselves. The physical sufferings and the material privations they had to endure under the new regime were as nothing to the tortures of the mind and the anguish of the soul—as leaders of a forlorn hope could not forget that they had called for useless sacrifices on the part of devoted followers. In addition all the things that they valued most highly, their ideals, their literature, their art were now denounced as the vile satisfactions of a selfish taste, as bourgeois vices. Theirs was a terrible dilemma ; to prostitute their talent and deny their gods or to remain silent for ever, unless there was another escape. It is to the lasting credit of the Russian Intelligentsia that when the choice had to be made so very few renegades were to be found in its midst. Those who were able to escape the living death at home and settle abroad could now endure penury and starvation with all the greater fortitude in that they could at least think, act and produce freely. In this way Russia lost such vital forces as the authors Bunin, Merejkovski, Kuprin, Remizov, Artsibashev; musical composers as Rakhmaninov, Stravinski, Prokofiev ; and artists as Somov, Bakst, Goncharova ; and many scientists.

The native soil had meant very much to the creative genius of these men. They had now to strike root in new ground. Long before this, in the '60's of 1800, Herzen had said : " For the Russian people emigration is a terrible thing. I am speaking from my own experience. It is not life. It is not death. It is something worse than the latter. It is a stupid, cramping numbness. . . . We are strangers in this world. We don't really live here but at home." But they are really living *here* now, each one justifying his or her existence on a foreign soil as a useful member of society. The Russian savant is doing good work in the learned institutions and universities abroad, and Russian literature has not died out in exile. There is now a more subtle refinement, a deeper note and a truer ring in the work of that marvellous story-teller Remizov—his style proclaims this to perfection. The beautiful creations of Bunin still delight and pain. The promise of the brilliant artist Aldanov in the field of historical fiction—*le roman documenté*—is being fulfilled. But where Russian literature has not yet won the need of recognition it deserves—few are the good translators and fewer still the enterprising publishers—the more direct appeal of Russian art and music has triumphed. France, the arbiter of all the artistic elegances, has taken to her heart the Russian painters, Mrs. Goncharova, Larionov, Yakovlev and Sorin, and the musical world proclaims Stravinski and Prokofiev as leaders of a great revival. The Russian ballet and theatre are now international institutions. All this has been achieved in exile.

At home the position of what remained of the Intelligentsia was very different. The Bolsheviks had made a clean sweep of the old culture and put in its place what they called the proletarian culture : wherein consists the superiority of that culture the leaders themselves are at a loss to explain. It is certainly not a distinction of sweetness and light. The reign of " proletarian beauty " and " proletarian truth " in Russia was inaugurated in the same forceful manner which had been so successful in the political field. Lunacharski was appointed Commissar for Public Instruction. Under his control were a number of different departments for science, art, music, literature, etc. A pure Communist was placed at the head of each department. The printing press was nationalized, the State alone had the right to publish anything. Thus was created the organization of the *Proletcult*.[1] Among the "creators" of the Proletcult invited to take the place of the older men now either driven into exile or forced to silence, there was a small group of "Bohemians," feeble imitators of the futurist Marinetti. There was no outstanding talent among them. They were more concerned with flashing effect than with sustained effort. They seized every opportunity to shock, *épater le bourgeois*, by deliberate rudeness, by trampling on every tradition of the past in art, by threatening to destroy museums, etc., etc. It may have been that in Italy the present was too much under the influences of a great past. This assuredly could not be asserted of Russia, which at no time had suffered from an overload of cultural tradition. That is why the futuristic movement in Russia had been looked on as a very artificial imitation which could never strike root in the Russian mind. Futurism as a whim had nearly died out in Russia before the Revolution. Its chance came once more under the Bolsheviks. The latter could make use of it—did not futurism stand for the negation of all the values of the past ? The noisy little clique was only too willing to serve and flourish gaily under a regime whose declared policy was one of complete destruction of the old superstitions. Futurism now became the officially-recognized art of the State. For three years Lunacharski gave it every support and encouragement. The streets were decorated with outlandish placards and uncouth statues. The new State publications and literature were full of the creations of these new "artists"—meaningless combinations of mere sounds without rhyme or reason. In 1920 the proletariat itself began to cry out against this senseless mystification. So strong were the protests that Lunacharski decided to give up the new experiment. Support and subsidies were withdrawn and futurism melted into thin air.

[1] It may be pointed out that contrary to general belief abroad, art collections and museums in Russia have been well preserved under the Bolshevik regime. In nationalizing private as well as public collections the Government was in position to maintain and organize new public galleries and museums. In this the Government was well helped by old scholars and art lovers, many of them former proprietors of famous collections, deeply concerned in preserving intact artistic treasures for the Russian people.

Lunacharski, however, did not give up hopes of finding new mediums for his purpose. Support was now given to writers and artists of pure proletarian origin, to those who had a good ear for the " music of the Revolution " and the " rhythms of the period," who could give the right translation for the ideals of the Revolution.

The New Economic Policy gave some hopes for a change in Lunacharski's experiments. Several private firms were now permitted to publish novels, poetry and musical compositions under strict•censorship. Exhibitions of painting were started by modern artists. In Moscow, 1924, a collection of essays and articles under the title *Writers on Art and on Themselves* was published. Among the contributors were Alexei Tolstoy, Pilniak, Zamiatin, Nikitin, Lidin, some of these now fervent Communists, others only Communists *pro forma*. All of these point out the poorness of the harvest garnered from the literature " that was to have taken the world by storm." " What we have written so far may be beautiful, but it is mere useless dust of the period," writes Nikitin. " All the same, our literature still remains that of yesterday," says another. " From the wealth and abundance of this literature of effect hardly anything will survive for coming generations," writes a third. Almost all these writers are of accord that it is impossible to create to order, and that the constant tutorship of the state is killing the soul and spirit of the literary man. " From every writer the authorities expect a symbol of faith. You must proclaim your faith in the proletariat of all countries or else you will be brought before the censor." " Real revolutionary writers cannot be brought up on the shouts of police and militia patrols." " If we writers are in fact no more than obedient fingers on an iron hand, anyhow we ourselves may not want to open and close them at the orders of only one index finger," protests Sobol. Pilniak is still more candid : " I don't recognise that it is necessary to gush when writing about the Russian Communist Party as very many, especially quasi Communists, do. . . I must confess that for me the fate of the Russian Communist Party is much less interesting than the fate of Russia."

Perhaps the reader will get a better representation of the

official point of view on literature in the U.S.S.R. from the following reflections. In a laudatory article on the " Party Poet," A. Bezimenski, which appeared in the *Pravda* of February 25 of this year, we read that the chief quality of this poet in that " he is *ours* in the full sense of the word. The Party, the Comsomol and all our great feats form the subject-matter of his poetry. . . It would seem that his example is one more proof of the well-known truth that the poets and writers who accept the Revolution can produce, quite apart from the talent they show, a great deal of matter of considerable social significance. Otherwise they are doomed to sterility." That is the official view. Here is what one of the novelists, Kasatkin, says : " October (*i.e.*, 1917) wholly banished the famous dead, all the fathers and grandfathers of Russian literature, in order to keep the proletarian culture pure." But soon it was evident that " even the victorious storm of Revolution could not destroy the law of literary succession, the development of one from the other. . . . The mirage was put before us (it is still being done) of the possibility of creating one single, whole, indivisible and constant proletarian culture. . . . In consequence on the literary ' fronts,' even the most left, we see walking about naked kings with an incredible conceit affirming that they are wearing the finest raiment." Another of these writers says : " Russian literature is bound to return from its wandering in chaos to the routes of Tolstoy and Dostoevski, and must leave off sneering contemptuously at the ' rotting west.' . . . We have yet much to learn and adopt from the culture of the west and from its creative discipline."

And so we see Russia coming back to the old ways, and not only in literature, but in music. The distinctive characteristic of contemporary musical composition in Russia is its detachment from the new departure in that field. Many composers are returning to the old traditions of Chaikovski and Glazunov, others to the sources of Scriabin's mystic inspirations. A striving for clarity and simplicity is very characteristic of the latest composers, A. Pashchenko, Miaskovski, Sabanéev, Alexandrov and Veprik. Similar tendencies are to be seen in painting. It is more difficult to speak about the movement of ideas among the people in general. The deadening censure continues to stifle all freedom of expression. At present we only hear the expressions of opinion —duly considered—of those who have passed this censure.

Two facts, however, stand out clearly from these and many other observations of cultural life in the U.S.S.R. to-day : (1) The attempt to create an artificial proletarian culture has been a failure ; (2) there is a pronounced tendency to return to the classic founts. Much clever striving for effect is still to be seen in the creations of the younger novelists like Pilniak and Zoshchenko, where realism passes beyond every limit and restraint of decency and loses itself in the most repulsive "naturalism." Essenin and Maiakovski continue to dissipate their undoubted poetic talent in graceless cynicism. These writers, however, merely reflect what has passed before their own eyes. They have seen but little else. Many others now feel the need of returning to healthier sources of inspiration than those that have served them so far. Among these is the young novelist, K. Fedin, whose first novel, *Towns and Years*, shows a conscious return to the traditions of the Russian novelists of the end of the nineteenth century. The subtle talent of the poet and novelist, B. Pasternak, strongly influenced by one of the greatest of Russian symbolists, Andrei Biely, reveals much promise. After a prolonged silence may be heard once more in Russia the voices of authors whose names were already known before the Revolution, such as the poetess, Anna Akhmatova, the brilliant *raconteur*, Zamiatin, and the ever-consoling and refreshing Boris Zaitsev. For these the fate of Russian culture is above that of the Communist Party. When we remember how Russia still lives and has its being in the U.S.S.R., we need not fear for the future of Russian culture.

CHAPTER XII

CONCLUSION

In this survey we have confined ourselves to an investigation of factors which may explain to a certain extent the economic, political and cultural developments in modern Russia and the crisis through which she is now passing. Let us rapidly summarize these and venture to estimate their significance for the future.

We have seen that Russian civilization, despite the presence of other elements, is essentially European. All the earlier history of Russia had no doubt been strongly influenced by the past. In Chapter I we have referred more particularly to the events which for so many centuries had isolated Russia from the rest of Europe, and had checked her development. It was only in the eighteenth century that Russia "returned to Europe," and only in the nineteenth century that she definitely joined the comity of European nations. Historical conditions, however, had left their stamp on the State structure which had become dangerously top-heavy, whereas the social foundation on which it rested was far from sound. The State power flourished excessively at the expense of the healthy growth of the social elements. Still, much had been done by the autocracy to create unity and cohesion in the State, and in the nineteenth century Russia was a powerful Empire. It was not a mere roughly assembled group of varied races, peoples and territories. It was (with the exception perhaps of Finland) a distinct cultural whole composed of parts which were very dependent one on the other economically as well as culturally. A very distinctive national type and mentality had meanwhile been evolved.

In the nineteenth century, in consequence of closer contacts with Europe, the era of industrial development started for Russia. New social and economic forces now came to the front. The spread of general culture was responsible for awakening great interest in political life among various sections of the people, who now began to seek outlets for the exercise of political activities. The ruling class of the nobility was gradually losing its economic significance, while that of the peasantry was forcing a recognition long denied it. The normal development of peasant economy had been considerably held back by serfdom, and even after the freedom granted to the serfs in 1861, the land reforms were quite inadequate to cope with what was now becoming an urgent problem for the State The almost complete isolation of the peasant in the State deprived him of the opportunity and the right of taking his proper place in public life, of exercising activities corresponding to his real significance.

In the second part of the nineteenth century a great revival of national sentiment started among the various peoples and races in the Empire. The repressive policy of the autocracy on the question of national rights accentuated and embittered this feeling which might have been turned to advantage in many ways. The autocracy only succeeded in converting it into resentment and even hostility.

Towards the end of the nineteenth century it was very evident that the highly centralized bureaucratic system of government was a great obstacle to the proper development of the State. Autocracy had proved incapable of adjusting itself to altered economic and cultural conditions, and of making timely and wise concessions. The same spirit was to be observed in its foreign policy—the old alertness in the national interest was lacking.

Partly under the direct influence of the peculiar political conditions, partly under the influence of advanced political ideas from the west, the Revolutionary and Socialist parties acquired a very special significance in the Russian liberative movement and in political activities. Under the repressive police regime political parties in Russia now took on a complexion very distinct from that of similar parties in western Europe. A crisis was inevitable. It was held up for a time by the Great War. But even this could not long prevent it. The autocracy was found to be unable to carry on the War and defend the country. In other ways it had completely discredited itself in the eyes of the vast majority of the people

What took place in February of 1917 was not a lucky stroke brought off by conspirators or political parties. It was a spontaneous movement of all the people, aiming at changing the existing form of government. It was in this way very much at the mercy of passions it had unloosed among all the elements of the population, and of forces foreign to all ideas of real progress, forces which might yet succeed in exploiting these passions to their own ends. The Revolution was not merely a political, but an agrarian revolution, complicated by such problems as the self-determination of minor nationalities and local self-government. In the period from February to October, 1917, it was thought that the solution of these problems was likely to be attained through a democratic republic, decentralization on the basis of self-government, federation of states, and land reforms on the basis of distribution of private land of landowners among the peasants. The Revolution accomplished what the Great War had already begun to do : it succeeded in shaking off the sluggish bear—the Russian peasant—who, like other social elements in the State, had at length been roused to action. It put an end to the outworn political system and social order unwilling to give place to the new. It swept away the relics of serfdom. It brought personal and national freedom which, once granted, cannot long be withheld from enjoyment by reaction and tyranny.

In every Revolution the appearance of destructive forces of all kinds is inevitable. They often succeed in holding back for even lengthened periods the development of the healthier forces in the country, thereby exposing the whole population to the greatest suffering. The conditions and circumstances at the start of the Russian Revolution in February, 1917, were particularly favourable for the growth of these destructive forces.

The immediate causes of the Revolution were the unsuccessful conduct of the War, a growing conviction that no good could result from it, and the break up of the economic life of the country. The demoralized soldiers of the rear and the industrial population of the great cities now became decisive factors in the situation. The predicament of the moderate Radicals and Socialists at the head of the Government was very awkward, obliged as they were to continue the War and to fulfil the inter-allied obligations and at the same time to start reconstruction at home and to endeavour to solve all the problems now before them. It was natural that the masses of the people utterly wearied of the War, hungered for peace and for the immediate satisfaction of their political and economic demands. These feelings were worked on by Bolshevik propaganda. Meanwhile the activity of militant reactionary groups played into the hands of the extremists by arousing fears of a restoration of the autocracy. The ill-starred revolt of Kornilov in August prepared the way for the successful *coup d'état* of the Bolsheviks in October, 1917.

When we come to the consideration of conditions and circumstances in Russia since the Bolshevik *coup d'état* it is much more difficult to gauge their real significance for the future. The sources of information are unreliable. Official information is that of a party organization in power which tolerates no opposition to its own views and policies. The general impression is created abroad that the only force that counts in the public life of the U.S.S.R. is that of the ruling caste, the Communist Party. That this force is not so supreme as it is represented to be is now very evident from the fact that the Communist Party has been compelled to alter its methods and modify its principles in so many directions. It has been difficult enough for the observer to follow the rapid changes in these principles and methods. One cannot help feeling, however, that the feverish energy and activity now being displayed by the Soviet Government and the Communist Party in no way reflect what is being slowly but surely accomplished by other stronger forces in Russia, which so far have kept in the background. There is no doubt, however, that the success of the Bolshevik *coup d'état* of October, 1917, is not so much to be ascribed to a fortunate conspiracy as to the considerable support of the people. War-weary and politically inexperienced and unorganized, these had been easily won over by the promise of immediate peace and plenty. In Germany, Austria and the other countries of Europe the same phenomenon was to be observed, but on a very much smaller scale, as was natural where the working classes were politically riper, more experienced and better disciplined and organized. In Russia the collapse of discipline in the army and navy had turned well-armed and equipped soldiers and sailors into emissaries of revolution. This immense mass making common cause with

the thoroughly roused workers became the ready tools of the
well-disciplined and organized Communist Party agitators.
But what was for these turbulent elements an end (peace,
land, etc.), was for the Bolsheviks merely a means for the
realization of aims quite foreign to the Russian workers and
peasants. This only became evident later. It has been said
that Communism had its echo in the soul of a large section
of the Russian people inclined to Messianism. The contradiction between this essentially religious sentiment and the
anti-religious materialism and militant imperialism of the
Bolsheviks soon revealed itself. In the reaction of these
influences we may find the explanation of much of the success
of the Communist policy which knows the market value of
illusions. It is not in Russia alone that the people are loth to
surrender their illusions.

The accession of the Bolsheviks to power led to the revival
of reactionary forces in Russia. Whatever might be the
immediate aims of the leaders of the White movement, this
movement, supported by foreign intervention and the blockade,
was considered by the masses of the people, especially the
peasantry, as anti-revolutionary and as a mere prelude to the
restoration of the old regime and its abuses. In the struggle
between the Whites and the Reds the peasantry generally
stood on the side of the latter, and only very seldom and
unsuccessfully took arms against either side in " Green
Risings."

The Communist Party made full use of these favourable
circumstances to strengthen its power. Under cover of the
dictatorship of the proletariat it had recourse to despotic
methods of the extremist kind. These methods could be easily
applied in a country where autocratic rule had been law for
a hundred years. Moreover, the Bolsheviks found ready and
willing servitors among the old police and bureaucratic officials
trained in the school of arbitrary rule. In this way arose a new
well-policed state under a highly centralized bureaucratic
system of government. The Bolsheviks were now in a position
to try out all their experiments on a well-prepared and isolated
field. Wholesale nationalization led to the creation of a vast
bureaucracy under the complete control of the Communist

Party, a close, ruling caste of officials determined to keep power at all costs.

The internationalism of the Communist Party soon proved to be aggressive imperialism. This was to be seen not only in the foreign policy of the Soviet Government, but in the attitude of the Comintern to non-Communist workers' movements abroad. Communism showed itself to be not only an anti-progressive and reactionary force in Russia, but " the greatest obstacle to the cause of the proletariat the world over." [1]

The blockade helped the Bolsheviks considerably in feeding the illusions : (1) of the Russian proletariat as to the spread of the proletarian revolution abroad, and (2) of the foreign proletariat as to the Soviet paradise in Russia itself. In 1920 the almost complete exhaustion of the economic life of the country and the resulting poverty of the people showed the failure of the Communist experiment. It was evident that the policy of the Government was in complete contradiction with the social and economic processes within the country. It was forced to compromise. Its programme was based on centralization. Various peoples were insisting on self-determination. It met this demand by creating a nominal federation which, as it turned out, put still more power into the hands of the central Government. The Soviet Government organized the policy of general nationalization and State control. Still the people kept on trading (everyone was trading) and had recourse to private enterprise. The Soviet power could not put down this " illegal " trade, and, indeed, had often to satisfy its own needs through it. Still more remarkable was the contradiction in agrarian policy. The peasant not only carried out the land redistribution according to his own ways and customs, which he would not change, but he offered such a sturdy resistance to the Communist policies *re* food, etc., in the village that in 1921 the Government was forced to alter its economic policy. The peasantry, having freed itself in February, 1917, began slowly to develop into

---

[1] " Greater than the shameful regime of Horthy in Hungary or of Mussolini in Italy," adds K. Kautski (*International and Soviet Russia,* 1925).

an anti-Communist political force. The process was much
hindered by the famine of 1921 and by the political oppression
of the time.

The advent of the Communist Party to power in Russia is
considered by many as being the most important event of
modern history. To form a proper estimate of its historical
significance we should, however, pay particular attention to
the period 1918–21 when the Communists on an open field,
with no one to gainsay them, had the opportunity of giving
the fullest expression to their aims and policies. What were
the results of their experiments during this period? What
contribution have they given to the world's progress? What
new prospects has Communism, according to the Bolshevik
interpretation, opened to the workers of the world?

As we have seen, Communism in practice as well as in theory
rests on unquestioning faith in the omnipotence of the State,
and in its ability to transform not only the social and economic
structure of a people, but its whole mentality by orders from
above. Herein the Communist finds a justification of the
principle of the despotic rule of a minority over a majority.
In reality under the cloak of Marxianism he merely repeats
the methods of the German war-lords in a most halting way
(wholesale militarization, etc.). One can understand the strong
appeal of this theory to restless and ardent spirits, and to
gamblers in a period of almost unprecedented upheaval such
as followed the Great War. A closer acquaintance, however,
with Soviet Communism at home, and especially with the causes
of the complete failure of its varied experiments from 1918
to 1921, should dampen the ardour of enthusiasts, for whom
even now the Russian Revolution of February, 1917, and the
Bolshevik *coup d'état* of October, 1917, mean one and the same
thing.

In our analysis of the theory of the Soviet State in
Chapters VIII and IX, we have pointed out how ancient, how
close to tradition, indeed we might say how true to type in
every respect, is this new Bolshevik theory of class despotism.
All the old arguments for absolute power are recapitulated,
all the old methods of arbitrary unconstitutional rule are
revived. The most obstinate reactionaries are now to be

found on the side of the Bolsheviks. In this connection the recently published book, *Das Land der Roten Zaren* (Hamburg, 1925), by Colonel Max Bauer, deserves attention. The Colonel, a friend and supporter of Horthy's, was one of the most prominent men in the secret German monarchist organization, " Konsul," which worked up the Kapp " Putsch " against the German Republic. From this book we see how remarkable is the similarity between reactionary German and Soviet methods.

The advent of Communism to power in Russia has, we think, definitely and for all time discredited absolutism as a principle of government, even when applied in the interest of the working classes. In the same way the Communist dictatorship has failed in its efforts to remould the mentality of the Russian people, to create a new " Communistic " culture in the U.S.S.R. The subordination of the purposes of education to the special aims of Communistic propaganda, the limitation of educational opportunities, especially in the universities, to the youth of proletarian origin professing the Communistic faith, have led to a distinct lowering of educational standards, to a great loss of intellectual life. This policy has already provoked strong opposition among the people, especially in the villages, who, as we showed, are now insistently demanding proper schooling and general education instead of mere propaganda. The Communists have also completely failed in doing away with the traditional culture and dismissing it as a bourgeois survival. Even among the more sincere Communists and their followers, the forced planting of the ideas and principles of internationalism and class - culture is now evoking strong opposition. A return to national culture and tradition in literature, art and music is very noticeable. Taking all these facts into consideration, one must come to the conclusion that the rising generations will derive but little satisfaction and inspiration from a study of the period of " pure Communism."

The N.E.P. was looked on by Lenin as a temporary withdrawal to catch one's breath and to collect one's forces. It offered at home a number of concessions under the pressure of economic reality, but on condition of the complete control of the Communist Party in the field of national economy as reminded us that " as long as the Bolshevik Party exists, as long as there is a real proletarian dictatorship, so long will the Party stand above the State apparatus, and guide and control it. It cannot be otherwise." And so long, we may add, will be continued the activity of the Comintern and the dual policy of the Soviet Government. Even though that policy has so far yielded no returns to the Communist Party it does not mean that the latter's activities will cease. " On the Western Front [*sic*]," says Zinoviev, " the advantage is on the side of the enemy : in a number of countries the Comintern is compelled to bring back its forces and its parties to the trenches. It is preparing for stubborn and prolonged trench warfare, and is in some places mining underground." The international aims of the Comintern have been well defined by Stalin, another member of the Politburo, the Triumvirate, in a speech at a meeting of a committee of the Comintern (*v. Pravda*, March 29, 1925). The Comintern cannot help interfering with the concerns of the various parties (in different countries) supporting the revolutionary elements and fighting against their enemies. In this connection the reader may be interested to hear the considered opinion of Chicherin in the last meeting of the general assembly of the U.S.S.R. Soviets, May, 1925. In answer to many criticisms from various quarters on the paucity of the results achieved by the Government's foreign policy, Chicherin declared that it was not of importance that one thing or another did not succeed. The question now was to what extent they could succeed in breaking up the united front against them which the most influential elements in the leading states were determined to create. Chicherin specified the aims of this " united front." Curzon, he said, insisted on a reduction of Communist propaganda by not fifty per cent but by one hundred per cent. Chamberlain followed the same policy. Chicherin's rejoinder was : " If they insist that all propaganda in general in the U.S.S.R. should be stopped, it means a demand that the Communist Party should cease to be the Communist Party. All hinges on the question shall we remain or not. We shall remain. *J'y suis et j'y reste*. The issue is now that of our relations to the capitalistic world."

Taking all these things into consideration one sees how great, how insuperable, indeed, are the difficulties in the way of establishing normal relations between the U.S.S.R. and other states. The realities of the situation at home and abroad compel the Soviet Government to make more and more concessions. And yet the ruling Party cannot allow this if it would continue to rule. It is only natural meanwhile that great divergences of opinion on all the questions arising from these contradictions should now be noted in the Communist Party. As, however, the Party is a ruling caste these divergences partake more of a personal character, and the outsider is often at a loss to understand their real causes. We know that they have become very pronounced since Lenin's death. The dismissal of Trotski [1] (who would grasp Lenin's sceptre) is a recent example of what is going on within the Party. There must, however, be something more serious behind these private differences of opinion. The Communists at present seem to have split up into three schools of politicians : (1) those still striving to continue the pure Communistic policy ; (2) those who realize more clearly the state of affairs in the country and abroad, and insist on a policy of large concessions, and (3) those who strive to reconcile these two elements and create a " united front " in order to preserve the supremacy of the Party and to maintain the activity of the Comintern abroad. Which of these tendencies will take the upper hand eventually it is hard to foretell. For the moment the reconcilers of the irreconcilables hold the balance. For the present the Soviet Government does its utmost to win the support of Soviet traders and capitalists. It now promises a number of concessions to the peasants such as the bringing up of the horse stock supplies to the normal requirements within the next five years (!) ; the development of the manufacture of agricultural machinery ; a reformation of land taxation, etc. It has now permitted " the right of criticism of our own internal affairs as long as it is meant for the improvement of our institutions." It further permits the employment of wage labour in agriculture, and the renting of land. (Resolutions of the General Assembly of the Soviets of

[1] The more recent recall of Trotski is evidently to be explained by the desire of Stalin to win the support of an able tactician.

Its disillusion is now almost complete. Unemployment is rife. Wages are being lowered. Labour trade unions are dependent on the Government, which is at the same time the largest employer of labour. But in this class we may already observe a greater spirit of independence and a soberer attitude to the problems of existence. The growth of strike movements and insistent political demands show this.

The N.E.P. has been responsible for the creation of another force in the U.S.S.R. that of a new trading and industrialist class. It is not strong enough to hold its own like the peasantry. But its claims to recognition as a highly significant factor in the coming economic developments of the country are being well maintained and successfully upheld.

Among the various nationalities of the U.S.S.R., the demands for local independence from the central power are becoming more persistent day by day. Under the highly centralized system of government these national forces are not developing outwardly in proportion to their real inner strength. But all these different forces are gathering strength and making headway, and give every reason for believing that in the near future they will compel the dictators to modify their policy towards them, or else make way for another government.

The Communist dictatorship is at present not only the greatest obstacle to the economic and cultural revival of Russia, but it is a menace to peace, order and economic stability in Europe. There is hardly any possibility of the restoration of the old autocracy in Russia. Autocracy would seem to have discredited itself for ever in the eyes of the Russian people. As regards reaction, Russia is passing through it now under the Bolshevik regime. A new Russia has been born from the War and the Revolution. She has seen the worst. There is now every reason to believe that she desires a sound democratic regime, that a federative system of government will arise, and that the present nominal federation will become a reality. It is hardly credible that the various peoples of Russia will surrender what they have already acquired, even nominally. On the other hand it would seem that the interests of the huge territory of Russia and of her varied peoples and races can best be served under a federative system of government. Moreover, the economic interests of Russia will demand in the future a closer alliance with a number of newly-formed states formerly part of the Empire. Mutual confidence between these and Russia will be fostered if the government system of the latter is democratic and federative. In this connection one fact should not be forgotten : the War and the Revolution—aye, and the Communist regime—have awakened among Russians at home and abroad a long dormant national feeling. This sentiment is particularly noticeable in the Intelligentsia of our day, which has learnt to tackle the more real problems of Russian life. In these years of hardship and trial it has entered more intimately into the life of the people. In literature, art and music it is ceasing to strain for effect. The tendency is now for greater simplicity and sincerity. Since the coming into power of the Communist Party many of the more educated elements have left the towns to settle in the country. On the other hand the cultural level, as also the political significance of the peasantry, has risen considerably during the period of the Great War and the Revolution. All this has helped very much in bridging the chasm between the people and the cultured classes. The Intelligentsia has undoubtedly a very important rôle to play in the restoration of Russia to healthier conditions. At the same time, greater opportunities for exerting direct influence on the Russian people are now being opened to the Churches. A distinct revival of religious feeling among all sections, the remarkable growth of religious activities are striking features of the post-revolutionary changes in Russia. The Mother Church, which had stood aloof for so long from the life of her children, is now coming nearer to their hearts. After sore tribulation she has found that only in the affections of the people can her influence be strengthened and realized.

These are some of the general conclusions which we consider may be drawn from the facts under investigation before us. We know perhaps too much about the present regime in Russia. About the new forces in formation there, we know too little. But from what we do know of them we have every reason to look forward to the complete restoration to health of Russia politically, economically and culturally. We believe the time is not far off when she will come into her own again. This, however, can only be achieved by the Russians themselves, by the Russian peoples living in Russia.

APPENDIX I

Centuries and Years.	
VIII c.–IX c.	Slav settlements in the basin of the Dnieper, and in the north along the rivers Volga and Oka. Trading centres and towns. Three chief centres of civilization : Novgorod in north-west, Kiev in south-west, Tmutarakan in south-east. Coming of the Norsemen.
IX c.–X c.	The Slavs with the help of Norsemen successfully repel attacks of wild tribes. The Norsemen supported by the trading towns and centres extend their principalities, that of Kiev being the most important. The Slavs advance to shores of the Black Sea and Sea of Azov. The river trading route from Novgorod to Kiev established. Slav settlements in direction of countries of Arabian civilization. Close relations with Byzantium.
987–989	
XI c.	*Adoption* of Christianity and of Greek alphabet.
	The Slavs spread over territory between the rivers Oka and Volga where a number of principalities and towns arise. In the first half of this century the Kiev State clears the south of nomadic tribes. In the second half of the century renewed incursions of other wild tribes.
about 1054	First collection of *Russian laws* (Russkaya Pravda). Free-lance, roving retainers of princes (Boyars), settle down as landed proprietors.
XII c.	Settlement of north-east Russia proceeds. A new centre is formed at Suzdal rivalling Kiev and Novgorod in importance. Change in routes of world trade from Eastern to Western Europe. Decline of the Kiev State.
1147	*First mention of Moscow.* Struggle for supremacy
1169	among the Russian princes. *Capture of Kiev* by Prince Andrei of Suzdal-Vladimir. Slav penetration eastwards. Development of the " folk-mote " institutions (*Veche*). Legendary poetry and church literature flourish. Rise of Moscow.
XIII c.	Decline of *Byzantium* adversely affects trade along the Novgorod and Kiev route. Territory around Kiev becomes devastated and from the time of the first Tartar
about 1224	invasion, when the hordes of Jenghiz Khan defeated the Russians at the battle of Kalka until the 15th century Kiev drops out of Russian history. Other centres in North-east of Russia assume growing importance,

	Suzdal, Tver and Moscow. The Novgorodians advance north and east to White Sea and Urals. Russia is now split up into a number of small principalities.
1237–40	*Invasion of Batu Khan*. Devastation of South-west of Russia. North-east Russia submits to the Tartar yoke. Development of popular institutions (*Veches*) in Novgorod. Novgorod, a Veche republic with a prince at head as leader of the military forces. In North-east Russia (Vladimir, Suzdal, Rostov, Yaroslav, etc.), the princes with help of the Tartars take upper hand over the Veches. Swedes advance to Novgorod after conquering Finland. German settlements on the Baltic. Lithuania forms an independent state partly on the ruins of South Russia. The Hanseatic League, a union of large trading centres of North-west German (Lübeck, Hamburg, Bremen, etc.), begin to trade with Novgorod.
XIV c.	Tartars hinder Slav settlement in the South and South-east of Russia. The Moscow prince becomes " the servant of the Khan " and with his support assumes title of Grand Duke. The unification of Russia proceeds. Moscow now the largest town after Novgorod and Pskov rivals Novgorod as centre for foreign trade, especially with southern countries and Middle Asia. After many unsuccessful efforts to free themselves from Tartar oppression the Russian princes under Dmitri Donskoi
1380	defeat Tartars at *Kulikovo*. Church becomes more and more national. Growth of her political significance. Appearance of *heresy*. Break up of the Golden Horde into three Khanates : Kazan, Astrakhan, Crimea. To
1386	the west of Moscow the newly-formed Polish Lithuanian Confederation is a menace. The Novgorodians penetrate to Siberia over the Urals in search of furs.
XV c.	The Moscow prince profits by the gradual weakening of the Tartar power, and extends his dominion northwards. The Kazan Khanate checks this movement in the east. In the north the Muscovites follow the old Novgorodian routes eastwards and cross the Ural Mountains into Siberia. Unable to free himself completely from the Tartar yoke the Moscow prince returns to the old policy of nominal submission and is thus enabled to extend his power over neighbouring territories. Ivan III (1462–1505). Break up of Tartar Dominion. A strong national stock—Great Russian—created. Moscow out-rivals Novgorod economically. *Riazan* and *Yaroslav*
1456, 1463	rivals Novgorod economically. *Riazan* and *Yaroslav* submit to Moscow. Series of wars between Moscow and
1470, 1485 1480	Novgorod ends by *submission* of latter. Submission of Tver.

	Growth of the Polish Lithuanian State. Muscovite advance to Finnish Gulf.
1499	Defeat of Lithuanians.
	The change of Moscow from a principality to a State and the " treachery " of Byzantium in recognizing the Pope's authority give rise to a new politico-religious theory of the State. Church teaches that centre of Orthodoxy is now Moscow—the third Rome. In consequence of the
1472	*marriage of Ivan III* with Sophia Paléologue, niece of the last Byzantine Emperor, the muscovite rulers consider themselves entitled to all the honours of the imperial dignity. The Church becomes their obedient
1497	servitor. New growth of heresy. *New codex of laws* (" Sudebnik.") Appearance of a new military landed class, nucleus of the future nobility, an offset to the old Boyar aristocracy. South-west Russia falls into the hands of Poland.
XVI c.	The Moscow State now covers the vast territory known later as the Governments of Moscow, Novgorod, Tula, Iver, Vladimir, Riazan, Nijni-Novgorod, Smolensk, Yaroslav, Archangel, Vologda, Kostroma. Moscow one of the largest towns in Europe. Direct relations with England during reign of Ivan the Terrible (1553–1584). Moscow drawn into trade between Europe and Asia. Unsuccessful attempt to reach the Baltic Sea. Livonian wars. Expansion eastwards and south-eastwards along the Volga and towards Steppes. Colonization becomes
1552	regular state policy. Capture of *Kazan*. Capture of
1556	*Astrakhan*. Colonisation leads to building of towns and fortresses. State colonization mostly follows on lines of settlements made by free Cossacks, runaway peasants and enterprising traders. Expansion beyond the Urals
1581–2	on same lines. Conquest of Siberia by *Ermak*. Aggravation of disabilities of peasants at home helps on colonization. Growing dependence on landlords. Efforts of latter to bind peasants more closely to the land. Clandestine flight of peasants to free lands. Advance to south meets with great opposition from powerful Crimean
1521, 1571	Khan. *Attacks* of latter on Moscow State. Moscow in danger. Tartar successes not followed up. Muscovite advance southwards proceeds. The old Boyar aristocracy descended from the ancient Rurik princes and their retainers, in endeavouring to maintain and strengthen its privileged position meets with vigorous opposition from the new military caste of landholders
1564	and the trading classes. The *Oprichina* of Ivan the Terrible. The Boyar Duma or Council loses significance.

	judicial administration. Economic revival. End of system of granting monopolies to individuals. The wealthy serf-owning nobility start many factories. About one-hundred-and-sixty-one of these in 1796. The bourgeois elements, merchants, etc., assert themselves.
1773–4	Abuses of serfdom. Sale of serf labour. *Pugachev Rising.* State power starts policing itself. Rights of the nobility
1796–1801	greatly curtailed under *Paul I.* Growing centralization. Under Catherine the Great a remarkable revival in cultural life. Western influences, French philosophy. Formation of Russian as a literary language. Liberal movement among the nobility. Formation of the Intelligentsia. Freemasonry. Religious movements : Schism and sects. Strong feelings of Intelligentsia *re* serfdom,
1790	police system, etc. Novikov, Radishtsev (*Journey to Moscow*).
1799	*First Anglo-Russian Alliance.* Participation of Russia in coalition against Revolutionary France.
XIX c. (First Half)	Extension of Russian territory unaccompanied by expansion of Russian population.
1801, 1803	Incorporation of *Georgia* and *Mingrelia.* Foreign policy of the Empire dictated not so much by Russian national interests as by the political sympathies and antipathies of autocratic rulers, by their desire to save " legitimate order " in Europe, to defend the old system against the new, and especially to prevent " the poison of the French Revolution " from penetrating into Russia.
1807	Anglo-Russian Alliance broken off on conclusion under Alexander I (1801–1825) of the *Treaty of Tilsit* when
1807–12	Russia was exposed to the so-called *Continental Blockade* of Napoleon. During this period Russia annexes Finland (1809) as far as the river Torneo granting her full administrative and political autonomy. Annexation of Bessarabia (1812), Imeretia (1810) and
1812–15	part of Trans-Caucasia (1813). The *National War*
1815	against France. Russian Army in Paris (1814) *Congress of Vienna* and the *Holy Alliance.* Further partition of Poland. The Russian Empire at the summit of its power in Europe. Nicholas I (1825–1855) wages war
1828	with Turkey (1826–1828) and with Persia. *Peace Treaties of Turkmanchai* with Persia (Russia acquiring
1829	Erivan and Nakhichevan districts), and of *Adrianople* with Turkey (Russia extending her territory to the north of the Danube ; to the Caucasian shore of the Black Sea, and in Transcaucasia), Serbia, Moldavia and Vallachia guaranteed autonomy. By the support of Russia, France and England, Greece becomes an

1839	independent state (1830). *Treaty of London.* Belgian
1849	neutrality guaranteed by the Great Powers. *Suppression*
1853–6	*of the Hungarian Revolt* by Russian forces. *Crimean War* ends with *Treaty of Paris.* Southern part of Bessarabia goes to Turkey. Russian fleet not allowed in the Black Sea. In the Baltic Sea Russia not allowed to fortify the Aland Islands.
	Home Affairs : Rise of industrial capitalism in Russia. Problems of serfdom, education and decentralization of
1802	administration. *Reform of the Senate* which now takes " the highest place in the Empire " after the Emperor. Creation of eight Ministries replacing the functions of the College system of Peter the Great.
	Alexander I puts an end to grant of serfs to nobility.
1803	*Ukaze* re *free peasantry* gave landowners right to liberate serfs. Four new universities founded, a number of secondary schools and primary schools. Autocratic reaction against principles of the French Revolution. Influence of Arakchêev (1814–1825). The ideal of Napoleonic France appeals to many higher officials. Speranski's Liberalism. The progressive Intelligentsia under the influence of French Revolutionary ideals.
1814	Secret societies : the *Order of Russian Knights, Union of Salvation, Union of Welfare* which split up into
1821	*Southern Society* and *Northern Society.*
Dec. 14, 1825	Outbreak of the *Dekabrist Revolt* on accession of Nicholas I to throne.
1830–1	*Polish Insurrection.* From this time Nicholas I adopts most reactionary policy. Creation of the Gendarmerie and of the Third Section.
	Growth of Russian literature and art. Griboyedov (1795–1829), Pushkin (1799–1837), Koltzov (1808–1842), Gogol (1809–1852), Lermontov (1814–1861), Shevchenko (1814–1861) ; Kuprenski, Brullov, Ivanov, Fedorov ; (artists) Glinka, Drogomijski, etc., etc. (musicians).
XIX c. (SecondHalf)	
1864	*Conquest of the Caucasus.*
1868, 1873	*Bokhara* and *Khiva* become dependent States.
1864, 1876	Acquisition of *Turkestan* and the *Fergan* region. Franco-German War gives Alexander II (1855–1881) opportunity
1871	of retrieving situation in the Black Sea (*London Convention*).
	Franco-Russian alliance replaced in 1863 by the Prusso-Russian entente directed against Austria and less openly
1873	against France. *Secret defensive alliance with Prussia.*
1877–8	*Balkan War* for the liberation of the Slav peoples from

APPENDIX II

BIBLIOGRAPHY AND REFERENCES.

(N.B.—Works marked with an asterisk * are in Russian.)

BIBLIOGRAPHICAL.

Bibliographie des questions ouvrières et sociales dans la Russie des Soviets.—(Genève, 1922.)

Labour Conditions in Soviet Russia. Systematic Questionnaire and Bibliography, International Labour Office.—(London, Harrison.)

Modern Social Movements. Descriptive Summaries and Bibliographies. —(The H. W. Wilson Co., New York, 1921.)

GENERAL.

DONALD MACKENZIE WALLACE : *Russia.*

Handbooks prepared under direction of Historical Section of Foreign Office : *Siberia, Ukraine, Caucasus, Don and Volga Basins, Estonia, etc.*—(London, 1920, H.M.S.O.)

A. RAMBAUD : *Histoire de la Russie.*—(Paris, 1900.)

HETTNER : *Russland.*—(Berlin, 1921.)

T. ENGELBRECHT : *Landswirtschaftliche Atlas des Russischen Reiches in Europa und Asia.*—(Berlin, 1916.)

* Professor S. PROKOPOVICH : *National Income of the Fifty Governments of European Russia for* 1906–1913 *years.*
   La Russie à la fin du 19ème *siècle.*—(Paris, 1900.)

* DOVNAR-ZAPOLSKI : *History of Russian National Economy.*—(1911.)

* Professor PICHETA : *National Economy of Russia in* 19th *and* 20th *Centuries.*—(Moscow, 1923.)

* Professor MENDELEEV : *Understanding of Russia.*—(1907.)

Professor KLUCHEVSKI : *A History of Russia.*—(London, 1911.)

* Professor S. PLATONOV : *Past of the Russian North.*—(1924.)

* Professor S. PLATONOV : *Period of Trouble.*—(Prague, 1924.)

T. G. MASARYK : *Spirit of Russia.*—(London, 1919.)

* Professor P. MILIUKOV : *Essays on History of Russian Culture.*

* I. BUNAKOV : *The Roads of Russia.* From Contemporary Annals.— (Paris, 1921–24.)

* Professor M. ROSTOVTSEV : *Origin of Kiev Russia.* From Contemporary Annals.—(Paris, 1921–24.)

* EFIMENKO : *South Russia.*—(1905.)

* M. OGANAVSKI : *National Economy of Siberia.*—(Omsk, 1921.)

OKAKURA : *Les idéaux de l'orient.*—(Paris, 1917.)

* I. GRABAR : *Introduction to History of Russian Art.*—(Moscow, 1910.)

* COUNT S. WITTE : *Memoirs.*—(Berlin, 1920.)

* V. NIKOLSKI : *History of Russian Art.*—(1923.)

* I. TOLSTOY and N. KONDAKOV : *Ancient Russia and its Art Relics.*—
(St. Petersburg, 1884-1899.)

* F. SHMIT : *Art of Ancient Russia—Ukraine.*—(Kharkov, 1919.)

* P. MURATOV : *Russian Painting to Middle of 17th Century.*—
(Moscow, 1915.)

MAURICE BARING : *Outline of Russian Literature.*

PRINCE MIRSKY : *Modern Russian Literature.*—(London, 1925.)

* Professor VENGEROV : *Heroic Character of Russian Literature.*

* Professor OVSIANIKO-KULIKOVSKI : *History of Russian Intelligentsia.*—(1914.)

Professor P. MILIUKOV : *Le mouvement intellectuel russe.*—(Paris, 1920.)

BOGUCHARSKI : *Active Narodnichestvo of the '70's.*—(1912.)

Rapport sommaire sur l'origine, le programme du parti socialiste-révolutionnaire de Russie.—(International Socialist Labour Congress, Paris, 1904.)

* MARTOV : *Russian Social Democracy.*—(Moscow, 1916.)

INDUSTRY AND TRADE.

The Industries of Russia. Official Edition for World's Columbian Exposition at Chicago.—(1893.)

Russia : its Trade and Commerce. Edited by A. Raffalovich.—
(London, 1918.)

* Professor TUGAN-BARANOVSKI : *Russian Factory.*

* Professor S. PROKOPOVICH : *Labour Question in Russia.*—(St. Petersburg, 1905.)

AGRICULTURE AND LAND PROBLEM.

* YAKOVLEV : *Outline of History of Serfdom up to Middle of 18th Century.*—(Moscow, 1911.)

* SEMEVSKI : *Peasant Question in Russia during 18th Century and First Half of 19th Century.*

* Professor A. CHAYANOV : *Sketches of Peasant Economy.*—(Moscow, 1921.)

* Professor N. MAKAROV : *Peasant Economy and its Evolution.*—
(Moscow, 1920.)

* Professor A. CHELINTSEV : *Agricultural Geography of Russia.*—
(Prague, 1924.)

* LENIN (ULIANOV): *Collected Works.*—(Moscow, 1923.)

Professor S. PROKOPOVICH: *Economic Conditions of Soviet Russia.*—(King, London, 1924.)

S. ZAGORSKY: *La République des Soviets, Bilan Economique.*—(Paris, 1921.)

H. BRAILSFORD: *Russian Workers' Republic.*—(New York, 1921.)

Hon. BERTRAND RUSSELL: *Bolshevism. Practice and Theory.*—(New York, 1920.)

* *The Land.* Collection of Articles edited by Commissariat of Agriculture.—(Moscow, 1922–24.)

* F. SHTSHERBINA: *Laws of Evolution and Bolshevism.*—(Belgrade, 1921.)

* Professor G. SHVITTAU: *Revolution and National Economy of Russia* (1917–1921).—(Berlin, 1922.)

* Professor A. MAKAROV: *Taxes in Kind and their Collection.*—(*Berlin*, 1924.)

Labour Conditions in Russia by the Russian Economic Association.—(P. S. King, London, 1922.)

Conditions and Prospects of Russian Agricultural Production and the New Economic Policy.—(*Russian Economist*, London, 1922.)

A. ORLOV: *Revival of the Co-operative Movement in Russia.*—(*Russian Economist*, London, 1922.)

L. TROTSKI: *Lessons of October.*

M. LANDAU-ALDANOV: *Lenine.*—(Paris, 1920.)

ROGER LEVY: *Trotski.*—(1920.)

K. KAUTSKI: *Dictatorship of the Proletariat.*—(Kansas, 1920.)

Professor S. MELGUNOFF: *Der Rote Terror in Russland.*—(Berlin, 1924.)

* S. MASLOV: *Russia after Four Years of Revolution.*—(Paris, 1922.)

G. A. PAVLOVSKY: *Russia's Current Monetary Problems.* From Economic Journal of the Royal Economic Society.—(London, 1923.)

Mrs. PHILIP SNOWDEN: *Through Bolshevik Russia.*—(London, 1920.)

EMMA GOLDMAN: *My Disillusionment in Russia.*—(London, 1923.)

B. MIRKINE-GUETZEVITCH: *La Constitution de l'Union des Républiques Soviétiques.*—(Paris, 1925.)

* *Administrative Division of U.S.S.R., May 1st,* 1924.—(People's Commissar for Foreign Affairs, Moscow, 1924.)

* *Statistical Information for U.S.S.R.,* 1918–1923.—(Central Statistical Bureau, Moscow, 1924.)

* *National Economy of U.S.S.R. in Figures.*—(Moscow, 1924.)

* *Production of Manufacturing Industry in U.S.S.R. for* 1912, 1920, 1921, 1922.—(Central Statistical Bureau, Moscow.)

* A. I. RYKOV : *Economic Position of U.S.S.R. and the real Problems of Economic Policy.*—(Moscow, 1924.)

* I. LARIN : *Intelligentsia and the Soviet Economy.*—(Bourgeoisie, Revolution, etc., Moscow, 1924.)

* A. RYBNIKOV : *Small Industry of Russia.*—(Moscow, 1924.)

* *Labour in U.S.S.R.* Statistical Economic Survey, 1922–1924.—(Moscow, 1924.)

* *Report of People's Commissar for Agriculture for* 1923 *in Eleventh Assembly of Soviets.*—(Moscow, 1924.)

* *The Land.* Collection of Articles, Nos. 1, 2 and 3.—(Moscow, 1921–2.)

* A. KONDRATIEV and OGANOVSKI : *Perspectives of the Development of Farming (Agriculture) in Russia.*—(Moscow, 1924.)

* J. YAKOVLEV : *The Village as it is.*—(Moscow, 1925.)

* J. YAKOVLEV : *Our Village.*—(Moscow, 1924.)

* A. GAGARIN : *Peasant Economy and Conditions.*—(Moscow, 1925.)

* *Foreign Trade of U.S.S.R. for* 1923. Collection of Articles.—(Moscow, 1924.)

* L. B. KRASIN : *Perspectives of Russian Export.*—(Moscow, 1924.)

* G. SOKOLNIKOV : *Finance after October.*—(Moscow, 1923.)

* *Money and Credit*, 1914–1921.—(Moscow, 1923.)

Also the Soviet Periodicals such as : *Economic Life*, Organ of the Supreme Council of National Economy ; *Izvestia*, Organ of Central Executive Committee of U.S.S.R., and *Pravda*, Organ of Central Committee of the Communist Party, etc., etc.